STRATEGIC

INVESTING

DOUGLAS CASEY

SIMON AND SCHUSTER
NEW YORK

Copyright © 1982 by Douglas R. Casey
All rights reserved
including the right of reproduction
in whole or in part in any form
Published by Simon and Schuster
A Division of Gulf & Western Corporation
Simon & Schuster Building
Rockefeller Center
1230 Avenue of the Americas
New York, New York 10020

SIMON AND SCHUSTER and colophon are trademarks of
Simon & Schuster
Designed by Irving Perkins Associates
Manufactured in the United States of America

10 9 8 7 6 5 4 3 2 1

Library of Congress Cataloging in Publication Data

Casey, Douglas R.
    Strategic investing.

    1. Investments—United States—Handbooks,
manuals, etc.   I. Title.
HG4921.C34   332.6′78   82-850
ISBN 0-671-43885-9   AACR2

Acknowledgments

I'd like to thank a number of friends, colleagues, and associates for their help, both direct and indirect, in getting this book together. Important among them are Richard L. Bast, Darrell Brookstein, Harry Browne, Bruce E. Greene, Frederic Hills, David Hudson, Robert D. Kephart, Tom Lipscomb, John A. Pugsley, and Robert Ringer.

More directly, the three people who helped pick apart the manuscript—and helped put it back together—in detail: Lee G. Lovett, who's at once a great lawyer, friend, and editor. The world will hopefully discover he's a fine novelist as well before 1982 is over. K. E. R., who insists on remaining "low profile" (must have something to do with Chapters 9 through 12 of the book), even though I might not have finished the book without her help. Jarrett Wollstein, who is full of fresh ideas, some of which have been developed here.

Last, but certainly not least important, my father, Eugene B. Casey, my mother, and my stepmother.

*To those who know that the Ascent of Man
will continue, and do their part to ensure
that it does*

Contents

STRATEGIC INVESTING

Introduction

This book is not about why an economic depression occurs and how to prepare for one. It's a little late for that,
I'm afraid. Instead it's about how you can survive and
profit from the one we're now in.

*The central proposition of this book is simply that the
world has already entered an economic depression of
unparalleled magnitude.* It's not just another recession,
soon to be followed by a quick recovery. Even the 1929
debacle looked like just a recession at the beginning.
That's the bad news. The good news is that you can
emerge from this depression very well off if you know
the right investments and act now to get into them.

When I wrote *Crisis Investing* in 1979, many of the
predictions I made seemed outlandish. Since many
things in this book will sound even more radical, I will
take the liberty of reviewing my own track record.
Below is a summary of how you would have fared financially if you had followed my advice in *Crisis Investing*.

• *Buy small energy stocks.* I listed 23 stocks selected by
the parameters; if an equal amount had been invested in
each stock, a $1,000 investment would have almost tri-
pled in value.

• *Sell bonds, especially municipals.* When *Crisis Investing* went to press, AAA corporate interest rates were
about 9 percent. They're now about 16 percent, and the
average bond has lost 30 percent of its nominal market

17

value and much more when inflation is taken into account.

• *Sell real estate.* In 1979, real estate brokers were insisting that the post–World War II real estate boom would continue indefinitely and that the price declines that had occurred in a few parts of the country were anomalies. Today the real estate market is crashing. Sales are off by an average of over 40 percent nationwide in the last two years, and prices are now dropping rapidly.

• *Buy gold and gold stocks.* Gold was $270 an ounce when I wrote *Crisis Investing* in 1979, and shot up to over $850 an ounce in January of 1980. Gold stocks did even better. The 40 South African stocks that I listed in *Crisis Investing* increased an average of almost 600 percent, with most paying more in dividends in a single year than they cost.

• *Buy silver and silver stocks.* Silver increased from $6.50 an ounce to nearly $50 an ounce at its peak—an increase of almost 770 percent.

• *Prepare for a stock market crash.* In real terms, stocks in early 1982 are at their lowest levels in thirty years.

• *Banks will fail.* In late September of 1981, 70 percent of all savings and loan companies were in the red, and many were failing. More banks than ever before are on the FDIC's "problem list."

The most unpalatable prediction in the book, however, was that another tremendous depression was about to begin—one that would have different, but in many ways greater, repercussions than the depression of the 1930s; all of my other projections were premised on the same theory that drew me to that conclusion. But now the "Greater Depression," as this one may someday be called, has begun, though we are still in its early stages and many areas of the economy have not yet been affected.

Everything I said in *Crisis Investing* is as true now as it was then, although financial conditions have changed;

the purpose of that book was not to sell readers on specific investments, but to give them the tools needed to figure out the way the world works. All the fundamentals I covered there are the same today, and for that reason this book is not a revision of *Crisis Investing* but a *sequel* to it, providing a practical strategy for how you as an investor can deal successfully with the present economic situation. Basic economics will not be explained here as in *Crisis Investing*. Rather, *Strategic Investing* will explain what the investment opportunities and dangers Americans now face are and why they are even greater than they were three years ago. In a nutshell, here are a few of the most important ones covered in the following pages, along with my predictions:

• *Money market funds*. While some are safer than any bank, recently returning yields of up to 18 percent, most are very dangerous. See pages 115 to 133. These funds will be the scene of a gigantic panic.

• *Business failures and opportunities*. There will be more failures than at any time since the 1930s, but each one presents the entrepreneur with a chance to build a mini-conglomerate with little or no cash. See pages 167 to 173.

• *The alternative economy*. This, particularly barter and unreported cash transactions, is the growth industry of the 1980s. The techniques of using it to earn, and save, thousands of dollars are detailed from pages 158 to 166.

• *Gold, silver, and foreign currencies*. All of these should be seen in a totally different way from that of only three years ago, even though the profit potential is still hundreds of percent. See pages 189 to 216.

• *Real estate*. The real estate crash won't bottom until at least 1984, and a new class of millionaires will be made in the next boom. See pages 236 to 275.

• *Stocks*. The bull market of the century will begin in the early 1980s. I detail how six different groups of stocks will perform from pages 302 to 357.

• *Commodities*. These have always been viewed as nothing more than a legal gambling casino in the past. From pages 369 to 411, however, I've outlined the techniques and commodities that will make it possible to multiply even a small amount of capital ten for one with low risk.

The overall economic scenario I anticipated for the 1980s is developing on schedule: We are witnessing the beginnings of massively reduced standards of living, titanically moving markets, huge government deficits, and much higher inflation.

To be financially successful in the 1980s you must be fully familiar with the financial and economic environment. You must understand it on a firsthand basis in its essentials in order to make your own decisions. It's not good enough to have a gut feeling that something's wrong with the world, and then react on the basis of whim or intuition. Nor can you rely on the advice of others without understanding the causes of the economic events that will shape the future. Acting on gut feelings is no better than gambling; and acting on advice that you don't understand is even worse.

It's not easy to give advice to an audience as broad as the one reading this book. Some of you are multimillionaires, some just getting by. Some of you are young, and willing to take risks; others old, and more concerned about income and security. But regardless of your personal situation, the depression will redefine the meaning of "good" and "bad" investments.

And the only good investment is one that gains in value regardless of the circumstances of the owner. The advice in this book, therefore, is generally applicable to all readers. Putting different people into different investments because of who they are is usually a mistake simply because *the investments don't know or care who owns them.* There is no stability among investments. You should be in situations that present *the lowest possible risks in relation to the potential rewards*—regardless of your personal circumstances.

Can I be saying that widows and orphans should buy penny mining shares? Well, I am, and they should. Of course, that prospect will send shivers down the spines of regulators, bank trust officers, and conventional advisers. But that's their problem. Just don't let them impose their judgments, fears, and prejudices on you.

You're not going to emerge intact from the 1980s by being conventional. These are most unconventional times, and to survive it's necessary to have an unconventional investment strategy.

A Plan of Attack

A strategy is an overall plan for accomplishing an objective. It's a word with military connotations, and that's appropriate, since you are engaged in a battle—at a minimum, the battle for investment survival. It's for that reason this book is entitled *Strategic Investing;* it lays out an overall plan to allow you to emerge a victor from the financial battlefield of the future.

The strategy is highly unconventional. It might seem a bit scary at first; that's because it's based on the current economic realities and they're none too cheery. But the strategy *works.* I can't offer the nostrums of establishment economists, but don't let it bother you. By disregarding their advice, you won't be charging into oblivion with the Light Brigade.

The strategy involves four steps: (1) *Liquidate,* (2) *Create,* (3) *Consolidate,* and (4) *Speculate.* It gives you a solid financial base of operations, while at the same time protecting your flanks from unexpected dangers and liberating you to move onto the offensive as a successful speculator. Let's consider the essence of each step.

1. *Liquidate.* It's pointless to talk about speculating without the cash to do it. This section of the book ex-

plores strategies for raising all the cash you can, getting the highest return on this money, and cutting expenses —including taxes. During this stage you'll marshal the resources you need to survive and neutralize any potential economic land mines under foot or financial time bombs about to go off in your path. By liquidating what you don't need you'll generate instant cash and put it in the right places.

2. *Create.* This depression, like the last one, will have massive unemployment. This part of the book explores strategies for earning more, including possibilities in the alternative (underground) economy, and the techniques of buying failing businesses. Here you'll ensure that cash reinforcements will be coming, in ever greater amounts, for the future. The worse the economy gets, the better you'll do.

3. *Consolidate.* This depression will be characterized by severe shortages of consumer goods, as well as by much higher inflation. This section defines the strategies for making sure you're unaffected by either—including the proper way to integrate gold and foreign currencies into your portfolio. Proper consolidation ensures safety in the midst of financial and social chaos in the years ahead.

4. *Speculate.* The financial markets of the 1980s will be the arena of the speculator. This section of the book covers the best high-potential investments in stocks, commodities, and real estate. The best defense is a good offense, and here you'll implement one. The battle for financial survival to be fought in the 1980s will eventually end like all battles. The victory will go, as it usually does, to the daring. In the financial world, that is the speculator.

The going will be tough in the years to come, but if you follow the strategy, and keep up your courage, virtually everything you've ever wanted can be yours.

What Lies Ahead

PART I

Chapter 1

What This Depression Will Be Like

People never believe in volcanoes until the lava actually overtakes them.
George Santayana

Great economic and social forces flow with a tidal sweep over communities that are only half conscious of that which is befalling them.
John, Viscount Morley

To successfully confront the environment of the '80s you need to be comfortable with the words that will be used to describe it. The most important of these words is *depression.*

It's a word that conjures visions of breadlines, Hoovervilles, and men selling apples on street corners; but those aren't valid images any longer. The word is used in a nebulous, almost purposely vague manner by most commentators; likely they don't understand the word themselves. The word is often used in ways that confuse and intimidate rather than illuminate.

The word "depression" may press a hot button for many people because of the associations it conjures, but it's just a word. In this book I'll use it, depending on the context, in one of three ways:

1. A period of time during which most people's standard of living goes down.
2. A period of time when distortions (misallocations of capital and malinvestments) that have been

built up in the economy by government intervention are liquidated.

3. A period of time when the business cycle climaxes
—the "bust" that inevitably follows an inflationary boom.

The Greater Depression of the 1980s has not yet been
formally acknowledged. But that's no surprise.

Three Scenarios

In 1929, 1930, or even 1931, many people didn't think
that they were in a depression; it took a while before
perceptions caught up with reality.

The situation is similar today. The Greater Depression has begun, but to many it looks like another temporary recession, which will pass in due time. But that's
quite unlikely at this point, and I explain why in the
next chapter. For now, it's better to examine how the
depression will likely evolve than to either hope it will
go away or pretend it doesn't exist.

There are many possible courses the depression can
take, depending upon how individuals, businesses, and
particularly the government react now to the first stages
of depression. The logical possibilities are: (1) the best
case—brief, sharp deflationary depression followed by
a very strong recovery; (2) the worst case—hyperinflation, collapse of the dollar, emergency regulations, and
authoritarian controls; (3) the most likely case—severe,
long inflationary depression, with recovery taking years,
perhaps decades. Below are images of three possible
futures. You will live through an approximation of one
of them.

Scenario 1: An American Renaissance

This is the best case: a brief, sharp deflationary depression.

October 1, 1983.   The Administration is in a self-described state of siege. Despite successful passage of the main features of the Reagan economic program in the spring and summer of 1981, inflation continues to exceed 10 percent annually and unemployment has crept over 11 percent. A compromise on Social Security cuts and deficit financing of new defense spending has resulted in increased "crowding out" of small and medium-sized businesses from the credit markets. Increasing bankruptcies threaten to push unemployment much higher. In a nationally broadcast speech to the nation, the President declares that the country is on the brink of economic disaster. He reaffirms more strongly than ever his commitment to reducing the burden of government, but states that previous gradualist methods simply will not work, given the political realities. He therefore declares a state of national emergency and uses the Presidency's existing near dictatorial emergency powers to make the following decrees:

1. The President announces the immediate abolition of the Federal Drug Administration, Securities and Exchange Commission, National Labor Relations Board, Federal Trade Commission, Interstate Commerce Commission, and a host of other government regulatory agencies. For the first time in over fifty years, common carrier rates, drug sales, securities transactions, labor negotiations, and other details of commerce will be determined by the free market.

2. To reduce the crushing weight of interest on the national debt (projected to absorb 20 percent of all government revenues by 1984) and the increasingly strapped Social Security program, the government will hold a public auction of all federal scientific, technical, and research and development agencies such as the National Aeronautics and Space Administration and the Smithsonian. In addition, all national lands in Alaska and the West will be sold to the highest bidders. All Postal Service assets will be included; the President si-

multaneously repeals statutes preventing private carriers from delivering the mails.

The proceeds of the sales will be used to permanently retire the national debt, Social Security, and other major government liabilities, although there will be an immediate drastic reduction in all transfer payments. The Social Security system—and its taxes—will be abolished, and everyone under age fifty-five henceforth will be responsible for his own retirement. Those between sixty and retirement age will receive 30 to 40 percent of their promised benefits; those between the ages of fifty-five and sixty will get 15 to 20 percent. In addition, the President announces he is calling for all states to ratify a modified "balanced budget amendment," which will prohibit the federal government from incurring any new peacetime national debt.

3. Explaining that the Federal Reserve is inherently an engine of inflation, the President announces that it will be abolished, and its assets used to further cut the national debt. The policing of fraud in the banking industry will be turned over to the Justice Department. In addition, gold and silver will be allowed to again circulate as legal currency in the United States and the government will auction off its reserves of gold and silver over a period of five years to ensure an adequate floating supply of the metals. Usury laws and all other banking regulations will be abolished. Henceforth interest rates will be determined by the free market.

4. The President announces that there will be an immediate across the board reduction of 25 percent in the federal budget including the Defense Department, whose mission will henceforth be to "protect the United States, not police the world." The President says he expects U.S. allies, including Germany and Japan, to pay for their own defense. Defense contractors will be allowed to sell arms without restriction at market prices, and without subsidized loans, since the Export-Import

Bank has also been abolished. Taxes will immediately be reduced by "at least 30 percent depending upon proceeds from the scheduled sale of government properties."

5. All government subsidies, price supports, and loan programs to businesses, local governments, and pressure groups will be abolished.

October 5, 1983. Several bills are introduced into Congress calling for the President's impeachment. White House security is beefed up after a member of the Weather Underground fires a bazooka from his van parked in front of Lafayette Park at the North Portico in hopes of touching off a violent revolution. The President is unharmed and damage to the White House is minor.

The financial markets and banking system start to brace for a runaway deflation and debt liquidation. The Dow Jones Industrials drop 150 points in one day.

October 7, 1983. In an unprecedented joint statement, the NAACP, AFL-CIO, American Federation of State, County and Municipal Employees, and the National Association of Manufacturers, declare the President's program to be a "return to the stone age, racist, and a threat to every man, woman, and child in America." The joint statement declares that Reagan's emergency declaration will be challenged in the Supreme Court and calls for a mass Halloween demonstration on October 31 in Washington, D.C., to denounce the President. On the same day, the Secretaries of State and Defense both resign, stating that the defense cuts threaten the security of both Europe and the United States.

October 30, 1983. In anticipation of the Halloween demonstration, the President moves up the first sale of government assets. The first round of sales nets $200 billion in anticipated revenue. The President declares the sale a resounding success, and declares that he expects taxes to be cut another 20 percent in fiscal 1984, while the government runs a massive surplus.

February 1984.   Titanic waves of buying and selling over the past months have sent some stocks soaring, but most have crashed; the Dow average breaks 400. The dollar, however, reaches a ten-year high against foreign currencies. Business bankruptcies have sharply increased since the President's emergency speech and will collapse some defense contractors and subsidized industries over the next year. Banks close by the thousands, and real estate is unsellable. Unemployment skyrockets, especially among large companies. But workers quickly start reorienting themselves to cash in on new opportunities that open up by the thousands because of an unprecedented influx of foreign capital in response to deregulation and new low tax rates which actually transform the U.S. into one of the world's outstanding tax havens. Scores of foreign companies announce plans to locate new factories in the United States. In the midst of a financial panic greater than 1929, some rays of hope are appearing, which makes it all the more confusing.

March 1984.   In a special message to the nation, the President announces that his recovery plan is succeeding. Inflation has not only disappeared; the Consumer Price Index (CPI) has dropped 15 percent in the last three months as scores of billions of dollars have been wiped out through bank failures, bond defaults, and the collapse of investment markets. Everywhere there is chaos and violence as many wonder where their next meal is coming from. The President affirms that the government will not provide any special welfare benefits or food stamps (as the government doesn't grow food) but it will maintain order and prevent looting.

He also states that federal spending and taxes will be

reduced another 25 percent in the coming eighteen months. Few, however, think he can retain office for the remainder of his term, as a fourth assassination attempt is narrowly aborted. Still, as bad as things are, there's no doubt the reduction in taxes has cushioned the radical drop in wages for workers who are still employed; the drop in prices is a boon to those who have kept some dollars in a safe place. And many failed businesses are taken over by speculators who, after buying them for pennies on the dollar, can sell products at the lower prices people can afford.

May 1984. The Dow Jones Average has bottomed at 200, but because consumer prices have fallen 40 percent in the last six months, it's not quite as bad as it could be. The huge deflation has curtailed borrowing and consumption, and scared people into getting back to work. Many welfare programs have gone bankrupt. The liquidation of many major companies has caused leading indicators of business activity to hit an all-time low. But as some assets are acquired for bargain prices and put back to work, some indicators surprisingly start to head back up. The major insurance companies that have survived the financial collapse are well on the way to offering practical alternatives to Social Security for most Americans.

Soviet leadership gloats on what appears to be the final collapse of capitalism with all its "internal contradictions."

November 1984. The President's actions polarize society into factionalized political parties which destroy any unified opposition to his re-election. Contrary to all expectations, Reagan is put back into office.

At the same time, the massive deflation climaxes and winds down. Most prices are down to 1950 levels in dollar terms and are still falling slowly as the money supply stabilizes. The supply of goods and services has started to increase radically. Inner cities, after extensive rioting, start experiencing a renaissance as domestic and foreign capital flows in to take advantage of the deflated assets and huge pool of unemployed labor. Crime rates drop radically. A dumbfounded labor leader comments, "This is the most unbelievable thing in history."

August 1985. The Department of Commerce reports that the average American has clearly experienced the first major increase in his living standard in the last ten years, although it was from the abnormally low levels of the preceding year. Everyone is amazed to find that nearly all of the real wealth in the world is still there, as are the desires of the people and their skills. Since it's impossible to collect unemployment or welfare, people go back to work. Entrepreneurs sense a bottom forming and ingredients for a boom building, and work to prepare for it by acquiring and revitalizing bankrupt businesses.

September 1986. The economy has turned around almost as radically as it collapsed three years earlier. Total federal spending is down an incredible 70 percent in three years, and is still dropping; the federal deficit has been abolished. The after-tax inflation-adjusted take-home pay of the average American returns to the 1981 level. A consensus to dismantle what little remains of the federal leviathan sweeps over Congress, despite the bitterest efforts of the collectivistic Old Guard. Senator Kennedy declares the recovery to be "a card trick, a cheap illusion that won't last." Nobody pays much attention to him. Within a few years the federal government will be reduced to little more than a court system of last resort and defense-oriented armed forces. It's increasingly evident, even to those who opposed the President's emergency action, that the depression has ended and a real boom, unparalleled in world history, has only just begun.

The President now calls himself a "moderate libertarian," but it is no longer important who is in the White House. People are too busy minding their own business and growing wealthy to care.

January 1987. The decline in government spending, taxes, and inflation has caused a new spirit of tolerance to sweep the land. Because of automated production and computer design, unhampered by building codes, regulations, and taxes, housing prices have dropped to an average of $30,000 1981 dollars for a three-bedroom home. Several U.S. companies are in the process of building hotels and manufacturing facilities in earth orbit. Socialist governments in Europe are being swept out of office and a revolution overturns the Soviet government as news of America's renaissance spreads. Competition for economic progress has begun to replace war as a means of rivalry among nations.

The brightest and wealthiest people from all over the world start flooding into America, adding to the prosperity. Americans are able to pick up assets in foreign countries for a song, and grow even wealthier.

Let's look at another equally possible scenario for the future course of events.

Scenario 2: Return of the Whip

This is the worse case: hyperinflation.

October 1, 1983. The Administration is in a self-described state of siege. Despite successful passage of the main features of the Reagan economic program in the spring and summer of 1981, inflation continues to exceed 10 percent annually and unemployment has crept past 11 percent. A compromise on Social Security cuts and deficit financing of new defense spending has resulted in increased "crowding out" of small and medium-sized businesses from the credit markets. Increasing bankruptcies threaten to push unemployment much higher.

In a nationally broadcast speech to the nation, the President declares that the country is on the brink of economic disaster. He states that while he is still "in principle committed to long-term reductions in government spending and taxes," practicality and impending economic disaster force him to now emphasize the short term. He therefore declares a state of national emergency and uses his existing near dictatorial emergency powers to make the following decrees:

1. The Federal Reserve, although technically independent of White House control, is instructed to ease tight money and cut interest rates in half. The national debt ceiling will be increased to $1.8 trillion.

2. A new federal Work Corps will be created to become an employer of last resort for the millions of unemployed. Work Corps members will be given jobs rebuilding abandoned housing in the inner cities, helping out in hospitals, and doing other "meaningful public-spirited work." Able-bodied welfare recipients will also be required to sign up, if they wish to continue receiving their benefits. As an alternative they can join the armed forces, as part of the massive buildup being planned to "roll back the tide of Soviet aggression, and stimulate the economy." The Soviet government sees this as a provocation and redoubles its own military programs.

3. To combat rising crime, the budget of the FBI will be increased by 50 percent and FBI agents will be authorized to assist local police forces in making arrests even in cases which do not involve federal crimes. Federal funding is provided to increase manpower in local law enforcement by up to 100 percent.

4. Income tax reductions passed by the 97th Congress will be suspended "for the duration of the emergency" and a new value-added tax (VAT) of 2 percent will be imposed on all commercial transactions, in an attempt to offset growing tax evasion. To ensure public compliance with the stiff new tax regulations, 50,000 new employees will be added to the IRS, including 10,000 additional field agents.

5. To "stabilize the economy, and give business and workers some breathing room," a program of subsidies and price supports is put in place. The President assures the nation it's only a stopgap "until the free market can once again be relied on to make business profitable."

6. To increase America's ability to protect friendly foreign governments, new federal subsidies will be available for arms sales to Europe, the Middle East, and Latin America.

October 5, 1983. The reaction of the public and Congress is mixed. The auto, defense, and real estate industries pledge to give the new program 100 percent support. Senator Edward Kennedy calls Reagan's decrees "tough, but fair and necessary." The ACLU calls his declaration of a national emergency "totally unjustified and ominous" and vows to fight it, although how the ACLU will do so is in doubt, because the authorizing legislation has been on the books for years. Wall Street is up sharply in heavy trading, in hopes the bold new program will turn around the collapsing economy.

March 1984. Inflation is up sharply, with the Consumer Price Index climbing to over 14 percent and accelerating. While the federal Work Corps has created some jobs, unemployment grows in many sectors, particularly among semi-skilled workers. With money more readily available, car and home sales are up. However, bankruptcies are also up among small and medium-sized businesses. Big business booms, but industrial production among companies without powerful lobbies drops sharply. The *Washington Post* editorializes that "the results of the President's plan are mixed to date, but there are some hopeful signs."

July 1984. Inflation is out of control. Consumer prices are now moving up at nearly 30 percent annually, according to the government's figures, which many question. After a six-month boom, real estate sales and auto sales are again in depression, with money again tight. New businesses are going bankrupt daily. President Reagan, confused and disheartened, suffers a nervous breakdown and is unable to continue serving. Vice President Bush takes the reins and vows to "make good on the promise of the new program with greater vigor." The crime rate skyrockets as more and more Americans are faced with either the Work Corps or theft. Gasoline again becomes scarce, and the acting President "reluctantly" announces allocation controls.

The bond market collapses totally, and the stock market fluctuates unpredictably. Banks and pension funds ask for, and receive, massive aid in order to stay above water.

August 1984. In a special meeting OPEC raises its prices 45 percent and a resolution to reject payment in dollars is narrowly defeated, thanks to pressure from Saudi Arabia, which is held together only by active American military involvement. Late in the month, a number of African and other Third World nations repudiate their debts to the West in protest over not receiving "enough" foreign aid and more loans. Most major U.S. banks teeter at the repudiation announcement. Deposits drop sharply, despite higher interest rates, as people panic. There's little new saving because of higher taxes and raging inflation.

The acting President raises income taxes 30 percent to "demonstrate fiscal responsibility," and the VAT is raised to 6 percent, which is needed to continue payments to current Social Security recipients, and justified as being only half the VAT rate in Europe.

Word leaks out that America's two largest banks are unable to meet current obligations and are seeking special aid in high-level meetings. Within days, 40 percent of America's banks announce that they will be unable to continue operations.

The Federal Deposit Insurance Corporation issues assurances that every cent of insured deposits will be covered. What it doesn't mention is how, since there is less than one cent on the dollar available for relief.

The acting President boldly proclaims that the federal government will issue a special class of bonds, "backed by the full faith and credit of the U.S. government," to pay off FDIC-insured depositors. Printing presses work around the clock turning out the new certificates. Scores of billions in the new currency substitute appear in a matter of weeks. The bond and mortgage markets totally collapse, wiping out the remaining capital of bankers, insurers, and brokers. A financial holiday is declared, and order in society starts to disappear.

September 1984.   Prices are out of control, and shortages of food, fuel, and consumer perishables become acute. An ounce of gold can purchase a car; twenty ounces a house. Workers demand payment in foreign currencies, precious metals, or consumer goods.

The economic and social fabric breaks down. Workers no longer report to the job, instead using the time to barter or steal what they need. Businesses fail en masse. Federal troops are detailed to guard food stores in face of wholesale theft and vandalism. Few people dare to leave their houses for fear of roving bands of thugs. Major riots occur in Chicago, New York, Detroit, Miami, and a dozen other U.S. cities; and both the Army and National Guard are called in. Organized armed groups begin taking "appropriate measures" against government agents; the government, in turn, takes its own countermeasures.

The acting President declares martial law with a nationwide curfew from sunset to sunrise. Police are ordered to shoot looters on sight. Food and gasoline are strictly rationed. There have been several instances of combat between American and Soviet "advisers" in Africa and the Middle East. Cuba and the U.S. are in an undeclared war throughout the Caribbean and Central American arena. The Secretary of State is given the post of Minister of Domestic Peace and Order, with special powers for the duration of the emergency, and he leaves no question about who is in charge.

By now, the condition of the stock market is the last thing on anyone's mind.

November 1984. Acting President Bush is overwhelmingly elected because of fears of "changing horses" in the middle of cataclysmic domestic and foreign crises.

January 1985. Civil disorder has been stopped by massive police and military efforts, but the President is forced to place a moratorium on all political activity until the economic situation is "normalized." To that end, a new currency is issued with one new dollar replacing a hundred old dollars. The Social Security system has been wiped out, but is replaced by a direct welfare scheme funded by the federal government for those most in need. Private citizens are prohibited from owning gold, silver, gasoline, or designated "essential commodities." An estimated 70 percent of the American work force is now directly dependent on the federal government. Large sections of most major metropolitan areas are rubble. In order to defend the national interests in the Middle East, the Caribbean, and Africa, the armed forces are mobilized and sent to defend "strategic resources" in those areas. The media and the telephone system are placed under the control of the Defense Department. President Bush assures his countrymen that after foreign and domestic dangers are neutralized, things will return to normal.

Many Americans seek to emigrate to quiet, secluded areas in Australia, the South Pacific, or the tip of South America, but getting assets out of the country is very hard and costly because of strict controls.

Scenario 3: The Dark Years

This is the most likely case: an acceleration of present trends leading to an inflationary depression.

October 1, 1983. The Administration is in a self-described state of siege. Despite successful passage of the main features of the Reagan economic program in the spring and summer of 1981, inflation continues to exceed 10 percent annually and unemployment has crept past 11 percent. A compromise on Social Security cuts and deficit financing of new defense spending has resulted in increased "crowding out" of small and medium-sized businesses from the credit markets. Increasing bankruptcies threaten to push unemployment much higher.

In a nationally broadcast speech to the nation, the President declares that the country is on the brink of economic disaster. He states that while he still is committed to reducing the federal deficit in the long run, mounting business failures and the sluggish U.S. economy require drastic action to solve the immediate problems. He has discussed the prospects with members of both Congressional parties, and has arrived at what appears to be a "viable compromise." He therefore is making the following proposals to Congress:

1. While maintaining the Federal Reserve policy of

tight money for consumer credit, the federal government will make special low-interest loans available to businesses. It's reasoned that this will increase the supply of goods, and hence decrease prices, so no compromise with "supply side" economics is made.

2. The FHA will reverse its previous policy and increase the availability of federal mortgage money for federally insured mortgages. Action will be taken to ensure that every American can own his own home, but only if the home is newly constructed and conforms to strict standards, and the purchaser's net income is within specified limits.

3. The federal debt ceiling will be increased to $1.4 trillion. Spending will be cut on federal research and development, scientific and technical programs, and the maintenance of public lands. As an economy measure, the Post Office will now deliver mail only four days a week in some areas. Spending continues to expand on social programs and the military.

4. Unemployment benefits will be increased to 52 weeks, and large tax credits will be given to companies that employ women, minorities, unemployed construction and auto workers, and other "hardworking but hard hit" pressure groups.

5. General tax revenues will be used to underwrite Social Security, but benefits will be reduced for those who don't have "real need." Social Security taxes are further increased in order to maintain "the integrity of the system," although it's deemed no longer possible to index benefits to inflation.

January 1984. A Congressional liberal coalition, having achieved a large majority in both houses in the 1982 elections, enact even more massive social spending and entitlement programs. Most of the President's compromise proposals are enacted into law, however, as "a step in the right direction."

The President still selectively vetoes some increased spending for food stamps, federal aid to education, and other programs, but his veto is frequently overridden and he finds himself in a Nixon-like adversary position with Congress.

The standard of living continues sliding down. After-tax after-inflation take-home pay of the average American has dropped to 85 percent of 1980 levels. Many consumers are unable to pay their debts, and there are housing repossessions.

The Dow Jones Average, washed out by the decline of 1981 and 1982, and at only 20 percent of its 1966 peak in real dollars, started a "surprising" upward move during 1983 and finishes the year at 1100, a new all-time high.

March 1984. Business and personal bankruptcies are at an all-time high. Chrysler is forced to declare bankruptcy despite car import quotas limiting foreign manufacturers to 65 percent of their 1979 import volume. Senator Kennedy declares "cheap foreign imports are responsible for the desperate position of many U.S. businesses" and proposes a host of new import restrictions. They pass after a bitter battle between Congress and the White House.

Inflation figures become less and less meaningful as many prices fall—bond prices, housing prices, and the inventory values of troubled businesses—but others rise dramatically—food, non-durable consumer items, and gasoline. Inflation is clearly getting worse, but at vastly different rates in different areas.

Housing sales are down 80 percent from their peak in 1978. Banks are allowed to pay market rates of interest on passbook savings in a desperate attempt to gain more deposits. Unemployment stands at 12 percent, but many who are collecting benefits are moonlighting in the underground economy at the same time. This causes a good deal of tension among different groups in society.

July 1984.   Radically dropping demand for oil causes the dissolution, for all practical purposes, of OPEC. The price of the liquid creeps up, however, because of the uncertainty of supply and reluctance of sellers to accept dollars.

As the Administration's policies reinflate the economy, but only with hesitation and delay, a number of "jumbo" certificates of deposit and several corporations' commercial paper go into default, causing a panic and run on the money market funds. Prompt action by the Fed prevents a collapse; the funds are now insured and regulated by the banking authorities as well as the SEC.

Defense spending is increased significantly to buoy corporate profits and to fight unemployment, which stands at 14 percent nationwide. Special federal "corporate aid" programs are passed. A number of large U.S. banks fail, but the FDIC, with aid from the Treasury, is able to cover insured accounts. The federal government is "forced" to impose strict controls on consumer credit in view of the large number of personal bankruptcies, which put severe strain on retail-oriented businesses and banks. Depositors are prohibited from removing more than 25 percent of their savings in any one month without special government permission.

The stock market starts to skyrocket as Americans look to get money out of dollars and into some type of equity.

September 1984.   Over weak Administration protests, Congress creates the Department of Employment, offering public service jobs to unemployed workers landscaping government parks, cleaning the streets, and renovating abandoned buildings.

Spot shortages of staples have led to the creation of a massive black market, despite fines for "hoarding" and "scalping." Further import of gold, which has passed $2,000 an ounce, is banned. This sends the stock market to 2500—a new all-time high. The U.S. balance of payments deficit is also at an all-time high, however, and the possession of foreign bank accounts accordingly is banned, and a "per diem" tax on foreign travel is enacted to discourage spending abroad. Federal subsidies are passed for General Motors and U.S. Steel, in addition to large new defense contracts. The average American now pays over 65 percent of his income in total taxes, and inflation is approaching 25 percent.

October 1984. Congress overrides a Presidential veto and enacts wage and price controls. Allocation controls on natural gas and oil are passed, along with a new windfall profits tax. Unemployment passes 15 percent, and 20 percent of all Americans are now eligible for food stamps. Both unemployment and inflation figures are becoming very arbitrary, though, since so many Americans are now part of the underground economy, often inadvertently. Prices move generally up, but with very unpredictable reversals as a government program or a liquidation sale of a business unexpectedly dumps large supplies of some items on the market. Gasoline lines reappear along with shortages of meat, milk, fresh vegetables, and household items; it's similar to, but worse than, conditions in 1973 and 1974. Hundreds of thousands of unemployed auto workers erect a tent city on the mall in Washington, D.C. demanding jobs.

November 1984. Senator Edward Kennedy is elected President of the United States on his platform of "Compassion and National Reconstruction." He promises new federal welfare programs to guarantee all unemployed Americans decent food, decent housing, and dignity. Inflation is over 30 percent, unemployment appears to have stabilized at 17 percent. There is no end to the Greater Depression in sight, but real estate—after a devastating bear market that wiped out many homeowners and naive speculators—starts to stage a strong recovery in anticipation of much, much worse inflation. Although many corporations are running large deficits and the profits of others are illusory, the stock market explodes to over 3000 and speculation is rampant in all areas of investment; fortunes are made by those who prepared properly.

The country has become polarized, and many Americans move to isolated rural areas and small towns. Although most people's standard of living is dropping radically, some maintain a relatively high standard of living and become rich in the midst of the depression.

Which Scenario?

The chances are quite small Scenario 1 will happen, but all logical extremes should be considered; a deflationary depression would be the best way the melodrama we'll all watch in the 1980s can end. The house of cards the government has built on a foundation of sand over the last fifty years is going to collapse eventually, and—as with a real building—it's best to bring it down before it collapses unexpectedly and uncontrollably by itself.

The 1929 unpleasantness was deflationary, but it was very messy because the government did exactly the opposite of what it should have under both Hoover and Roosevelt: it increased taxes and regulations and tried to reinflate the currency. Instead of taking advantage of the liquidation to set the stage for real prosperity, it initiated a dismal chronic depression that lasted until the extraordinary controls and debt financing of World War II turned it around—and got things rolling toward this depression.

The chances of Scenario 2 coming to pass are, hopefully, small, but nonetheless significant. It's the way a hyperinflationary depression would probably unfold, and it's the worst thing that could happen short of another war. Unfortunately, it's also the type of thing that tends to set the stage for wars. In any event, it has happened elsewhere scores—perhaps hundreds—of times throughout history. By far the most likely scenario for the next ten years is the third one.

Inflation and Deflation—Together

The critical question that has been posed for the last fifteen years has been: Will the depression be inflationary like 1923 in Germany, or deflationary like 1929 in the U.S.? Observers tend to come down strongly on one side or the other of the issue. They say either the present debt-credit structure must collapse in a deflation, or it definitely will be hyperinflated, as if the two possibilities were mutually exclusive.

They're not. Just as it's possible to have the best of all possible worlds, it's also possible to have the worst.

The "inflationists" say that the government will never allow a '29-style collapse to happen again, and they're half right; the government will do its best to prevent it. But there's no reason to assume the government will be any more competent at preventing a deflation than there is to assume it can run the Post Office or Social Security or a war in Southeast Asia without nasty surprises.

The "deflationists" recognize that the government will continue trying to "stimulate" the economy by fiddling with bank reserves, tax laws, and deficit spending; they know the bottom line is more inflation. But they point out that the size of the debt and financial activity in the private sector is still so much greater than in the public sector that the government's efforts might prove futile if it doesn't stimulate at just the right speed and in the right way. And they're right, too.

The government certainly didn't want the crash of the

real estate and bond markets since 1979 to happen, but it did. The government can prevent a deflationary financial collapse only by literally creating scores of billions of dollars. And it's afraid to do that because that would cause even more inflation.

In a nutshell, it's a battle of the free markets, which are attempting to deflate and liquidate, against the state, which continues to inflate and prevent the collapse.

Scenario 1 covers the best case for a constructive deflation; Scenario 2 the worst case for a destructive hyperinflation. Both are possibilities; but, since trends in motion tend to stay in motion, Scenario 3, with both inflation and deflation at once, is the most likely.

The collapse of real estate, stock, bond, and mortgage prices is deflationary. When a house, for instance, which was valued at $200,000 is sold at $125,000, that's $75,000 of inflationary funny money that's, in effect, disappeared.

Like many things in the economic world, deflation and inflation appearing at the same time is a paradox. High interest rates are deflationary, but they are a direct result of high inflation. While inflation drives up the price of assets, high interest rates tend to drive them down. The current value of bonds and mortgages decreases in direct proportion to higher rates; higher rates increase the cost of holding real estate and other hard assets, and force their values down.

Inflation, in other words, is deflationary—a bit of a paradox. It creates an inherently unstable situation.

In practical terms, it means that while government is "forced" to continue inflating in the '80s, the free market will deflate financial assets in response. But that doesn't mean prices of the things most people want and use from day to day will fall; to the contrary. As inflation bankrupts businesses and unemploys workers, the supply of goods and services will drop, and that lower supply will place upward pressure on consumer prices. And

although the drop in the value of financial assets reduces the supply of money substitutes (anything that can be quickly converted to cash is a money substitute), the government's inflation acts to increase the spendable (i.e., M-1 and M-2) money supply.

Because both are happening at once, the Greater Depression will have cyclical times when deflation or inflation is the greater danger, and others when they will occur *simultaneously* in different sectors of the economy. Housing prices drop in Detroit: deflationary. At the same time the increased money supply raises food prices at the checkout stand in the same city: inflationary.

Although the danger of a quick deflationary or hyperinflationary collapse is ever present, the chances are the trend of the last two decades will continue.

Eventually inflation will destroy the currency, even if there is a deflation first along the way. There's a *cyclical* danger of a deflation every few years, but the *secular* long-term trend is clearly for more inflation.

In the recessions of 1970, 1974, and 1979, any of which could have snowballed into a full-fledged deflationary depression, each time the inflation rate crested at a higher peak. That trend is likely to stay in motion for the reasons covered in Chapters 2 and 3.

That's one of the major differences between the Great Depression of the 1930s and the Greater Depression of the 1980s. "Depression" is not the opposite of inflation; the two can and will co-exist.

Bet On

- *An inflationary depression.*
- *Sporadic periods of deflation within the longer inflationary trend.*
- *More government intervention in the economy, despite political rhetoric.*

Chart I

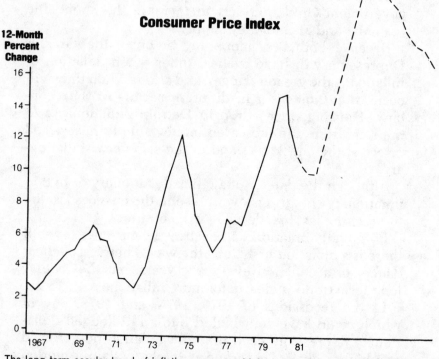

Consumer Price Index

The long-term secular trend of inflation goes ever higher, with short-term cyclical declines every few years. The recessions are brought on by high interest rates and price increases.

Chapter 2

Comparing the 1930s and the 1980s

The fact is that the Great Depression, like most other periods of severe unemployment, was produced by government mismanagement rather than by any inherent instability of the private economy. . . . Similarly today, governmental measures constitute the major impediments to economic growth in the United States.

Milton Friedman

If we do not halt this steady process of building commissions and regulatory bodies and special legislation like huge inverted pyramids over every one of the simple constitutional provisions, we shall soon be spending many billions of dollars more.

Franklin D. Roosevelt

We go downhill very fast over here. The full impact of the Depression is just beginning to be felt. Until lately, thousands of people were able to get along on their savings, but now their savings begin to vanish. . . . The cities are going broke one by one. . . . I doubt that the big railroads will last beyond the Spring. . . . The industrials have all gone to hell, and so have the mortgage bonds. For the first time in my life I begin to give serious thought to money; it is a new experience for me. . . . I hope to continue to eat.

H. L. Mencken

To properly weigh and analyze the three scenarios in the last chapter, you'll want to consider how this depression compares to the last one. You've heard the axiom "History repeats itself." It does, but never in exactly the same way. To apply the lessons of the past, we must understand the differences of the present.

During the American Revolution the British came prepared to fight a successful war—but against a European army. Their formations, which gave them devastating firepower, and their red coats, which emphasized their numbers, proved the exact opposite of the tactics needed to fight a guerrilla war.

Before World War I, generals still saw the cavalry as the flower of their armies. Of course the horse soldiers proved worse than useless in the trenches.

Before World War II, in anticipation of a German attack, the French built the "impenetrable" Maginot Line. History repeated itself, and the attack came, but not in the way they expected. Their preparations were useless, because the Germans didn't attempt to penetrate it; they simply went around it, and France was defeated.

The generals don't prepare for the last war out of perversity or stupidity, but rather because past experience is all they have to go by. Most of them simply don't know how to interpret that experience. They are correct in preparing for another war, but wrong in relying upon what worked in the last one.

Investors, unfortunately, seem to make the same mistakes in marshaling their resources as do the generals. If the last thirty years have been prosperous, they base their actions on more prosperity. Talk of a depression isn't real to them, because things are, in fact, so different from the 1930s. To most people a depression means '30s-style conditions, and since they don't see that, they can't imagine a depression. That's because they know what the last depression was *like*, but they don't know what one *is*. It's hard to visualize something you don't understand.

Some of them who are a bit more clever might see an end to prosperity and the start of a depression but—although they're going to be a lot better off than most—they're probably looking for this depression to be like the last one.

Although nobody can predict with absolute certainty what this depression will be like, you can be fairly well assured it won't be an instant replay of the last one. But just because things will be different doesn't mean you have to be taken by surprise.

To define the likely differences between this depression and the last one, it's helpful to compare the situation today to that in the early 1930s. The results aren't very reassuring.

CORPORATE BANKRUPTCY

1930s   Banks, insurance companies, and big corporations went under on a major scale. Institutions suffered the consequences of past mistakes, and there was no financial safety net to catch them as they fell. Mistakes were liquidated and only the prepared and efficient survived.

1980s   The country's financial institutions are in even worse shape than the last time, but now the ethic of the country has changed and everyone expects the government to "step in." Laws are already in place that not only allow but require government intervention in many instances. This time mistakes will be compounded; and the strong, productive, and efficient will be forced to subsidize the weak, unproductive, and inefficient. It's ironic that businesses were bankrupted in the last depression because the prices of their products fell too low; this time, it'll be because they went too high.

UNEMPLOYMENT

1930s   If a man lost his job, he had to find another one as quickly as possible simply to keep from going hungry. A lot of other men in the same position competed desperately for what work was available, and an employer could hire those same men for much lower wages and expect them to work harder than was the case before the depression. As a result, the men could get jobs and the employer could stay in business.

1980s   The average man first has at least 180 days of unemployment insurance; after that he can go on welfare if he can't find "suitable work." Instead of taking whatever work is available, especially if it means that a white collar worker has to get his hands dirty, many will go on welfare. This will decrease the production of new wealth and delay the recovery. The worker no longer has to worry about some entrepreneur exploiting (i.e., employing) him at what he considers an unfair wage because the Minimum Wage Act, among others, precludes that possibility today. As a result men stay unemployed, and employers will go out of business.

WELFARE

1930s   If hard times really put a man down and out he had little recourse but to rely on his family, friends, or local social and church group. There was quite a bit of opprobrium attached to that, and it was only a last resort. The bread lines set up by various government bodies were largely cosmetic measures to soothe the more terror-prone among the voting populace. People made do because they had to, and that meant radically reducing their standard of living and taking any job available at any wage. There were very, very few people on welfare during the last depression.

1980s   It's hard to say how those who are still working are going to support those who aren't in this depression, because 35 percent of the country is already on some form of welfare. But food stamps, aid to families with dependent children, Social Security, CETA, and local programs are already collapsing in prosperous times; and when the tidal wave hits they'll be totally overwhelmed. There aren't going to be any bread lines, because people who would be standing in them are going to be shopping in the Safeway just like people who earned their money. Perhaps the most dangerous aspect of it is that people in general have come to think that these programs can just magically make wealth appear and expect them to be there, while a whole class of people have grown up who have never learned to survive without them. It's ironic, yet predictable, that the programs which were supposed to help those who "need" them will serve to devastate those very people.

REGULATIONS

1930s   The U.S. economy had been fairly heavily regulated since the late 1800s, and those regulations caused distortions which added to the severity of the depression. Rather than allow the economy to liquidate, the Roosevelt regime added many, many more regulations—fixing prices, wages, and the manner of doing business in a static form. It was largely because of these regulations that the depression lingered on until the start of World War II, which "saved" the economy only through its massive reinflation of the currency. Had the government abolished most controls then in existence, instead of creating new ones, the depression would have been less severe and much shorter.

1980s   The scores of new agencies set up since the last depression have created far more severe distortions in the ways people relate than those of fifty years ago; the potential adjustment needed is proportionately greater. Unless government restrictions and controls on wages, working conditions, energy consumption, safety, and such are removed, a dramatic economic turnaround during the Greater Depression will be impossible.

A choice confronts the government. It can free up the economy or it can redouble its efforts to hold the old order of things together by literally Sovietizing the economy.

Government actions during the 1980s will probably be the same as those in the 1930s in many ways. In other words, it will do the most expedient but least desirable things possible under the circumstances; that's just the nature of politics.

TAXES

1930s   The income tax was new to the U.S. in 1913, and by 1929, although it took a maximum 23.1 percent bite, that was only at the $1,000,000 level. The average family income then was $2,335, and that put average families in the ¹⁄₁₀th of 1 percent bracket. And there was still no Social Security tax, no state income tax, no sales tax, and no estate tax. Furthermore, most people in the country didn't even pay the income tax, because they earned less than the legal minimum, or they didn't bother filing. The government, therefore, had immense untapped sources of revenue to draw upon to fund its schemes to "cure" the depression. Roosevelt was able to raise the average income tax from 1.35 percent to 16.56 percent during his tenure—an increase of 1100 percent.

1980s   Everyone now pays an income tax in addition to all the other taxes, and there's been enough resistance, evasion, and protest that in 1981 the government started cutting them. For that reason, it's unlikely direct taxes will go much higher, but inflation driving everyone into constantly higher brackets will have the same effect.

A person has had to increase his income faster than inflation over the last ten years to compensate for taxes.

Whatever taxes a man does pay will reduce his standard of living by just that much, and it's reasonable to expect tax evasion and the underground

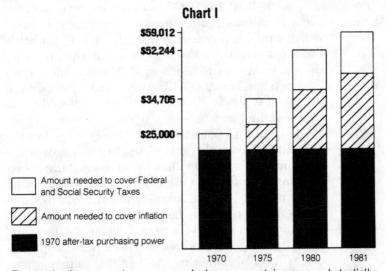

Chart I

To stay in the same place, a person's income must increase substantially more than inflation.

economy to boom in response. That will cushion the severity of the depression somewhat, while it serves to help change the philosophical orientation of society.

PRICES

1930s   Prices dropped radically because billions of dollars of inflationary currency were wiped out through the stock market crash, bond defaults, and bank failures. The government, however, somehow equated the high prices of the inflationary '20s with prosperity, and attempted to prevent a fall in prices by such things as slaughtering livestock, dumping milk in the gutter, and enacting price supports. Since the collapse wiped out money faster than it could be created, the government felt the destruction of real wealth was a more effective way to raise prices. In other words, if you can't increase the supply of money, decrease the supply of goods.

Nonetheless, the 1930s depression was a deflationary collapse, a time when currency became worth more and prices dropped. This is probably the most confusing thing to most Americans, since they assume—as a result of that experience—that "depression" means "deflation." It's also perhaps the biggest single difference between this depression and the last one.

1980s   Prices *could* drop, as they did the last time, but the amount of power the government now has over the economy is far greater than was the case fifty years ago. Instead of letting the economy cleanse itself by allowing the financial markets to collapse, the government will probably bail out insolvent banks, create mortgages wholesale to prop up real estate, and have the Federal Reserve buy bonds to keep their prices from plummeting. All of these actions mean that the total money supply will grow enormously. Scores of billions will be created to avoid deflation. If you find men selling apples on street corners, it won't be for five cents apiece but five dollars apiece. But there won't be a lot of apple sellers, because of welfare, nor will there be a lot of apples, because of price controls.

Consumer prices will probably skyrocket as a result, and the country will have an inflationary depression. Unlike the 1930s, when people who held dollars were king, by the end of the 1980s people with dollars will be wiped out.

THE SOCIETY

1930s   The country was largely rural or small-town. Communications were slow, but people tended to trust the media. The government exercised considerable moral suasion, and people tended to support it. The business of the country was business, as Calvin Coolidge said, and men who created wealth were esteemed.

All told, if you were going to have a depression it was a rather stable environment for it; despite that, however, there were still plenty of riots, marches, and general disorder.

1980s   The country is now urban and suburban, and although communications are rapid, there's little interpersonal contact. The media are suspect. The government is seen more as an adversary or an imperial ruler than as an arbitrator accepted by a consensus of concerned citizens. Businessmen are viewed as unscrupulous predators who take advantage of anyone weak enough to be exploited.

A major financial smashup in today's atmosphere could do a lot more than wipe out a few naives in the stock market and unemploy some workers, as occurred in the '30s; some sectors of society are now time bombs. It's hard to say, for instance, what third-generation welfare recipients are going to do when the going gets really tough.

THE WAY PEOPLE WORK

1930s   Relatively slow transportation and communication localized economic conditions. The U.S. itself was somewhat insulated from the rest of the world, and parts of the U.S. were fairly self-contained. Workers were mostly involved in basic agriculture and industry, creating widgets and other tangible items. There wasn't a great deal of specialization, and that made it easier for someone to move laterally from one occupation into the next without extensive retraining, since people were more able to produce the basics of life on their own. Most women never joined the work force, and the wife in a marriage acted as a "backup" system should the husband lose his job.

1980s   The whole world is interdependent, and a war in the Middle East or a revolution in Africa can have a direct and immediate effect on a barber in Des Moines. Since the whole economy is centrally controlled from Washington, a mistake there can be a national disaster. People aren't generally in a position to roll with the punches as more than half the people in the country belong to what is known as the "service economy." That means, in most cases, they're better equipped to shuffle papers than make widgets; even "necessary" services are often terminated when times get hard. Specialization is part of what an advanced industrial economy is all about, but if the economic order changes radically it can prove a liability.

THE FINANCIAL MARKETS

1930s   The last depression is identified with the collapse of the stock market, which lost over 90 percent of its value from 1929 to 1933; a secure bond was the best possible investment as interest rates dropped radically. Commodities plummeted, reducing millions of farmers to near subsistence levels. Since most real estate was owned outright and taxes were low, a drop in price didn't make a lot of difference unless you had to sell. Land prices plummeted, but since people bought it to use, not unload to a greater fool, they didn't usually have to sell.

1980s   Since the peak of 1966, stocks have already lost 70 percent of their value in real after-inflation terms. That means the greater part of the crash has already occurred and with it a great deal of the risk. This time stocks—and especially commodities—are likely to explode on the upside as people panic into them to get out of depreciating dollars in general and bonds in particular. Real estate will be—next to bonds—the most devastated single area of the economy, because no one will lend money long-term. And real estate is built on the mortgage market, which will vanish.

Everybody who invests in this depression thinking that it will turn out like the last one will be very unhappy with the results. Being aware of the differences between the last depression and this one makes it a lot easier to position yourself to minimize losses and maximize profits.

So much for the differences. The crucial, obvious, and most important similarity, however, is that *most people's standard of living will fall dramatically.*

In 1980, the real gross national product dropped by 1.6 percent, and the income of the average American worker fell by 5.5 percent in *real* terms—by far the largest amount since World War II. *The Greater Depression has started.* Most people don't know it, because they can neither confront the thought nor understand the differences between this one and the last. So far, it's been a gradual process; there's been no cataclysm to announce the arrival of the Greater Depression.

But as a climax approaches, many of the things that you've built your life around in the past are going to change, and change radically. The ability to adjust to new conditions is the sign of a psychologically healthy person.

Look for the opportunity side of the crisis. The Chinese symbol for "crisis" is a combination of two other symbols—one for danger and one for opportunity.

The dangers that society will face in the years ahead are regrettable, but there's no point in allowing anxiety, frustration, or apathy to overcome you. Face the future with courage, curiosity, and optimism rather than fear. You can be a winner, and if you plan carefully you will be. The great period of change will give you a chance to regain control of your destiny. And that in itself is the single most important thing in life. This depression can give you that opportunity; it's one of the many ways the Greater Depression can be a very good thing for both you as an individual and society as a whole.

Bet On

• *A depression much different from that of the 1930s.*

Chapter 3

Why a Financial Collapse Is Inevitable

We are presently in the middle stages of a runaway inflation that began accelerating in the 1970s and which is irreversible in the 1980s. Informed, intelligent observers should not be deceived by interludes of moderation in price inflation rates into believing that the long-run acceleration toward hyperinflation has been halted or reversed.

Jerome F. Smith

Evidence that the Greater Depression has begun is apparent everywhere. Whether or not people have come to prefer small cars, they can no longer afford large ones. For the first time in decades, the average new house is shrinking in size, and clothes washers, dishwashers, and air conditioning are options, not standard features; notwithstanding these changes, housing sales dropped over 50 percent from 1979 to 1982. The government's figures only serve to underscore day-to-day observations. Unemployment is nearly 9 percent nationwide (and will go much higher), while it's 50 percent or more among black urban teenagers.

Even though the Greater Depression has already begun, the financial collapse is yet to come. It's important to explore what form it will take, what its effects will be, and what the government is likely to do in response.

Boom and Bust: A Financial Phenomenon

A depression is primarily a financial phenomenon. The physical world will change very little because of it, although the way people relate to the world will change greatly. Somehow when we speak of real estate collapse people get the impression of buildings tumbling down. They won't, only their prices will. Just because corporations are bankrupted doesn't mean the factories they owned will vanish, or that their employees will forget all their skills and knowledge. Just because governments default on their bonds or the currency becomes worthless doesn't mean "the country" is bankrupt. It just means those who bought the bonds or held the currency are poorer.

In other words, all the real wealth will still be here, only its ownership will change, and some things will become more (or less) valuable relative to other things.

The people who wind up owning the most valuable things as the depression unfolds will, predictably enough, be those who understand what's going on and why. A grasp of the "business cycle" is essential to that understanding.

The Business Cycle

The most destructive single consequence of inflation is the business cycle. The business cycle is the process in which the economy is artificially expanded by increases in the money supply, followed by its uncontrolled contraction. In other words, it's the cycle of "boom and bust," which has been touted as one of capitalism's "internal contradictions" since the time of Karl Marx.

Like most of Marx's theories, however, his explanation of the business cycle is nonsense. The business cycle would not exist in pure capitalism. There could be no inflation, since the money supply—gold—would be constant relative to everything else. And with no inflation there would be no business cycle—and no inflationary booms. Depressions would be rare and localized events that occurred only during war or a severe natural disaster.

The best way to understand the business cycle is to follow through a specific example. Suppose, for a moment, that Los Angeles is not quite as prosperous as some people think it ought to be. Many people desire a $10,000 swimming pool in their back yards, but can't afford to put one in because they're spending so much time thinking about movie deals, talking about real estate, or playing racquet ball. People decide it would be nice if the government gave them the money they need to buy the pools.

Bowing to the voice of the people, the government credits the bank account of every Angeleno with $10,000. (The idea isn't as absurd as it may seem. In 1968, presidential candidate George McGovern proposed crediting every American's savings account with $1,000 for much the same reason.) Things would change rapidly. Although the morning after the government credited the bank accounts there would be no more real wealth in the world than there was the night before, there would be a lot more money. Everybody would feel $10,000 richer. And in the best Keynesian tradition, the economy would be "stimulated."

The first business to prosper as a result of the government's new monetary policy would probably be the telephone company, because the next morning all the phone lines would be jammed with Angelenos trying to call the local swimming pool construction company to place their orders. Shrewdly sensing increased consumer demand for telephone service, astute phone company executives make plans to put in more lines and hire more operators.

But the telephone company's expansion won't be nearly as dramatic as that of the swimming pool construction industry, which is soon swamped with orders. With demand skyrocketing, pool companies raise prices to take advantage of the situation, then run down to their bankers to borrow to expand capacity.

Because the banks have just taken in billions of dollars on deposit courtesy of the government's action, they will have plenty of money to lend, and at very low interest rates. "Interest" is the price of money, and with money in such ample supply its price is cheap. In order to build the swimming pools, the construction companies would contact their suppliers of concrete, copper pipe, and bulldozers, who would go out and do exactly the same thing.

All of these companies now have a labor shortage and have to raise wages to overcome it. Throughout Los Angeles, people will soon stop parking cars, pumping gas, and washing dishes to take advantage of the enticing offers from the swimming pool construction industry. The places where they were working are going to find all of a sudden that no one wants to work at menial jobs; good help, as it were, becomes hard to find. Late night television is deluged with ads from schools promising big money to those who train at driving bulldozers, pouring cement, or laying pipe. All this activity doesn't escape the notice of would-be entrepreneurs. Soon the family leisure van and custom surfboard are put up for collateral at the bank, and new swimming pool companies are formed. Some people even become millionaires overnight.

Boom, Boom, Boom

The newly created class of swimming pool construction millionaires and their highly paid employees increase their standards of living commensurate with their new incomes. They drive Mercedes cars, smoke Davidoff cigars, and wear Gucci shoes. Gold chains and silk shirts proliferate. People in general and the swimming pool contractors in particular, newly rich, work less and play more.

After a while, however, everyone who wanted to buy a swimming pool has placed his order, and sales taper off. People also start to notice a disturbing trend: Prices in L.A. have gone up, as they must whenever the supply of money around increases without a corresponding increase in goods and services. (What about all the new pools, you might ask? No new wealth has been created, just different—and more visible—types of wealth. Everyone who started making swimming pools used to make something else, something that's not being made now. Net production is the same.)

If the government's munificence increased the money supply by 20 percent, then prices will have gone up by almost that much. However, not all prices will go up by the same amount. Some particularly desired goods— like swimming pools, water to fill them, and chlorine— will have gone up much more than 20 percent. And other prices will have gone up less. People who spent their $10,000 to get a swimming pool may find that the price of water has gone up so much they can no longer afford to fill the pool, and the price of labor has gone up so much that they can't afford to maintain it. Since most people are consuming more and producing less—as people are likely to do when they feel wealthy—there is, in many ways, even less real wealth to spend money on than there was before the magical bank deposits transformed the way the world worked.

People have acted in ways they would not have had the government not debased the currency. Inflation has encouraged them to produce things that would not have been produced otherwise (such as swimming pools) and not produce things that would have. It becomes impossible to have a plumber visit your home to fix a leak, because his time has become so much more valuable installing drainage pipe for the pools. Doctors no longer care to make house calls, because they've made millions by investing in the stock of newly floated companies in the swimming pool business. And of course when you visit the gas station, you have to pump your own gas, because the kid who used to do it is now in the contracting business.

Even though everyone has a big swimming pool, his standard of living has started to go down in subtle ways.

Bust, Bust, Bust

Soon, swimming pool companies find that orders drop off to less than before the boom started. The situation is even worse, as there are many more companies competing for the business. They have to start laying off employees, and many have trouble paying their loans at the bank. The copper company and the cement company feel the ripple effect, and so do the silk shirt and gold chain retailers. Doctors fret as they see their swimming pool stocks plummet.

The Los Angeles economy is now experiencing a recession, which is simply a mild depression (the difference is one of semantics and degree). At this point the government could admit that giving everyone $10,000 was a stupid idea; people haven't improved their standard of living, they've just changed their consumption patterns. And it's at this point that the government should let the extra swimming pool companies go bankrupt, let the shareholders of the banks eat their loan losses, foreclose on the vans and surfboards they held as collateral, and let the misdirected tycoons go back to parking cars and pumping gas. But if the politicians did this, they would become very unpopular and would have to find a new line of work themselves come election time.

Government to the "Rescue"

No politician wishes to be blamed for a recession. Moreover, there are now strong vested interests for keeping the "swimming pool boom" going. The Association of Municipal Swimming Pool Builders, for example, declares it would be "economically disastrous and a criminal disregard of their sacred public trust" for the government officials to let the industry collapse. The Greater Los Angeles Water Authority suggests it would be in the public interest for government to subsidize water for swimming pools. The Silk Shirt and Gold Chain Retailers Association proclaims that "the city could never recover from the blow if the swimming pool industry is allowed to fail." The telephone company declares the government simply must get the economy moving again, and recommends tax credits for calls to swimming pool companies as a reasonable way to get things started.

A deflation could easily begin. Millions of dollars of loans the banks have made could be defaulted on, and that much currency would be wiped out. The stocks and bonds of failing companies would become worthless, destroying that much more. The value of all the thousands of newly built pools would plummet, simply because the supply had increased so dramatically, so quickly.

You can bet that everyone in society will be screaming at his elected representatives to bring back the good old days, and they will if they care to be re-elected and don't want to be blamed for a depression. This time, however, it might take $12,000 deposited in everybody's bank account to have the same effect, as the dollar might by now have lost 20 percent of its value.

A full business cycle has been completed. Stability, followed by inflationary expansion, followed by deflationary contraction. The contraction will be called a recession if the government acts quickly and reflates the currency in time to prevent a complete collapse; it will be called a depression if the government decides not to act, or acts too late. In other words, it will be a depression if the government allows the economy to liquidate the distortions that have been created; it will be a recession if the government steps in before the liquidation is complete.

But even if the government does act in time, things will be different the second time around. People have seen inflation and are therefore much less anxious to save money and much more anxious to borrow it; interest rates go up because of supply and demand. And because the government averted a depression by inflating the money supply again, prices stay up as well.

Businessmen and consumers start planning on higher prices, so everybody buys as much as he can to beat them. Everybody sees the fortunes made during the last boom, and even more people get into the game. More construction companies, more houses, more extravagant lunches at the Polo Lounge to celebrate success. People consume more than ever, and most investment is directed to cater to these higher levels of consumption.

The longer this goes on, the more convinced people become that the government actually can create prosperity and "fine tune" the economy. They also start thinking it should, because if it doesn't there's going to be a depression. The economy becomes shakier and more unstable because it's increasingly dependent on government policy, and how effectively that policy is implemented, rather than on natural market forces. If the government had ended the game the first time around, the economy would have had only a mild, short depression. The longer it keeps going, the greater the inflation, the distortion, and the resulting depression.

To be sure, the only way the government can keep

things together is by pumping ever more money into the economy, but the more it does so the higher prices and interest rates will go. The very thing that causes the boom absolutely guarantees the bust. After a while people see both inflation and recession at the same time. The standard of living starts to decline noticeably, despite the existence of more swimming pools, factories to build them, and expensive restaurants in which to discuss pool deals. The financial markets grow chaotic and unpredictable.

The longer this inflation continues, the more unhappy the eventual ending. Once the engine of inflation gets under way, the government is like the driver of a powerful car with a stuck throttle; if it stamps on the brakes to slow it, the car will spin; if it doesn't, the car will run off the road. Of course the driver wants neither to happen, so he uses "moderation," stepping on the brakes, but then releasing them before the car spins. The ride inevitably gets wilder and crazier. First to ten m.p.h., then back to five. Then to twenty and back to ten. To forty m.p.h., then a disinflationary "bust" back to thirty m.p.h. As the inflationary gas takes the car to a hundred, it's only with a bit of panic that the government's application of fiscal and monetary brakes can take it back to seventy-five m.p.h. Throughout 1979 and 1980, the car accelerated to 120 and at this point is careening wildly about the road. The issue is still in doubt whether the government will be able to slow it down without going into a deflationary collapse. But even if it can, the next step is 160 m.p.h., and the car is not in the hands of A. J. Foyt.

Inflation and Government

Things would be bad enough if inflation in Los Angeles were the sole problem and government caused it only by depositing equal amounts of cash in everyone's bank account. That would create a business cycle, with all its distortions, but there wouldn't be any special automatic beneficiaries. Unfortunately, that's not the way it works in the real world. In the real world it's worse.

The government creates new money by selling its debt to the Federal Reserve, which credits the government's accounts with Federal Reserve notes (a.k.a. dollars) at various commercial banks. The government doesn't distribute them equally, or even at random, but spends them in specific ways. The money is spent with some people and industries first. In other words, the government acquires the dollars at zero cost, and is able to trade them for real wealth at face value; the state benefits directly and drains resources from the private sector to itself through inflation.

The second rank of beneficiaries are those who receive the government's grants, transfer payments, and orders for goods and services; they can spend the dollars they receive at close to their old values, before the dollars filter down and prices start rising in response. The beneficiaries at this level are those closest to government—Big Business, Big Labor, and the Establishment. (More on the fate of these groups in the Epilogue.)

Those groups are firmly in control of the nation's political process as well, so it's a bit problematical for that reason to look to the political process for constructive change. Nonetheless, politics is so entwined with economics that the likely actions of the federal government bear closer scrutiny.

Bet On

- *A climactic bust of the long-term business cycle that began at the bottom of the last depression.*

Chapter 4

Political Solutions?

Men who have greatness within them don't go in for politics.
Albert Camus

People always have been and they always will be stupid victims of deceit and self-deception in politics.
Nikolai Lenin

Virtually everything politicians, government intellectuals, a majority of economists, and most members of the media tell Americans about inflation is not only false, but the exact opposite of the truth.
Robert J. Ringer

As inflation gets worse and the depression deepens, there will be a growing public outcry for government to do something, anything, about it.

People will join political action committees, lobbying groups, and political parties in hopes of gaining leverage to impose their will on the country at large, ostensibly for its own good.

Possible government "solutions" will include wage and price controls, credit controls, restrictions on changing jobs, controls on withdrawing money from bank accounts, import and export restrictions, restrictions on the use of cash to prevent tax evasion, nationalization, even martial law—almost anything is possible. None of these "solutions" addresses the root cause of depression—state intervention in the economy. Each will just make things worse rather than better.

What these solutions all share is their political nature; in order to work they require that some people be forced to obey the orders of others.

Whether you or I or a taxi driver on the street thinks a particular solution is good or not is irrelevant. All of the problems that are just beginning to crash down around society's head (e.g., a bankrupt Social Security system, federally protected banks that are bankrupt, a monetary system gone haywire) used to be solutions, and they must have seemed "good" at the time, otherwise they'd never have been adopted.

The real problem is not what is done but rather *how* it is done: that is, through the *political process* or through the *free market*. The difference is that between coercion and voluntarism. It's also the difference between getting excited, frustrated, and beating your head against a wall and taking positive action to improve your own standard of living, to live life the way you like it, and, by your own example, to influence society in the direction that you'd like to see it take—but without asking the government to hold a gun to anyone's head.

Political action can change things (Germans in the '30s, Chinese in the '40s, South Vietnamese and Cambodians in the '70s certainly discovered it can); it's just that the changes usually aren't very constructive. That's the nature of government; it doesn't create wealth, it only allocates what others have created. More typically, it either dissipates wealth or misallocates it, because it acts in ways that are politically productive (i.e., that gratify and enhance the power of politicians) rather than economically productive (i.e., that allow individuals to satisfy their desires in the ways they prefer).

It's irresponsible to base your own life on what 200 million other people and their rulers may or may not do. The essence of being a free person is to be *causative* over your own actions and destiny, not to be *the effect* of others. You can't control what others will do, but you can control yourself.

Perhaps that's what the persistent decline in the number of voters since 1960 means. The percentage of those voting has dropped every year, and over the past twenty years has fallen from 62.8 percent to 51.8 percent. That may be because of a commitment to libertarian princi- ples on their part. If so, it's cause for optimism. But more likely people are abstaining because they see voting as a poor way to spend a day, or don't care to get into an- other government computer bank, or don't care to en- courage the politicians, or just believe their vote doesn't count.

If you're counting on other people, or political solu- tions of some type, most likely it will make you unwary and complacent, secure in the hope that "they" know what they're doing and you needn't get yourself all flus- tered with worries about the collapse of the economy. If you think the government can solve most of the prob- lems ahead, then you don't need this book. If you're beginning to have some doubts they can pull it off, keep reading.

Reaganomics, Nixonomics, Supply Side Economics, etc., etc. . . .

A case can be made that in response to the recurring crises of the 1970s things changed radically with the 1980 election; that a corner was turned and a new begin- ning made. Even so, we can't afford to plan our lives around it. Even a President who believes in the free market can't easily undo the damage done over the last fifty years; his popularity wouldn't last long enough.

That's perhaps one reason why all the supposed free marketers involved in politics never advocate the sim- ple abolition of state intervention. Instead the Republi- cans come up with jury-rigged gimmicks of some type, which are repeatedly hauled out as cures for the prob- lem. Nixonomics, Kemp-Roth, supply side, monetarism, and Reaganomics are all simply variations on the same theme; all endorse some measure of state control over the economy, just a different type than propounded by the Democrats, who gave us the New Deal, the Great Society, and the New Frontier.

In some ways the new "supply side" proposals are even more inimical to individuals than are overtly collectivist ones. The supply siders hope to increase government revenues by decreasing taxes, when the optimum for society is to decrease both taxes and government revenues.

In many ways, Reagan's election is an unfortunate thing. He has "positioned" himself, in the parlance of the ad industry, as the defender of free enterprise and traditional American values. As the standard of living inevitably decreases during his term, disaffection with him—and what he is perceived to represent—will grow. In the process, he will devalue free market arguments and discredit true advocates of laissez-faire. The voting public (by definition those who accept the political process as a valid way of structuring the world) will confuse the Republican half-measures with laissez-faire. At the end of Reagan's term, the American people will be told that freedom was tried and failed. Economically speaking, in 1980 the ticking bomb was passed to the new President. If it explodes in his face, as I expect, it will give collectivist politicians someone to run against for decades.

While Reagan will be largely blameless, there's every chance that he will have the bad luck to be the one who reaps the whirlwind for the sins of the last fifty years. Ironically, his programs of deregulation and tax reduction will allow the distortions of the last fifty years to begin to unwind. Although these programs are the only way to straighten out the economy, they are exactly what will precipitate a depression in the short run. As unemployment, inflation, and bankruptcies skyrocket while the general standard of living declines, he could wind up being the most hated man in the country by 1984.

The only real choice he can make is whether we'll have an inflationary or a deflationary depression. Let's examine each possibility.

Reaganomics and a Deflationary Depression

The second definition of a depression is: A period of time when the distortions and misallocations of capital in an economy are liquidated.

Every administration for the last fifty years has been confronted with the choice of either propping up the economy to give the impression of more prosperity or allowing it to collapse and liquidate so things can restructure themselves. That, however, would cause bankruptcies, unemployment, and a lot of unpleasantness; it would certainly raise a cry that whoever was President had "caused" the collapse. And it would certainly appear that way. So instead of precipitating a depression, administrations always move the problem further into the future.

The outstanding feature of Reaganomics and supply side is the reduction of taxes, debt, inflation, and regulations. To the extent it succeeds in that objective, it's going to reverse a trend of the last fifty years, when the entire economy has been structured around high levels of all four. When any of them decreases, distortions and malinvestment are liquidated, and the people and institutions that have grown to count on them will be hurt.

It's ironic that the only thing the government can really do to create prosperity in the long run—the total elimination of government intervention—is the very thing that will cause a depression in the short run.

It seems likely the Reagan Administration sees only the good things that eliminating government intervention will bring; paradoxically it sees only the indirect and delayed effects of its programs and is overlooking the direct and immediate effects—exactly the opposite of what politicians usually do.

A look at what would happen if taxes, regulations, debt, and inflation were eliminated reveals a picture of a deflationary depression.

Taxes. Someone receives each of the tax dollars the government confiscates from someone else. Thus, if taxes are cut back, government employees and welfare recipients of all types will feel the pinch. Every industry the government buys from will be hurt, many bankrupted, and their employees laid off, starting a domino effect.

And that's just the most obvious direct effect of a tax reduction. Taxes cause people to consume fewer of the things that are taxed; the industries manufacturing them are therefore smaller than they would have been in a free market. Other products have been subsidized; in response the industries making them have grown, a bit like cancer cells, absorbing resources that would have gone elsewhere. If subsidies are withheld, recipient industries will contract or be bankrupted. If taxes are ended, others will boom.

Regulations. Reagan's intention is to roll back regulations and reduce the number of government employees.

All regulations, regardless of whether you approve of the intentions behind them or not, cause people to change their actions. Some regulations have spawned whole industries employing millions: bureaucrats to regulate and tax; lawyers to litigate; accountants to keep records; and all the little folks behind the scenes to lend support. If the regulations are ever abolished, all those people will have to find new lines of work.

Debt. There have been lots of complaints about high interest rates since 1979, and they've intensified since the 1980 election. The government can't control all interest rates, because it can't control how many people choose to buy and sell bonds and mortgages in the free market, or how many foreigners choose to hold dollars at interest. But through the Federal Reserve, the state can establish a monetary policy to manipulate the reserve requirements of the banking system (i.e., the amount of loans it can make), and manipulate the discount rate (i.e., the interest rate at which commercial banks can borrow money from the Fed). And the state also sets a fiscal policy, determining how large a deficit it will run, and whether it will borrow the money required from the public or from the Fed.

Consumer debt is another problem. There are three basic ways someone can get money to raise his standard of living: steal it, earn it, or borrow it. Earning it is hard

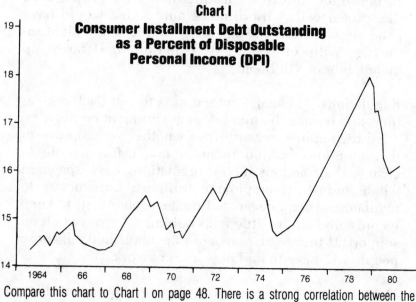

Chart I
Consumer Installment Debt Outstanding as a Percent of Disposable Personal Income (DPI)

Compare this chart to Chart I on page 48. There is a strong correlation between the amount of consumer debt and increases in the CPI.

work, and stealing is dangerous, so many have borrowed as much as possible over the last thirty years.

Borrowing makes people feel wealthier than they are. Debt can certainly raise the standard of living, but only until it has to be paid back with interest.

The high interest rates and general disinflation favored by the Republicans stand to break the bubble of false prosperity fostered by the last thirty years' orgy of debt.

High interest rates encourage savings and discourage borrowing; that's good in the long run. Those high interest rates, however, also stand to collapse industries—such as housing, autos, appliances, and banking—which were built around artificially cheap money. By adopting policies that discourage debt, the Administration will remove the major support underlying the country's present "prosperity."

When enough people are unable to pay their past debts and can't afford to borrow to refinance them, the result could be a 1929-style deflation and a debt liquidation.

Inflation. Every president says he's going to "fight inflation," but, if he does, it will cause a credit collapse exactly like that in the Los Angeles Swimming Pool Case.

The whole country has geared itself to inflation over the last twenty years and has leveraged itself up to "profit" from yet more. If Reagan doesn't take immediate, decisive, and wholehearted action to reinflate, the whole debt pyramid could come crashing down and end the business cycle in a deflationary depression. The Administration economists think they can go between the horns of the deflationary-inflationary dilemma, and engineer a "soft landing." While an unintentional deflation is a real possibility, they'll try to forestall it with more government intervention, if only to "buy time"—

and the result will be more inflation. And if deflation does occur, they'll undoubtedly try to cushion it with some form of intervention. The end result will be an inflationary depression.

Reaganomics and an Inflationary Depression

The Reagan Administration has cut taxes, but hasn't cut spending by the same amount; the result is higher deficits. The overall impact of higher deficits is inflationary.

Programs enacted into law long ago must be paid for out of the current budget. Interest on a government debt of well over a trillion dollars must be serviced.

The deficit itself doesn't directly cause inflation, but its method of financing does. There are two places the government can obtain the money: from the marketplace (i.e., you and me) and from the Fed (i.e., creating money by monetizing the debt).

In view of the fact that spending is not dropping, just growing less rapidly under the new Administration, the trends illustrated in Charts II and III are likely to stay in motion.

When interest rates are already at back-breaking levels, as they now are, and the entire economy is so leveraged with debt that it has to borrow yet more to pay off the old, the trend of government deficits is of critical importance. You can assume that from now on the majority of them will be monetized by the Fed, simply because there is no other choice.

Regardless of whether we have a deflationary collapse along the way, evidence is very strong that we will have an inflationary depression. The government has legal commitments to massively increase expenditures in Social Security and other unfunded liabilities in the coming years, regardless of who is in the White House. Higher federal budgets are virtually mandated by law.

Chart II

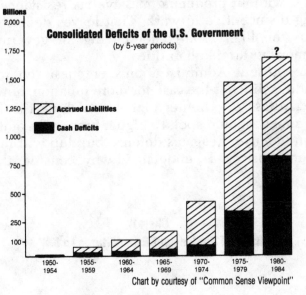

Chart by courtesy of "Common Sense Viewpoint"

Chart III

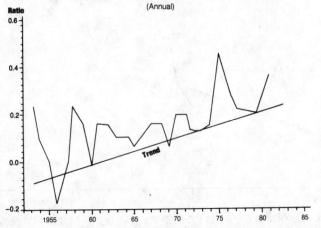

Chart II shows the trend of deficits in absolute dollars. Chart III shows the trend of these deficits relative to other borrowing in the economy.

It is doubtful that direct taxes can be increased much further without producing massive tax resistance and a strong disincentive to work. That leaves deficit financing as the likely source for paying for government's enormous unfunded liabilities.

The present Administration's emphasis on military spending clinches the case for more inflation, however.

Regardless of whether or not you think the federal government should spend a higher proportion of its budget on defense, Reagan's defense buildup will increase consumer prices. To understand why, consider the eco-

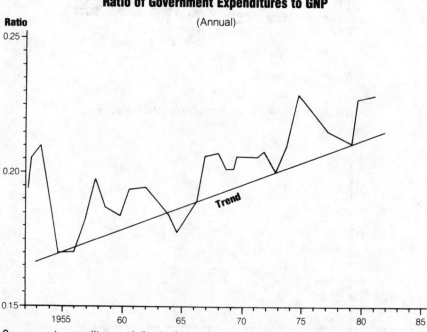

Chart IV
Ratio of Government Expenditures to GNP

(Annual)

Government expenditures relative to the economy have been increasing for decades, as this chart shows. But the government is now forced to finance those expenditures by monetizing its debt, which will cause inflation to go much higher.

nomic difference between taking $1,000 from me and giving it to a person on welfare and giving the same $1,000 to the Pentagon.

I might spend the $1,000 to buy a new TV or some other consumer item. If the government takes that $1,000 from me and gives it to someone on welfare and he buys a TV or some other consumer item with it, the total demand for, and subsequent production of, consumer goods has not changed. But if the $1,000 is given to the Pentagon instead and is used to buy a bomb, the total demand for, and subsequent production of, consumer goods falls by that much.

There are two primary ways consumer price inflation occurs. If either (a) the money supply increases or (b) the supply of consumer goods decreases, consumer prices will rise. So when massive funds are shifted from social to military spending, the end result is that a larger portion of the country's productive capacity is used to produce non-consumable weapons, leaving less consumer goods for people to use. This is highly inflationary for consumer prices.

Despite everyone's desire for the government to solve all the problems confronting them, and the government's best efforts, there's nothing it can do.

Bet On

- The failure of Reaganomics and supply side economics.
- New, desperate efforts to stabilize the economy, which are foredoomed to failure.
- Yourself, not any collective political action.

The Importance of Liquidity

PART **II**

Chapter 5

Generating Cash

Economy is in itself a source of great revenue.
Seneca

A man is rich in proportion to what he can do without.
Thoreau

The Chinese coolie lives in a palm-thatched hovel on a bowl of rice. When he has risen to a higher occupation—hawking peanuts, for example, from a barrow—he still lives on rice and still lives in a hovel. When he has risen farther—to the selling, say, of possibly stolen bicycle parts, he keeps to his hovel and his rice. The result is that he has money to invest. . . . As a success technique this is well worthy of study.
C. Northcote Parkinson

First things first. The liquidation phase of this strategy amounts to marshaling your resources so you know what you've got to play with before the game begins. The first stage of liquidation is to generate cash now tied up in non-earning assets, and cut back on expenses that are depleting assets; that's the subject of this chapter.

The next three chapters cover the tactics of managing that cash—borrowing, lending, and predicting the interest rates that determine which you should do. The point of liquidating is to ensure quick adjustment to change, something there'll be no shortage of.

The investment markets are going to be more treacherous and the economy more chaotic in the 1980s than at any time since the Civil War. You are going to have to be very quick on your feet to survive financially.

Most people alive today have grown up in an environment of ever increasing prosperity, and naturally enough they've planned their lives around the prospect of more of the same. Whenever people project the past into the future, however, they are constructing a mental Maginot Line for themselves. The future always attacks them from an unexpected direction and overwhelms their position.

Liquidating Your Mistakes

Work on the assumption that many of the things you've been doing in the past—that have served you well—are going to become liabilities and mistakes in the future. When the times change, so must the strategies of those who want to survive. To win the battle for investment survival in the '80s, the strategies that worked in the '60s, or even the '70s, won't do.

A lot of people are at least unconsciously counting on the government to bail them out if something goes wrong in their lives in particular or the world in general. Many think the UN will save the world from war, the FDIC will save the banks from failure, and the U.S. government will somehow set the economy right. It's never been prudent to believe that others will take as good care of your interests as you yourself will, though. And until the President says he'll take personal responsibility for balancing my checkbook I expect to retain that responsibility. The more you depend on preconceived concepts and the open-ended promises of others the more you've lost control of your life. Don't expect Reagan, or any of his successors, to "kiss it, and make it better."

Remember, the broadest definition of a depression is a period during which most people's standard of living goes down. The key phrase there is "most people," and you don't have to be one of "most people" if you act intelligently. The program laid out below is not one "most people" are going to take seriously, or have the fortitude to follow. But that's why they will always be "most people"; it's why they aren't as happy, wealthy, or successful as they'd like to be.

The way to keep your standard of living from declining is by investing your surplus capital now, and if you don't have any, getting some. You may have little or no surplus capital at present. If you come to grips with the principles in this book, that need not be a great problem.

The question for many is how to get the capital to invest in the first place. If you don't have some money put aside now to absorb the financial shocks that will hit, not to mention the money to capitalize on the opportunities that come along, your life in the future will be a lot less pleasant than it could be. And *you may always regret the fact that you knew the depression was coming, and knew what to do, but didn't put yourself in a position to take advantage of it*. There are, fortunately, several courses open to get investment capital.

The three-point strategy laid out below may seem radical and won't be easy, but it's going to be a lot easier than life in the next few years if you don't employ it.

1. Sell what you don't need.
2. Cut back your consumption.
3. Earn more money and pay less taxes, which are the subjects of Chapter 10.

Sell What You Don't Need

This section could save you $500 to $5,000 or more. If that figure is significant, read on. If not, skip to page 89. Everybody has unused articles lying around. You may have an extra radio, television, or electric blender. Since you're reading this book, you may have other books you've bought and read that are now sitting on the shelf, or perhaps some unwanted pieces of furniture, artwork, or jewelry. All those things—in fact most things you own—have a market value, a value to someone other than yourself.

First, inventory your possessions. Everything you don't need should be liquidated. "Need," of course, is a relative term; you may figure you need almost everything you have, plus a lot more. A necessity isn't the same as something nice to have, or a convenience item. "Need" means "essential to get by from day to day." Don't be deluded by what the neighbors do or by what advertisers promote. They've turned yesterday's luxuries into necessities. And all those extraneous things cost money to maintain. They must be stored, cleaned, and repaired. They may consume electric power. Sell the second car, as well as the vacation condo, and look at a smaller house. By liquidating them, you'll not only generate cash but reduce expenses—the next step of the plan.

Use classified ads to sell big-ticket items, and contact friends who might need what you don't. Unload what remains at a pawn shop, a yard sale, an auction house, or a secondhand store. And don't pay any attention to the opinions of others, unless you value their opinions more than your own welfare. When the process is over you'll be free of possessions that were probably just weighing you down and making it hard to maintain an "air mobile" mental attitude, while they took up valuable storage space and tied up precious capital.

As a practical matter, you're never able to sell everything that got hauled out of the closets, attic, and garage. Nobody else wants that ugly tie or those old paperbacks either. Not to worry; it's an opportunity to realize some tax savings. Contribute the leftover goodies to your favorite charity and take an itemized tax deduction.

There are over 300,000 tax-exempt organizations and a great many of them are happy to get secondhand goods and contributions. Of course, the IRS likes you to think it keeps a close eye on secondhand donations which you appraise yourself, but if the deductions are legitimate, don't hold back. It may not be cash in your pocket at the yard sale, but it will be worth cash next April 15. Depending on your tax bracket, those junk items could save up to 50 percent of the top dollar you were asking for them. Those salvaged tax dollars should be placed immediately into the investment program outlined later in this book.

After getting rid of all that accumulated junk, you'll feel as though you've just completed a good diet—light, trim, and ready for action. You'll have freed yourself mentally as well as physically.

But the psychological benefits are simply a bonus. The main idea was to generate tax-free cash—$500, $5,000, or $50,000—the amount depends on your position. And properly invested that money could multiply by ten, while the things you sold would continue to depreciate. If you want those things again in the future, you'll be able to buy them, and much more, and still have money left over.

At the same time you're doing this, begin step two of your liquidation plan: Cut back your level of consumption.

Cut Back Your Consumption

Not spending money is actually twice as important as either earning it or saving it. Every dollar you don't spend is in effect saving about two dollars in before-taxes income. Don't think about what something costs; consider rather how much time it takes you to get the net money to buy it. A dollar saved in today's tax environment is really the equivalent of two dollars earned.

Many of the suggestions that follow may smack of a New England miser's philosophy. But, as one wealthy man said when asked why he was comparison shopping for groceries: "This is how a man like me got to be a man like me."

The only way you can grow in wealth is by producing more than you consume; and unless you're already on the borderline of malnutrition, you can cut back on consumption. Over the last few decades of conspicuous consumption and rising expectations, most people have gotten used to living up to and beyond their means. Change that now while you're still in control of the situation, rather than later when lack of planning and precautions could force you into a corner. Every dollar cut from consumption can be allocated to your investment program. Examples? Here are just a few of the thousands of possibilities:

Communication. Whenever possible don't make a long-distance call, write a letter. Use UPS instead of the U.S. Postal Service for sending packages; UPS is usually cheaper (and invariably faster and more reliable).

When making a long-distance call, dial direct after rates drop in the evening or on weekends. If you make a number of long-distance calls, do so through a private microwave network such as MCI (1151 Seven Locks Road, Rockville, Maryland 20854, [800-638-8505] or Sprint (SP Communications Co., 3600 Telegraph Road, Birmingham, Mississippi 48010, [800-521-4949]. Both have minimum-usage bills, but can cut costs 50 percent or more in some cases.

Transportation. Unload that prestigious high-profile expensive car and get an older, cheaper model. Selling your $12,000 Buick for an old $3,000 Chevrolet puts $9,000 in your pocket, even if the fuel bill is somewhat higher. It needn't be that much higher, though, if you use part of the difference to buy a bicycle or small motorcycle for local commuting; and you can always exercise the discipline of walking a mile to the store rather than riding. It takes about fifteen minutes, and over the long run will mean fewer medical bills as well.

Whenever it makes financial sense, use public transportation. The time you're not busy driving can be used to bone up on an interesting or potentially profitable subject. If you do drive, keep your car properly maintained and the tires properly inflated; both can reduce fuel consumption. When you have to fly, plan in advance and use the airline's discount fares; when you can, take a night flight.

Food. It's estimated the average American household literally throws out over $120 a year in edible food, just because of poor menu planning; buying more selectively is the first way to save money on food. Another is to grow and/or preserve your own. The whole process is educational and, as the success of magazines like *Mother Earth News* and *Co-Evolution Quarterly* prove, even fashionable. You'll never starve if you know how to grow food; too bad about the neighbors.

Energy. Need I even suggest that you reduce your consumption by saving on energy? Even if you've heard about the advantages of converting to wood heat, buying a solar collector, insulating the home and reconditioning its heating system, as well as simply lowering the thermostat on the hot water heater, you may not have done it. Now's the time to put all that good advice into effect wherever possible.

Children. If you have children, it's wise to let them in on the shape of things to come so they will willingly contribute to the effort. It is difficult to cut back your consumption when your ten-year-old wants the latest $200 video game and your teenage daughter insists on $49.95 designer jeans. Don't feel guilty about putting your foot down and closing your wallet. You don't owe them frivolous luxuries. The sooner you start treating them like responsible adults, the sooner they'll become responsible adults.

It is an opportunity to give your children an understanding of basic economics. If your child wants something, let him figure out what he's going to do or create to get it. The process will increase his street smarts and improve his ethics, while he can get what he wants without pressing you. Everybody wins.

For perspective, don't forget to mention that in your time the baseball bubble gum cards cost only ten cents (or a nickel, or was it two cents?). It's an American tradition to regale the kids with stories about how cheap things used to be.

Explain that price increases affect your salary the same way, and the family must pull together. You're all in the present economic jackpot together. They'll appreciate your confidence and trust.

Entertainment. This is a stickler, because you don't want to take the fun out of life, but this can be a major expense. An evening of drinking in a bar, a restaurant meal, and incidentals can set you back a mini Krugerrand or 1,000 shares of a penny stock, either of which could earn you ten for one in short order. When you make it a night on the town, you're choosing the one over the other. Entertainment doesn't have to be expensive. Movies can be seen on television rather than at the theater, and both HBO and cable television are much less costly, per movie, than theaters. Cancel magazine and newspaper subscriptions and find out where the library is. Keep reading, but buy used books or go to the library. Going to the racetrack and pumping quarters into video games are out, and so are lottery tickets. Not only does the state rake off about 50 percent (the local bookie only takes one-third for the so-called "numbers racket"), but taxes are due on your winnings, and all that money goes to the state. It's silly to enrich your greediest adversary in the process of losing money.

It doesn't cost anything to play local sports—softball, soccer, and touch football. Take up hiking, backpacking, or bicycling; all those things will improve your health while costing little or nothing. The exercise might induce you to quit smoking, which at a pack a day runs close to $300 a year before taxes, and really costs you closer to $600, because that's what you have to earn to support the habit. The indirect economic benefits will be lower doctor bills and higher productivity.

Learn to amuse yourself, and get out of the habit of paying others to do it for you. It'll not only save money, but will help put you in an active, causative frame of mind instead of one that's the passive result of whatever some entertainment entrepreneur lays out.

While liquidating past financial mistakes and cutting back on consumption, you can take two more steps to generate cash: borrow to generate more capital, and keep your own money working as hard as it can.

That, of course, is what interest rates and the next chapter are all about.

Required Actions
- *Liquidate all non-essentials.*
- *Cut expenses radically.*

Chapter **6**

Predicting Interest Rates

*The chief value of money lies in the fact that one lives in a
world in which it is overestimated.*
H. L. Mencken

The first considerations about debt are psychological,
not financial. What might be objectively the best plan in
the world may turn out to be the worst one for you if
you're unable to bear the risks of putting it into effect.
Freedom is the main reason why you may want to have
nothing to do with debt.

Money represents freedom, and when you're in debt
you are not free. Cash assets liberate their owner; debt
imprisons. The time you spend working is not yours,
because the fruits of your labor go to your creditor. Debt
is a shackle that weighs you down, and in the '80s you
want to be able to float like Muhammad Ali's butterfly
so that you're free to sting like a bee when the time
comes.

Your flexibility decreases with debt. When you're already borrowed to the hilt and an investment opportunity presents itself—and there will be some incredible
ones in the years ahead—you may not be able to take
advantage of it.

Most people have hardly given the idea of debt a second thought over the last thirty years as the U.S. developed an enormous credit economy. People buy houses,
cars, and furniture on credit. Plastic money takes care of
clothes, meals, vacations, and incidentals. And if the
burden of finally paying for it all becomes too great, the
debtwise consumer simply activates his line of credit at

94

the bank, borrows more to pay off the other borrowings, and even has a bit of cash left over. That game, however, is rapidly coming to an end because of high interest rates.

Inflation or Deflation?

The question of whether to be a net borrower or a net lender in the '80s gets us back to the question of whether the depression will be inflationary or deflationary. Since it will be inflationary, you would do well to owe as much as possible, since the dollar will eventually die; but there are so many permutations of how its death will occur that, unfortunately, the path to profits is not as simple as just staying in debt and counting on the incompetence of the government. You could be hurt badly waiting for the currency collapse if it takes a little longer than we anticipate. So even if you can get down not only what is going to happen, but the sequence, and the proper time frame, you've got to predict the level of interest rates accurately while all this is going on.

Interest Rates

Debt has been the road to riches—or at least to living above one's means—over the last thirty years. That's because inflation has generally been higher than interest rates. In real terms it cost nothing to borrow money, because principal was losing value faster than interest was adding to costs. But the amount of debt can't continue rising forever; it will eventually self-destruct. Interest rates will have a lot to do with how that happens.

The government can control interest rates in three major ways: by having the Fed decrease bank reserve requirements (the percentage of assets commercial banks must keep on deposit with the Fed), by selling its debt to the Fed (which increases the money supply), and by having the Fed lower the discount rate. Each of these actions increases the money supply. In the short run, interest rates, which are the price of money, go down simply because more money is available; so the direct, immediate consequence of an increase in the money supply is lower rates. The delayed consequences of it, however, are always even higher rates.

Interest rates reflect four basic factors: (1) *the demand for credit;* (2) *the amount of saving;* (3) *the rate of inflation;* and (4) *the creditworthiness of the borrower.* Each of these factors is closely, and subtly, related to the others.

The Demand for Credit

The more that individuals, corporations, and governments borrow, the higher the price of money—interest—will go. That's why recessions usually lower interest rates, because consumers stop borrowing to buy and corporations stop borrowing to expand in response; instead they pay off debt and save for fear of hard times.

The wild card is government. As the economy slows in a recession, its tax revenues drop, and that alone would force government to borrow more, even if its spending remained the same. But since government has given itself the mandate (e.g., the Full Employment Act of 1946) to create make-work jobs and fund welfare programs for ailing corporations and the unemployed, its spending actually rises during a recession today. Recessions, as a result, have become an opportunity for the state to absorb an even larger portion of the nation's production.

Deficits have ballooned during past recessions and will grow even further in the future. Those deficits, however, have to be financed. The demand for credit from government alone will put ever increasing upward pressure on interest rates.

The Amount of Saving

Saving is the setting aside of present production for future consumption. It's real wealth represented by money. If people stop saving, the government can print up all the money it wants, but it can't replace the real wealth people aren't saving. This is the distinction between "credit" and "savings." The government can create credit by simple bookkeeping entries, but only private individuals who create real wealth can save. There's very little incentive to save when prices are rising rapidly. If a currency is stable, most people prefer to save a portion of their income because it leads to a higher standard of living. They can draw upon what they've saved, plus the interest that it's earned, and it's worth their while to defer consumption. A high rate of savings works to reduce interest rates by increasing the supply of capital that can be borrowed. If inflation is high enough, however, people have no incentive to save —and there's nothing to lend.

The creation of credit through state action (i.e., manipulation of fiscal and monetary policy) can give the appearance of saving by driving down interest rates. But creating more credit actually just further discourages real saving by exacerbating inflation. Higher inflation causes lower savings, which in turn results in higher interest rates. Inflation also causes savers to demand a compensatory interest premium.

The Rate of Inflation

Inflation is the creation by fiat of new currency and credit; price rises are the result of inflation, not its cause.

As the government increases the supply of credit to hold down interest rates, savers demand a premium to compensate for the resulting inflation. Interest rates are, therefore, a function of inflation.

Unfortunately for savers, however, high interest rates are no guarantee of a good real return. Anybody who wants to can get 40 percent bank interest rates in Iceland, 100 percent rates in Israel, or 120 percent rates in Argentina. The problem is that interest is paid in local currency and those rates only approximate the domestic inflation rates in those countries. You still wind up losing money. In Germany in 1923, interest rates of many thousand percent were available, but of no avail as the mark became totally worthless.

Nominal interest rates, for that reason, can be a dangerous illusion. At the same time, chasing after high real rates can be just as dangerous; the risk doesn't normally carry an adequate reward.

The Creditworthiness of the Borrower

Interest rates also compensate for the risk of lending, the danger of the borrower's default. That's why AAA-rated bonds yield less than B-rated bonds.

The less debt a borrower already has, the less risky he is; the more debt he carries, the greater the danger of default. It's been very smart to borrow to the hilt over the last thirty years, but all that borrowing has not only helped drive rates to where they now are but has made the borrowers uncreditworthy. As business slows, many will need new loans just to pay off debts incurred when they were expanding during good times. There could be dozens of defaults among Soviet bloc and Third World countries, scores among well-known businesses, and hundreds of thousands among consumers and real estate speculators.

The risk premium will skyrocket across the board, driving interest rates to very high real levels. Only borrowers with very large profit margins will be able to afford to borrow.

What You Should Expect

The bottom line is that you shouldn't expect interest rates to go down (other than for brief periods) until the market pressures for high rates (all four of them) moderate. The government was able to keep interest rates at artificially low and stable levels for decades by manipulating the money supply; the consequence of that is today's abnormally high and very unstable rates. They will come down only through a drastic liquidation of all the debt outstanding, the elimination of inflation, and a basic reorientation of the structure of society itself. That's part of what the Greater Depression is all about, and part of why, in the long run, it will prove a good thing. For decades people got used to low rates and considered them part of the cosmic landscape; now they seem to think they'll stay high forever as well, although they're not quite as happy about it. People will once again get low rates, but not, unfortunately, in the way they expected. Both real and nominal interest rates will fall when the long-term business cycle begun at the bottom of the 1930s depression climaxes.

It's going to happen at the point when the government can neither restimulate the economy for fear of hyperinflation nor stop stimulating for fear of a deflationary collapse. In other words, exactly where we are right now. The situation is very dangerous for borrowers because the whole thing could get out of control in a deflationary credit collapse, and for lenders because it could escalate into a hyperinflation even if loans don't default. The traditional solution to this dilemma has been to stay in cash, but that won't work today.

Today it's foolish to have more than a minimum amount of cash on hand for everyday expenses. Unless you keep all your money in $100 bills tucked under your mattress (a sure losing proposition), you've got to lend your surplus to someone, at least in the short term between investments. In an environment as turbulent as today's, you're between a rock and a hard place. You need a strategy.

There are two possible logical responses to the situation. One is to neither borrow nor lend dollars; neither save nor use credit. That goes between the horns of the dilemma and effectively insulates you from the problem. The other workable alternative is to be both a borrower and a lender—but of different types of debt, on different terms.

The long-term trend is for higher inflation and interest rates. Nevertheless, even though that trend is almost certain to continue, it's dangerous to bet everything on it, because the cyclical downturns that come every few years are becoming more likely to turn into a full-blown deflation each time. The proper strategy is built around this pattern.

In brief, *borrow all that you can, on long term, with fixed interest rates wherever possible. Lend only for the very short term, so that you can move with fluctuations of the rates*. The reasons for that will become even more apparent after you've read Chapter 17 on real estate.

The next chapter covers borrowing—or strategic debt management; Chapter 8 covers lending—or strategic cash management—specifically money market funds. Together they'll allow you to put an understanding of the credit markets into profitable practice.

Bet On ⎯⎯⎯⎯⎯

- *Interest rates to remain high, and go higher, until the entire financial system restructures.*
- *In the long run, debt will either be defaulted on or paid back in worthless dollars, or both.*

Chapter **7**

Strategic Debt Management

I just read an article the other day where they estimate that there's less than one half of one percent of people who can lay their hands on $50,000 liquid cash overnight.
Jimmy Hoffa

Any debt you incur in the years ahead should comply with the following five rules:

1. Borrow Only for Capital Goods or Investments, Not Consumer Goods

It's a good idea to define the key terms of that piece of advice, to head off any misunderstanding.

A *capital good* can be defined as anything that produces more wealth, from a business typewriter to a steel mill. A loan for capital goods—a business loan—should be self-amortizing, i.e., it should pay itself off with the increased profits it generates.

An *investment* can be defined as anything that will maintain or increase its value over time. A loan for the types of investments recommended in the rest of this book is worth considering, but with the understanding that there may be substantial fluctuations in their value. Loans for expensive cars (such as Mercedes and Rolls) and houses are not investment loans. These things have resembled investments because they've kept pace with the depreciation of the dollar in the past, but that's not likely to continue. They're just fashionable consumer goods whose prices have been driven up by the influx of a lot of borrowed money, and are at artificially high levels for that reason. At this point you can win only if the money you borrow to buy them (plus interest) loses value even faster than they do.

A *consumer good* can be defined as anything which you own primarily to increase your standard of living.

Disposable consumer goods like clothes, furniture, and vacations have little or no value to others, so it's almost always a mistake to buy them on credit. If you can't afford to pay cash for consumer goods, then you simply can't afford them. It's a rare person who can keep track of what he can really afford (for cash) once burdened under a bunch of revolving charge payments. If you're that rare person, go ahead and buy consumer goods on credit, but it's not a good policy.

2. Borrow on the Longest Terms Possible

A thirty-year fixed-interest loan on a house or anything else is literally a gift, since the dollar may not even survive for another ten years in its present form. The longer the terms, the more time is on your side.

3. Borrow at a Fixed Interest Rate

If there's a choice between a floating-rate and a fixed-rate loan, always take the latter even if it costs more. If interest rates drop, you can always pay off the fixed-rate loan early, but if they rise it's the lender's problem.

4. Don't Go Overboard

A lot of people have taken out loans expecting inflation to bail them out. It will in the long run, but they may not last that long. Any and all loans you take out should be comfortable to service from your regular income alone. Don't count on investment appreciation, or inflation, or a government imposed debt moratorium, or an inheritance from your rich uncle to bail you out. Things just may not turn out as you plan. First things first, and that means making sure you can survive regardless of what happens. The profits that "would have, should have, and could have" been won't mean much if you're forced into receivership before they mature.

5. Don't Be a Lender

Not lending is an obvious corollary of all the above, but some people will undoubtedly fail to make the connection.

The best general rule is to lend money only if you don't care whether or not you get it back. Only two things can happen: You'll get back less valuable dollars, or you won't get them back at all. Don't be deluded by a high interest rate, since you'll be paying taxes at ordinary income rates on it.

Just so there's no confusion, I don't consider money market accounts or bonds to be loans within this context, because they are liquid and you can get out of them instantly. And bonds offer speculative opportunities from time to time. Forget other loans.

Just as some reasons for borrowing are better than others, some sources are better as well.

Where to Borrow

There are six main sources of credit that most people can tap to generate capital:

1. Life insurance.
2. Real estate second mortgages.
3. Margin borrowing.

4. Credit cards.
5. Loans by mail.
6. Overdraft accounts.

Life Insurance

The cash value from a whole-life insurance policy offers the least costly way to borrow. If you have such a policy, the loan interest rate will probably range from 5 to 8 percent. When about double that is available from U.S. Treasury securities and even more from top-grade corporate bonds, it's ridiculous to leave the cash with an insurance company. Borrow it all, and do it now. It's a long-term loan on which you are *never* obligated to repay the principal, only the artificially low interest. Buying cash-value insurance may have been a mistake in the first place, but a 100 percent policy loan will help recoup some of your losses.

Of course, if everyone takes that advice, then the insurance companies are in serious trouble. (You don't have to feel guilty about it, because insurance companies are in serious trouble anyway. Their bond and mortgage portfolios have been crushed by interest rates, and inflation will ultimately destroy those assets totally. The real estate they own is yet another problem.) It won't be long before the public figures that out and panics; no one wants to be last in line in a run on the bank or, in this case, insurance company. The insurance companies have safeguarded themselves to some extent by including a provision in all cash-value policies giving them the right to delay granting a loan for up to six months if they choose, and most will be forced to exercise that provision in the near future. And that certainly won't increase the public's confidence in them. So even if you don't currently need the money in your insurance policy, it's wise to borrow it immediately. Act now, and beat the last minute rush.

Real Estate Second Mortgages

It may be a better idea to sell your house than borrow against it; I cover this in the real estate chapter. If you can't sell the house, though, at a minimum borrow all the equity out of it. That way if the housing market collapses, it's the lender's problem more than yours. There are much more rewarding, and safer, places for your home equity than tied up in your home.

Margin Borrowing on Securities

Unlike the "margin loan" you can take out on your house, brokers' margin loans are no bargain.

First, the interest is at or above the market, and it fluctuates with the market. Second, should the securities you borrow against drop in value, you'll have to post more collateral. And if the stock market crashes, you're personally liable for the loan. By contrast, real estate loans are usually for a fixed interest rate, and are generally non-recourse (in other words, if the payer defaults he cannot be held personally liable for the amount of the debt).

Brokers' loans are useful in playing the securities market but not for generating capital.

Credit Cards

If you have ever used a fifty- or a hundred-dollar bill in a store or restaurant, you know the look of skepticism that can cross the proprietor's face. He seems to be asking himself whether you're a counterfeiter, a drug dealer, or a successful income tax evader. Avoiding such confrontations is just one reason to observe the first rule of credit cards, which is simply to use them whenever possible—but only when you're not concerned about privacy, because each use leaves a paper trail and compromises your privacy.

A better reason to use credit cards is that they let you borrow interest-free for at least a few weeks. Interest is the time value of money, and the money a credit card "fronts" to the merchant frees your cash to earn at the high rates easily available today in money market funds. By the time you get the bill and wait the maximum time to pay it—before incurring finance charges—the money owed will be worth 2 or 3 percent less, discounting current interest rates. The name of the game is "cash management," which is to say, "Collect by airmail, pay by dogsled." For that reason you want to avoid widely advertised "credit cards that act like a check," which debit your bank account almost immediately.

Credit cards are a phenomenon. There are at least 8,000 separate banks in the U.S. offering American Express, Visa, or Mastercard; and until 1980 all of them were interested in distributing as much plastic as possible, to anyone who would take it. That mania, of course, has ended and the banks will eventually have huge consumer loan losses to remember it by; but it was fun while it lasted. A California pharmacist (Walter Cavanaugh) holds the world record for credit-card acquisition with more than 800 cards; many of them are Mastercards and Visas issued by different banks. There is no legal limit on the number you can get, just a practical limit to the number you can carry around and use. Each card usually offers an additional line of credit as well, and you never know when that could come in handy. For that reason, it might be wise to contact as many banks as possible and arrange as many credit cards as possible. Don't use them; simply treat them as an insurance policy of credit.

Loans by Mail

You have probably seen those intriguing advertisements in newspapers' financial pages offering to lend up to $20,000 unsecured, and strictly by mail. Anyone who has a good credit rating, a reasonable income, a few assets, and the ability to fill in an application can get such loans from several companies that I'm aware of. Interest rates are quite high, and vary with the amount borrowed and the length of the repayment schedule. But it costs nothing to apply, and when you need money it's only a telephone call away once you've been approved.

Terms are similar with all the companies, and both the credit limits and repayment schedules are more liberal than those offered by local small loan companies. The companies in this business feel that the approximately 50 to 100 percent premium they can get over market interest rates compensates for the increased risk and transaction costs. Maybe it does, but I'd prefer not to be one of their shareholders when the business cycle comes to a final climax.

Use one of the following firms:

Beneficial Executive Loans, 2858 Stevens Creek Boulevard, San Jose, California 95128.

Commercial Credit, P.O. Box 1990, Bellaire, Texas 77401.

Dial Financial Corporation, P.O. Box 2321, Santa Ana, California 92707.

Postal Thrift Loans, 703 Douglas Street, Sioux City, Iowa 51102.

Overdraft Accounts

Banks provide the best way of borrowing money, through automatic overdraft accounts. It's one of the more interesting things to have happened to money since the invention of the printing press.

Not too long ago, when banks were simply warehouses for the storage and transfer of money, there was no such thing as a "consumer loan." Before the days of the Federal Reserve and the Federal Deposit Insurance Corporation, the main way a banker lured in depositors was by showing how conservative and prudent he was, not what a nice guy he could be. Loans were generally made only on projects that guaranteed the principal would be paid off at the end of a short term—like financing the completion of a building or the costs of marketing a crop. But as America has transformed itself from a society of producers to one of consumers, the banks have flowed with the tide.

You may recall the Norman Rockwell painting of the young married couple, conservatively dressed in the fashions of the '50s, with their eyes turned humbly toward the floor as they supplicate before a glassy-eyed loan officer, offering him all sorts of co-signatures and security. In those days, visiting a bank was a serious endeavor—the place looked like a mausoleum—and speaking to a banker was like counseling with one's confessor, except that the banker wanted more information and thought that the fact that you were borrowing was in itself sinful.

That, however, was before the age of rock-and-roll banking. The folks who lend money are no longer conservative gray-flannel-minded types. Banks lend money the way Mad Man Muntz used to sell TVs.

The millennium in consumer banking arrived in the early 1970s with the automatic overdraft account. Banks call such accounts Chextra, Ready Reserve, Cash Advance, and other catchy names. They're the next best thing to a second job for someone who needs money.

Today, through the mails, it is not hard to establish a line of credit for from $500 to $20,000 or more with most banks. It is unquestionably the neatest, cleanest, and most flexible way you can borrow; in fact, it's probably all you really need to know about the subject of credit. There are several reasons why you should have one or more of these credit lines:

- *They are easy to get.* I still remember a conversation with one naive banker in 1980. "Almost anyone can get one of our overdraft accounts," he said in explaining how financial irresponsibility may even be helpful in getting credit. He'd just granted one to a woman because she had recently bounced several checks, and he felt it would keep her from doing so in the future. One would think that a reason to close her account rather than to offer her a loan.
- *The credit is available anytime.* Once an application is approved, all you have to do to get a loan is write a check. No waiting for credit approval, no loitering around a banker's office while the papers are drawn up. A loan is as close as your checkbook.
- *The credit is available anywhere.* If you need a loan in Pittsburgh, or Paris, you have it.
- *The credit is available for any reason.* Ask a banker to lend money specifically to buy stock, and, by law, he can advance no more than 50 percent of its value, and then only if the stock is deemed suitable. If you need a loan to make a quick speculation in the commodities market, you probably won't get it at all. *But an overdraft account is, literally, a blank check.* A stock speculator can legally borrow $10,000, for instance, from an overdraft account to purchase stock, and let the broker lend another $5,000 with the stock as security.
- *The credit is available at fixed interest.* Once activated, overdrafts usually run at a fixed rate of interest. That may change as the financial markets get crazier, but banks are usually at least six months or a year behind the times.

How can banks afford to do this? In a sound banking environment they couldn't. If the Federal Reserve were abolished, banks could only issue bank notes or make loans for as much as had been deposited with them for that purpose. If a person deposited $1,000 (i.e., $1,000 worth of gold) the bank might guarantee him 3 percent for one year and act as a broker to lend the money to someone else for 6 percent for the same period, reaping a 3 percent profit. Because there is a fixed underlying amount of gold that only one person has the right to use at a time, there can be no inflation. Today, it's legal for a bank to lend over 80 percent of a deposit to someone. When that money is redeposited, it, in turn, may be used as a "reserve" for another loan, and so forth. This is one of the ways the money supply is increased and inflation is caused. It is also one of the reasons banking can be so profitable—and why banks still lend for 15 to 18 percent in the face of 15 percent inflation; they are able, in effect, to lend the same money multiple times. It's also one of the many reasons why you should borrow money from banks but never deposit it with them.

An overdraft is in some ways better than money in the bank. With an overdraft, the money is available when you need it and doesn't cost a thing until you do. Depreciation of the dollar works for you, not against you. Inflation can play tricks with both accounting and values.

One of the more bizarre characteristics of these overdraft loans is that they never really have to be paid off. There are two variations on this theme. In the first, suppose your credit line is $2,000 and you borrow $1,000. Some banks simply increase your loan by the interest costs from month to month (i.e., next month you owe $1,020, then $1,040.40, and so on). Not until compound interest reaches your credit limit need you post any real cash.

Most banks, however, require the cash repayment of some portion (generally about one-twentieth) of the loan each month, either by writing a check to them, or allowing them to debit your regular checking account. But nothing stops the customer from borrowing that same amount back the same day, perhaps by just activating his overdraft at another bank. He needn't ever get off the credit merry-go-round.

If nothing else, borrowing heavily makes good sense for tax reasons. After federal and state levies, many people reading this book may be near or above the 50 percent bracket. Since interest is tax deductible, that effectively cuts the cost of borrowing in half, and with it your risk. There is still a risk, though. Deflation.

Deflation and Debt

If the government doesn't manipulate its fiscal and monetary policies properly to keep the economy and credit expanding fast enough, the daisy chain of debt could easily break. Peter can't pay Paul, Paul can't pay the bank, and the bank can't pay the depositors. It's 1929 all over again.

That's because, unlike the collapse of 1929, everybody is in debt this time, not just the stock speculators and farmers who borrowed on future crops. Almost everyone who could possibly get a loan to buy a house has done so. Everyone who has credit cards has used them to buy in the expectation (hope?) that inflation will drive prices even higher. Most large stores offer charge accounts. All banks have overdraft checking. The government itself has vast numbers of programs to lend out the taxpayers' money, often intentionally to those least able to repay it.

These things are new and different since the last depression, and they're part of the reason why if there's a credit collapse, as there was in '29, it will be different. When everybody is a debtor and nobody can afford to pay, the government will find it "politically impossible" to allow a default. (Whenever that catch phrase is used, it is usually a variation on the theme "Since everybody is stealing, let's make stealing legal, since we can't put everybody in jail.") Rather than see houses repossessed by the townful and bankruptcies swell the court dockets, the government will probably place a moratorium on debt repayment until it can figure out what to do. So while being in debt was the worst thing possible during the last depression, it could turn out to be a non-problem during this one, since the debt probably won't have to be repaid. Which is really a shame. Instead of letting the shaky debt structure collapse, the government will create even more problems by propping it up. Rather than let high-living debtors and foolish creditors take their lumps, the government will win the votes of the debtors through a loan moratorium and a write-down of some sort and then win the gratitude of the creditors by a bailout of some type. That, of course, means not only more government controls but much, much more inflation to finance the bailout. Your moral obligation to repay the debt you incurred won't be removed, but your legal obligation probably will be. When you consider "the political realities," if you can stay in debt long enough, it's almost a risk-free proposition. There is, however, another alternative should the burden grow too great for most people: bankruptcy.

Bankruptcy as a Cop-Out

If inflation is too slow to bail them out and the government doesn't step in wholesale, many people will declare bankruptcy. It's a growing trend. (Personal bankruptcies in 1981 were at the highest level since 1969—a total of 452,145.) The advantages of going bankrupt are certainly well promoted; many unscrupulous financial advisers and shyster lawyers make a lucrative business of encouraging people to take advantage of their "constitutional right" to discharge their debts every seven years. But just because it's constitutional or legal doesn't mean it's ethical. Voluntary bankruptcy is theft, pure and simple. If you borrow money you are obligated to repay it. If you're foolish or incompetent or unlucky and find yourself unable to meet the debt when its due, that's not an excuse.

If someone gets over his head and can't pay, one may lose a little respect for his ability. Respect for his character, however, can only grow if, despite difficulties, he arranges to make good on the debt in the future. But if someone hides behind the law to engineer a default, then it's impossible to respect either his ability or his character.

At present the bankruptcy laws allow a person to default on his obligations every seven years. Suppose they were changed to allow it every three years, or every year? Could organized society continue?

Bankruptcy laws allow people to escape responsibility for their actions and, further, let them feel it's okay to do so. The laws are dehumanizing and destructive. But you'll see plenty of bankrupts in the years to come as people rise or sink to their natural level.

It's dangerous to do business with a bankrupt, because if a person is capable of using the law to defraud those who've trusted him with their goods or money, then he's capable of other destructive, anti-social acts. Bankruptcy is a legal option when dealing with debt, but one I hope you don't consider. The debt structure is a fact of life. It's too bad that a lot of innocent people will be hurt when it collapses.

Whatever happens, though, having regrets about it won't do any good for anyone. We don't make the rules, we just play the game. The chips will fall where they may, and under the circumstances you'll do well to grab as many as you can when the game comes to an end. If the thought makes you feel guilty, you can always redistribute your wealth to those you think are more deserving at some point in the future. If you let the opportunity offered by smart debt management evade you, however, you may have to rely on others redistributing their assets to you if they feel you're deserving. Pay your money, as it were, and take your choice.

The first part of your cash management strategy was to borrow properly; the second part is to lend properly. That's where money market funds come in.

Four Fundamentals of Strategic Debt Management

- *Even if the economy experiences a deflationary collapse, it will remain wiser to be a net borrower rather than a net lender.*
- *Borrow only for self-liquidating business deals and low-risk investments.*
- *Borrow on the longest terms possible.*
- *Borrow for a fixed rate, even if it's higher than a floating rate.*

Chapter 8

Money Market Funds

Given the political, monetary and economic outlook in the world today, the "full faith and credit" of the government of the United States and that of other major nation-states isn't worth the paper it is printed on.
Jerome F. Smith

The cure for evil and disorder is more liberty, not suppression.
Alexander Berkman

Money market funds are mutual funds that invest in large-denomination short-term money market instruments issued by the Treasury, government agencies, banks, and corporations. In practice, they are much more than just another type of mutual fund.

Money market funds are the free market's answer to a banking system at the point of collapse. They're one of the most prominent ways in which the Greater Depression is equalizing the average man with those who have Big Money. High inflation and interest rates spurred development of the funds, and the funds offer a perfect example of the government causing the problem and the free market presenting a solution. Since the development of the funds there is no longer any reason to keep money in a bank beyond what's needed for day-to-day convenience.

The first money market fund (MMF) was started in 1972. The assets of all funds together totaled only $4 billion as late as September 1977, but from there they've grown hyperbolically to approximately $200 billion in over 110 funds today.

Chart I

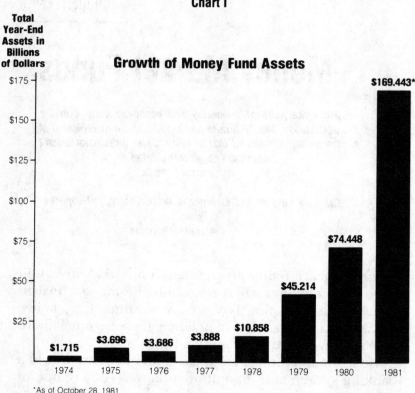

Total
Year-End
Assets in
Billions
of Dollars

Growth of Money Fund Assets

$169.443*

$175 —

$150 —

$125 —

$100 —

$75 —

$74.448

$50 —

$45.214

$25 —

$10.858

$3.696 $3.686 $3.888

$1.715

1974   1975   1976   1977   1978   1979   1980   1981

*As of October 28. 1981

For years Americans had no choice but to accept the niggardly few percent available on savings accounts because of a law known as Regulation Q. Like a great many laws, it was passed with the connivance of industry to keep costs down. Instead of competing with one another on interest rates banks competed on the number of clock radios, toasters, and electric blankets they could dispense to new accounts. High market rates of interest were always available for U.S. dollar deposits from banks in Canada, Switzerland, the Bahamas, and dozens of other countries; but few Americans knew about it because the laws also prohibited foreign banks from soliciting retail accounts in the U.S., while Treasury reporting requirements discouraged Americans from investing overseas. The entrepreneurs who started the money market funds executed an end run around the overregulated and dangerously illiquid banks.

The money market funds came to the rescue of the small saver who never before had had enough money to buy the government's Treasury bills (minimum $10,000) or the banks' large certificates of deposit (minimum $100,000), which carry market rates of interest. They've done so in four significant ways.

The Advantages of Money Market Funds

There are four major advantages the funds can offer over banks: (1) *higher yields;* (2) *instant liquidity;* (3) *more safety;* and (4) *more privacy.* Each of these advantages, however, is potentially a double-edged sword. There's never a free lunch in the investment world, but by choosing a money market fund responsibly, you can have higher yield, more liquidity, more safety, and more privacy than banks offer, with few attendant disadvantages.

Yield

The interest available on savings accounts isn't even worth considering. Even the bank's widely touted small certificates of deposit pay rates several percent below what's available in the MMFs, and impose penalties for early withdrawal. They can get away with it partly because of the public's ignorance and partly because banks are insured by the FDIC, which makes people feel safer. The appearance of extra safety seems to make the disadvantages worthwhile to some.

The money market funds offer among the highest yields available today anywhere, on the most liberal terms. Deposits earn interest from day of deposit to day of withdrawal, with no penalty for early withdrawal.

By using an MMF, the small saver can reap a yield only ½ percent less than someone with millions to invest. And he needn't tie up money for any specific period in order to do so. That's what liquidity is all about.

Liquidity

All bank certificates paying more than the standard passbook rate carry some type of penalty for early withdrawal. In most cases, the bank isn't even obligated to cash a CD until maturity; passbooks from savings and loan associations usually allow the institution to require up to six months' notice before returning funds. In the chaotic markets of the '80s, anyone who lends his money under such terms will deserve whatever he gets (or doesn't get).

A money market fund offers the best combination of high liquidity and high yield. The typical fund's portfolio matures in less than thirty days, which theoretically means that even if there was a panic, shares could be redeemed within at least that time. That, unfortunately, is not really a safe assumption, as we'll see in a moment. Nonetheless, an MMF's assets are much more liquid than those of the banks and thrifts, who have made thirty-year loans with money they may have to make good on overnight.

In the event of a financial accident, a properly chosen MMF will more likely be able to redeem your deposit than the banks. Since most offer checking privileges and the automatic telephone transfer of funds, you can withdraw money almost as easily as well.

Safety

Some of the funds are safer than the average bank— and this is perhaps the most ironic point. Many otherwise sophisticated people have come to think of banks as being the safest—even if not the most rewarding—place for their money. Of course, safety is relative, but things have changed over the last few decades. Banks are more dangerous today then at any time since the 1930s.

The argument can be made that deposits in the banks are protected by the FDIC (up to $100,000), while there's no government insurance for money market funds. But the fact is that the FDIC is no better prepared to meet its obligations in the case of a major upset than Social Security. If there were a run on the banks—a financial panic—the $100,000 would be hard to deliver. It is estimated that in this case only about 2% of all bank deposits could be paid off under the guarantee. On the other hand, shares of a money market fund invested solely in U.S. government paper are in effect backed by the folks who actually print the money. There's no better assurance that when you ask for a dollar you'll get a dollar. There's no assurance what the dollar will be worth, of course, but that's the point of getting high interest rates in the first place—which brings us full circle. For practically every safety reason, you're better off using a properly selected money market fund.

There are all manner of important questions that can be raised regarding what your bank may have done with your money, the answers to which could result in banks closing wholesale on any morning. It's bad enough that banks are illiquid; but if realistic accounting were done, many or most would prove insolvent as well.

Bad loans are the most direct reason a bank can go under. All of the loans to the Soviet bloc and Third World countries, as well as many consumer loans, real estate loans, and corporate credit lines fall in this category. But even if we lived in a fantasy land where loans were actually going to be repaid, today's high interest rates alone are enough to do the banks in; as interest rates rise, the current value of fixed-rate loans and bonds drops proportionately.

For instance, if a bank buys a $1,000 thirty-year bond with an 8 percent coupon and interest rates double to 16 percent, the bond's current value will fall to about $500 (making its current yield competitive with new 16 percent issues). That means that even the "secure" assets of banks have a market value much less than their acquisition cost. Of course, the bank's capital and retained earnings must be exhausted before depositors' money is at risk, but the average U.S. bank today has a capital-to-asset ratio of only 1 to 20. That means that if only 5 percent of its loans default or if the market value of its loans and investments decline only 5 percent, the depositor is at risk dollar for dollar.

The situation is even more critical at savings and loan associations. At the end of 1981, thrift institutions held about $600 billion of mortgages and bonds, but the market value on them was probably only about $400 billion, which leaves a shortfall of about $200 billion. Unfortunately for the thrifts, that's about $170 billion more than the industry's net worth (about $30 billion). It's also unfortunate for depositors, as the Federal Savings and Loan Insurance Corporation has assets of only about $6 billion—or 3 percent of the amount of the shortfall, and only a small fraction of insured deposits. When the public starts to realize the size of the problem, it could easily set off a wholesale run on the banks. During 1980 alone, the FSLIC paid out $1.3 billion in connection with only eleven problem institutions; during its entire prior existence, from 1934 until 1980, it paid out a total of only $815 million. The fund will probably evaporate in the next few years.

Frankly, it's impossible to know what kind of trouble your banker has gotten himself into over the years. Owing to the regulatory agencies' protective policies, you can't assess the maturity dates of his loans, their likelihood of default, or the true strength of his capital position. Further, the FDIC's assets are totally inadequate to cover losses except in isolated instances. It will probably be able to borrow enough money from the Treasury or the Fed to make good, but why put yourself in a position where you have to rely on them for your solvency? Even if they do make good, you might be forced to wait months.

Rather than trust to the prudence of your banker or the benevolence of the regulatory authorities, the money market funds allow you to take responsibility for what happens to your money. By selecting a fund with the proper assets and maturity dates, you can not only cut out the middleman but actually increase your safety while reaping a higher yield.

But while what the fund is doing with your money can't be kept a secret from you, your dealings with the fund are easier to keep private. (That word sounds more legitimate than "secret.")

Privacy

By law (the Orwellian Bank Secrecy Act of 1970), commercial banks must keep microfilm records for at least five years of any checks over $100 that you write. Since it isn't practical to separate out small checks, all checks are microfilmed. Ostensibly for your safety and convenience, it's an effective way of monitoring your activities. Checks establish a very accurate record of personal finances, beliefs, friends, desires, and mode of living. Every check gives an investigator the name of a person who can supply more information about your life. A check to an airline or a hotel discloses where you went and for how long. A check to a liquor store, a gun store, a political book club, or a pharmacy can be interpreted and used.

With Big Brother anxious to look over shoulders on

every occasion, you're well advised to control the information that is available.

MMFs with checking privileges microfilm your checks, like banks, but don't have the sophisticated filing and retrieval systems that banks do. In addition, whereas most banks require a positive identification before they'll open an account, an MMF will usually accept whatever information you disclose on your application. These MMFs, which are not bank accounts, give you an added bonus of greater privacy—in addition to higher yields, better liquidity, and greater safety.

The advantages the funds present are compelling, but there are very substantial risks involved with most of them. In order to analyze them, you must understand the type of things in which they invest. Remember that money market funds are still mutual funds, only they invest in short-term debt, not stocks. The stocks that some funds buy fluctuate, and the issuing companies can go bankrupt; the paper an MMF buys can default. The difference is only the type and degree of risk.

Where the Funds Invest Your Money

The seven classes of money market fund assets are listed below in order of increasing yield, increasing risk, and, in today's world, decreasing desirability.

U.S. government and federal agency debt is the most secure. That's because the government can tax and print up currency to any extent necessary to prop itself up.

1. U.S. Treasury Obligations

In general these are T-bills or T-notes with short maturities. It's hard to conceive of them defaulting unless there's a violent revolution or the government loses a major war. The fact that they are intrinsically worthless (i.e., they're only redeemable in paper currency, which is itself intrinsically worthless) is beside the point. If you want to maintain the illusion of a moving paper fantasy, you've got to pretend these are as "good as gold," as it were. These are the safest ways to own dollars.

2. U.S. Government Agency Obligations

Government agencies, such as the Small Business Administration (SBA) and Government National Mortgage Association (GNMA), sell their own securities in the market, much as would a private corporation. The debt is not technically the Treasury's (one reason why the national debt and annual deficits are always understated), but it is guaranteed by the Treasury, so for all practical purposes it's as good as Treasury debt, although it offers a higher yield.

If you're cautious, you won't go beyond the first two instruments.

"Repos" and bankers acceptances are the next most secure class of debt because they are backed both by some type of collateral and the credit of a financial institution.

3. Repurchase Agreements (Repos)

Banks and brokers keep long-term debt instruments in inventory the same way a clothier stocks garments. Occasionally they must borrow money to finance this inventory. A repo is a loan made to a financial institution with a debt instrument for collateral. If the underlying instrument defaults (most are Treasury paper, so this is unlikely) or drops sharply in market value (long-term bonds have shed well over 30 percent since 1979), your fund's security could melt away. Of course, the institution it loaned that money to must stand good for it anyway, but that's exactly the type of situation that could cause the borrower to collapse as well.

4. Bankers Acceptances

Banks finance inventory for commercial businesses through bankers acceptances. The loan is secured first by the value of the product, second by its producer, and often by a party who has contracted to buy it. When times are good, it's a secure piece of paper. During a credit collapse, however, the inventory could fall drastically in value, and as a result the buyer and/or seller could go into default. If that happens, your fund is left holding the bag.

Bankers acceptances are the last class of paper worth considering. Beyond this, things get really risky. CDs, ICDs, and commercial paper are all unsecured loans. These will be the first to go, and any fund holding them should be scrupulously avoided.

5. Certificates of Deposit (CDs)

These are CDs of over $100,000 issued by domestic commercial banks. They are not covered by FDIC insurance; and if the bank gets in trouble, as many will, the only thing standing in back of them is the bank's assets. Of course, if the bank's assets were any good in the first place, the bank wouldn't be in trouble. The Federal Reserve or the government may or may not directly bail out a given bank when it fails. Holders of CDs will probably have to wait until the receiver divvies up assets to collect whatever they can, or else rely upon the munificence of the government.

6. International Certificates of Deposit (ICDs)

These are CDs issued by foreign banks or by foreign subsidiaries of U.S. banks. This is a likely area for massive defaults, because the banks (and their subsidiaries) in this market are the ones making wholesale loans that will never be repaid—loans to places like Zaire, Peru, Poland, Brazil, and the U.S.S.R. Because the Eurodollar market (of which ICDs are a part) is a truly international unregulated market, it's unlikely the Fed or the Treasury will step in to bail out the unlucky lenders when the music stops in this game of musical chairs.

7. Commercial Paper

This is the unsecured promissory note of a commercial corporation. Granted, some issuers are pretty creditworthy—like Chrysler and International Harvester *used* to be.

Corporations have turned increasingly to this source of money, and the money market funds have made it available to them. As the economy slows down, businesses are going to have a hard time paying the freight on their short-term paper and will probably be almost as sorry they borrowed as the lenders.

About 36 percent of money market funds' assets are currently in commercial paper, 37 percent in CDs, and 10 percent in ICDs. The fund you invest in should have 0 percent in any of them.

Nobody knows where this moving paper fantasy is going to end, but a $200 billion marketplace where the entire amount has to be rolled over every twenty-three days on average at 15 percent to 20 percent interest rates is inherently unstable. It's a disaster waiting to happen.

But it doesn't have to happen to you. It's possible to limit your risks by sticking scrupulously to only certain types of funds. "Choose wisely, Grasshopper."

Which Fund?

The following table lists the only funds I would now consider acceptable. My sole criterion is simple: they must have 100 percent of their assets invested in either

Treasury, federal agency obligations, or repos backed by them. Their yield is generally a bit less, but it would be tragic if you traded safety for a few points of yield today. As a side benefit, some of the funds listed are completely exempt from state and local tax, and that's worth over ½ percent of yield to most people in most states. The numbers listed under the "Approved Investments" column correspond to the seven categories of assets listed earlier.

Apart from portfolio composition, different funds offer different features. Choose those that fit your requirements. All the headings are self-explanatory with the exception of the fund exchange privilege. MMFs with this feature will allow transfer of all or part of your credit balance into designated stock or bond mutual funds. If you want to move with the flow of the other markets, you can simply move your money into the appropriate fund at the appropriate time. If the MMF you choose is run by a brokerage firm, it's possible to transfer funds in and out of stock or commodity accounts with only a call to your registered representative.

Risks of Money Market Funds

The managers of money market funds are compensated by a fee of about ½ percent of total assets in the fund. That's a powerful incentive to increase the size of the fund, because it doesn't cost much more to manage a billion dollars than it does a million, but the manager makes a thousand times as much.

Most investors seem to think that the money market funds are riskless, and they don't really understand the differences between classes of assets they invest in. The managers are encouraged, therefore, to invest in high-risk, high-yield paper if they want their money to grow. The public thinks the "best" fund is the one that pays the highest yield, and it's no coincidence that that's usually the riskiest fund. Once again, the public will be taken to school and given a lesson it won't soon forget.

The money funds have grown like Topsy for over four years. Their growth can't continue at its present frantic pace, for within a few more years the entire net wealth of the U.S. would be tied up in short-term obligations. It's going to end. The only question is whether it will be with a whimper or a bang. My guess is the latter.

It will be interesting to see what happens when a few funds (actually it's likely to be more than a few when it happens, since most hold the same type of paper) experience some defaults. After some assets are wiped out, the public will start redeeming en masse, which will have unpleasant consequences for the banks and corporations that have been counting on this pool of funny money to keep rolling over their paper. The default of a few borrowers could cause a credit crunch of unbelievable proportions as other corporations looking to the funds for cash find there's none available. And that would bring on more defaults, which would bring on even more, and so on, ad bankruptium.

Even though there's less money involved, a collapse of some MMFs could be more devastating than the collapse of the real estate market, because it couldn't be disguised. One result would be a paper blizzard of unbelievable proportions as shareholders and borrowers both panicked. There's no telling how much money could be misplaced through bookkeeping errors alone in the ensuing chaos.

There's also no way of telling what shareholders would do with money they salvage from troubled funds under those circumstances, but it's unlikely they'll put it back in the banks; more likely they'll try to cash their redemption checks for Federal Reserve notes at the teller window, which will further compound the crisis, since banks don't keep a lot of cash on hand. If the Fed

Table I MONEY MARKET FUNDS

Name Address Phone Number Date Started	Approved Investments *	Assets (Millions) As of 12/30/80	Minimum Investment: Initial/ Subsequent	Checking/ Minimum Check	Fund(s) Available for Exchange Privilege
Capital Preservation Fund, Inc. 755 Page Mill Road Palo Alto, CA 94304 800-227-8380 800-982-6150 (CA) Started: Oct. 1972	1, 3	$775.6	$1,000/None	Yes/$500	Capital Preservation Fund II
Carnegie Government Securities Fund, Inc. 831 National City Bank Building Cleveland, OH 44114 800-321-2322 216-781-4440 Started: April 1980	1, 2	$21.7	$1,000/500	Yes/$250	Liquid Capital Income, Inc.
First Variable Rate Fund for Government Income, Inc. 1700 Pennsylvania Ave., #270 Washington, D.C. 20008 800-424-2444 202-328-4010 Started: Feb. 1976	1, 2, 3	$426.5	$1,000/250	Yes/$500	None

* See pages 122–25

128

Franklin Money Fund II 155 Bovet Road San Mateo, CA 94402 800-227-6781 800-632-2180 (CA) 415-574-8800 Started: May 1980	1, 2, 3	$20.6	$500/100	Yes/$500	All funds in the Franklin Group of Funds
Fund for Government Investors, Inc. 1735 K Street, N.W. Washington, D.C. 20006 202-861-1800 (Collect) Started: March 1975	1, 2, 3	$400.7	$2,500/500	Yes/$500	None
Fund for Ready Income 2100 M Street, N.W. Washington, D.C. 20063 800-424-2881 202-872-5310 Started: Sept. 1980	1, 2, 3	——	$1,000/100	Yes/$500	None
Hilliard-Lyons Cash Management, Inc. 545 South Third Street Louisville, KY 40202 502-583-6651 Started: Feb. 1981	1, 2, 3	——	$3,000/500	Yes/$500	None

Table I MONEY MARKET FUNDS (continued)

Name Address Phone Number Date Started	Approved Investments *	Assets (Millions) As of 12/30/80	Minimum Investment: Initial/ Subsequent	Checking/ Minimum Check	Fund(s) Available for Exchange Privilege
Merrill Lynch Government Fund, Inc. 165 Broadway One Liberty Plaza New York, NY 10080 800-631-0749 212-637-6300 Started: Sept. 1977	1, 3	$156.5	$5,000/100	Yes/$500	None
Midwest Income Trust/Short-Term Government Fund 522 Dixie Terminal Cincinnati, OH 45202 800-543-0407 513-579-0414 (Collect) Started: Dec. 1974	1, 2, 3	$125.3	$1,000/50	Yes/$250	Midwest Income Trust/ Intermediate Term Government Fund
Principal Protection Government Investment Fund, Inc. 327 South LaSalle Street Chicago, IL 60604 312-939-5575 (Collect) Started: Nov. 1980	1, 3	$.2	$2,500/100	Yes/$500	None

* See page 122–25

Shearson Government Agency, Inc. Two World Trade Center 106th Floor New York, NY 10048 800-221-7136 (ME, VT, NH, MA, RI, CT, PA, NJ, DE) 800-221-2990 (Other states) 212-321-6554 Started: Oct. 1980	1, 2	$88.6	$5,000/1,000	No	None
Sigma Government Securities Fund, Inc. Greenville Center 3801 Kennett Pike Wilmington, DE 19807 800-441-9490 302-652-3091 Started: Sept. 1980	1, 2, 3	$1.2	$500/100	Yes/$500	All funds in the Sigma Group except Sigma Tax-Free Bond Fund
Steadman Federal Securities Fund 1100 17th Street, N.W. Washington, D.C. 20036 800-424-8570 202-223-1000 Started: Jan. 1980	1, 2, 3	$7.8	$500/None	Yes/$500	All funds in the Steadman Group of Funds

responds by printing up enough currency to meet demand, what started out as a 1929-style deflation could end up as a 1923-style hyperinflation. Either way, shareholders of the wrong funds will become bagholders. At that point, holders of dollars in any form won't do too well.

The whole idea of "cash" may be overturned in the next few years, anyway. All of the government's debt—the Federal Reserve's unbacked paper currency and no one really knows how many trillions of dollars of bonds, mortgages, notes, bank credit, Eurodollar deposits, second trusts, and consumer credit loans, just to name a few things—could vanish tomorrow morning under a variety of circumstances.

All or most of those pieces of paper could again become simply pieces of paper, and no more. The scene has become so surreal that even the paper holders might be luckier than those whose money exists only in a computer memory, with no actual certificates issued. Treasury bills, for instance, are no longer physical certificates but computer balances. And a couple of nuclear explosions in the ionosphere which could send electromagnetic charges through electric lines that would erase data storage banks—forget about a few hundred at ground level—could erase memory of those funds. Where would all that money go? Perhaps if someone pulled the big computer plug in the sky, it would just die and go to money heaven. If you think balancing your checking account is hard, that would keep every accountant in the world busy for the next thousand years. The end result could be revolution, hyperinflation, credit collapse, deflation, or any combination of them at the same time.

This is not just idle speculation. It could happen. Since your life savings could be wiped out ("misplaced" or "forgotten") that easily, perhaps you should consider making a few changes. You don't want to be left standing there with a blank Garp-like stare on your face if the unlikely, unbelievable, or unthinkable happens.

But if you have liquidated the way I've discussed in Part II, you're now ready to advance to the next level of strategic investing. You're ready to Create.

Rules of the Funny Money Game

- *Never leave any significant amount of money with a bank or thrift institution.*
- *Be careful in choosing a money market fund; only one in ten is suitable.*
- *Money market funds are only a short-term parking place for your capital. Serious money belongs in the investments discussed later in this book.*

Creating Money

PART III

Chapter 9

Earning a Dollar or a Million

It has often been found that profuse expenditures, heavy taxation, absurd commercial restrictions, corrupt tribunals, disastrous wars, seditions, persecutions, conflagrations, inundation, have not been able to destroy capital so fast as the exertions of private citizens have been able to create it.
Lord Macaulay

A good player quits a game that is not financially worthwhile or that conflicts with a more profitable game.
Frank R. Wallace

A man is never so harmlessly occupied as when he is making money.
Ben Jonson

The best way to get the money you need for an investment program is to earn it.

It may be a purifying experience to liquidate possessions, and it may be character building to cut back on your consumption, but it's not most people's idea of fun. Moreover, there's clearly a limit to the amount of capital you can put together just by liquidating and saving. In the right line of work, though, the sky is the limit.

Obviously, it's better to make more money by working smarter; but until you figure out how to do so, you'll just have to work harder. A stopgap alternative might be to get a second job. It will automatically increase your income, you'll double the number of business contacts you make, and you'll enhance your experience. It might be either a sideline business you start yourself or a regular part-time position working for someone else.

There's no reason the extra job has to be a dead end. Hobbies that once seemed like only entertainment can be quite remunerative—things like computers, mechanics, woodworking, and electronics. If you lose your present job, they can provide a backup system. You won't need an employer, and it's an ideal opportunity to make your avocation your vocation.

Although it may not seem like a benefit at the time, working two jobs will automatically cut down on your consumption level, since you won't have the time to spend the money you earn. The best way to fight temptation is to eliminate it.

Years ago, everybody worked sixty hours a week because they had to. If you get in the habit of doing that now, while you don't have to, you're less likely to be forced into it in the future, on less favorable terms.

Working hard is a good way to earn more money. Working smart is a better way.

How to Earn More Money

There's a great deal more to becoming rich than buying the right investments and hoping for the best. The most important element in your strategy to win the battle for investment survival is your own psychology. You've heard that your attitude helps your health and your golf score; it'll also improve your earning power.

It's not enough to liquidate your past financial mistakes; it's more important to liquidate counterproductive attitudes, approaches, and methods of dealing with problems. The results that anyone can achieve in life are an indication of how sound his approach toward life is. A sound philosophy of life gives good results. People with chaotic, unproductive, unhappy lives usually don't have anyone to blame but themselves. They don't even have a strategy for living, and thus have no foundation on which to build a strategy for investing.

There's plenty of good advice available on the subject. Marcus Aurelius's *Meditations*, Ben Franklin's *Autobiography*, Norman Vincent Peale's *Power of Positive Thinking*, Frank Bettger's *From Failure to Success in Selling*, and Maxwell Maltz's *Psychocybernetics* are all helpful.

One of the important things about the Greater Depression is that it will give you a chance to put your philosophy of life as well as the approaches detailed in this book to the test. Almost anyone can get by in good times, but the 1980s will separate the real winners from the losers. Many will taste the thrill of victory or the agony of defeat firsthand; they won't need the vicarious pleasure of Saturday afternoon TV sports to experience life. There is, of course, no guarantee that just because you've developed a workable strategy you won't still be a casualty in the battle for financial survival. There is such a thing as plain bad luck. But, as Damon Runyon said, the bread may not always go to the wise, nor the race to the swift, nor the battle to the strong—but that's the way to bet. Tilt the odds in your favor by developing pro-survival attitudes, and the law of large numbers will take care of the rest.

There is, of course, an almost infinite number of valid attitudes. Anything that works for you is as good as anything that works for me. But since the next step—consolidation—in the strategy deals with gathering physical goods, I don't want to leave any false impressions. You may be able to salt away ten bags of silver, a thousand Krugerrands, and enough food to open a restaurant chain, but that's not nearly as important as knowing how to get them all back again if you should lose them for any reason. That's one thing no one can ever take away from you, and you can never lose.

Scrooge McDuck had that attitude.

The Right Attitude

One formative book I've read was an Uncle Scrooge comic book written in 1953 by Carl Barks at Walt Disney Studios.

It finds Scrooge McDuck at play in his binful of money, diving and wallowing in it, doing what he likes best. As he leaves the bin to go out for his daily constitutional, his nephew, Donald Duck, decides to play a prank by putting a fake newspaper on the park bench with the headline "Coins and Banknotes Now Worthless . . . Congress Makes Fish the New Money of the Land."

Scrooge sees it and is stunned. All his cash is worthless. He plops against a tree thinking that he hasn't even one little minnow with which to buy a crust of bread. By the next frame of the comic book, however, the courageous old duck has picked himself up and is ready to get back in the race, saying, "Well, there's no use crying over bad luck. I'll get a job and start life all over again."

Soon we find him down at the waterfront talking to a fisherman. He offers to paint the man's boat for a sackful of fish. Scrooge earns his fish and takes them to a clothing store where business is bad. He trades the fish for a raincoat. Back at the waterfront, he trades the raincoat to another fisherman for *two* sacks of fish. Since the fish is getting heavy to carry around, Scrooge trades the two bags to a farmer for an old horse, then trades the horse for *ten* sacks of fish. By the end of the day, Scrooge has a mountain of fish—three cubic acres. As much of the new money as he had of the old. He looks at the cold, clammy fish and asks himself how to count the new money, by the pound or by the inch? How to keep it? And how to spend it fast enough before it goes bad? Sorrowfully he realizes that the fish isn't as nice to play with as his old money. Fish don't feel good, and they smell bad. All of a sudden he doesn't want to be rich any more. He hires a trucking fleet to take the mountain of fish to Donald, who always wanted to be rich. Donald's house is buried under dead fish.

Donald's joke backfired, but Scrooge proved his point: You can start from scratch if you have the right attitude and come out ahead if you play your cards right. Scrooge didn't have a fish to his name when he had to start over, a lot less than you'll have if you liquidate as the previous section explains.

The next step in your plan is to start earning to add to your grubstake—that is, create more money. It was the key to Scrooge's second fortune, and it's the key to yours.

But it's necessary to have skills to provide goods and services to others. Scrooge made his fish fortune by skills at business, but there are thousands of others.

Gaining Skills

One of the most important parts of taking control of your own life as a step to prospering in the years to come is to educate yourself and gain skills. That means a lot more than just logging eight years in high school and college.

Going to college may be necessary for those who wish to learn a trade such as doctoring, lawyering, or engineering. Those are all formal disciplines which are not only easier to learn in a structured environment but require a formal degree in order to enter practice. But you or your children can't count on somebody else for education; it's necessarily self-taught.

Sometimes going to college is actually a disadvantage. Some professors teach because they have trouble performing in the real world; they prefer to isolate themselves in an ivory tower. Learning an academic subject is one thing, but learning to make money is something else again.

A lot of people seem to think that simply going to college will bestow an education. Eric Hoffer, the San Francisco longshoreman who never completed high school but has written such profound books as *The True Believer,* is an outstanding example of the difference between going to college and getting an education. Practical, marketable skills are often better acquired in trade schools, through self-teaching efforts, and through experience working from the bottom up in a field. A lot of teachers who finished first in their class couldn't run a successful hot-dog stand and are hardly in a position to help their students learn survival skills.

It would be a tragic mistake to devote all your resources to accumulating gold, hoarding commodities, devising clever tax schemes, and speculating—to the neglect of much more basic intangibles. The government may succeed in negating a lot of your efforts through its inflation, taxes, and regulations. And even if you overcome them, market risks—a bad judgment, an unexpected development, a failed brokerage house—can wipe you out. As can fraud, theft, a fire, a flood, or a war.

And in the environment coming up all of those things and many others like them will be greater dangers than they have been in the past. The only thing that's permanently secure is what you carry in your head—the intangibles you accumulate.

Who knows what skills may be required in the years to come? What you're doing now—teaching school, practicing law, laying brick, or selling insurance—may be in low demand. But preparing French cuisine, fixing autos, keeping books, or offering financial counsel may be in high demand. Or perhaps the other way around.

The single wisest thing you can do with your money is not buy gold or any of the things in this book. It's to take courses, and acquire knowledge in other fields, as unrelated to what you are now doing as possible. Anything related to science, and in particular, technology, would seem especially suitable. Computer science, medicine, mechanics, agriculture, and electronics are all going to remain in demand. In the TV series *Star Trek* it was the supremely knowledgeable Mr. Spock who bailed the crew out as often as anyone. It's hard to imagine him unemployed, for that reason. More knowledge can only increase your understanding of the way the world works now, and if it stops working the way it presently does, you'll be able to continue. It will then no longer be the end of the world if you lose your present job. And a lot of people will.

Unemployment and Using Your Skills

Your present job may exist only because of the artificially high standard of living that we've had over the last few decades; that's why it's important to gain new skills and perfect old ones to be in a strong bargaining position.

Ten years from now many of today's industries will be the equivalent of the horse and buggy business sixty years ago, and their workers will soon have to find something else to do for a living.

To start with, it's a bad idea to think in terms of a "job." The concept implies dependency on somebody else's munificence. Rather start thinking about what goods and services you can provide to the other four billion people in the world, regardless of what happens to the economy.

There are infinite job opportunities, because people have infinite desires; and work is simply the act of satisfying the desires of other people. You don't need anybody else to give you a job; create one.

People will always need certain things no matter how bad the economy gets. People will still want to eat, to travel, to be entertained, to be clothed; the problem is to determine which services to provide to which people. That's what entrepreneurs do for a living, and it's a lot more fun than trying to extract as much salary as possible in return for as little work as possible.

An entrepreneur is in control of his own fate, unlike an employee, whose fate is determined by the whim, competence, or luck of some employer. When the going gets tough, if you can't count on yourself, it's hard to count on someone else.

The depression will certainly cause unemployment, but it will also create numerous job opportunities. Many businesses will fail, but that does not mean that the services of the workers won't still be in demand. For instance if an automobile dealer goes out of business—something which is likely to happen on a large scale in the years to come—his mechanics will become unemployed. But cars will still break down and need repair. Rather than seeing unemployment as a disaster that will put him in the welfare lines, the mechanic should view it as an opportunity to solicit the customers who were going to the dealership and to cut out the middleman. Of course, he's now got to act as a salesman and a business manager as well as a mechanic, but his income will now be limited only by his own ability, not by the ability of the bankrupt dealer. He's got to be better off, because if the dealer had had any real ability he wouldn't have gone bankrupt.

The depression will bring out the best in some people. Many times people who can do something won't do it simply because they don't have to. It's much like a champion swimmer who never would have become a champion if his father hadn't thrown him screaming into the pool when he was a child.

An employee who loses his job in this depression will be forced to sink or swim under similar circumstances.

Most of them will not only stay afloat but will strike out strongly for shore and make it in grand style. There's a lot of hidden entrepreneurial capacity in Americans, suppressed by nine-to-five drudgery.

Since the last depression a lot of people have grown up with the idea that the real wealth in the world appears through magical hocus-pocus. That's because they can't look at things in non-monetary terms. Money tends to confuse the form with the substance. Nobody really wants money per se; they want the things money can buy. If you want real wealth from other people, you have to barter real wealth in exchange; money is just a form of indirect barter, and a lot of people are using barter to become more self-sufficient. In some cases they're doing it voluntarily; in others, they're forced into it because they simply don't have any cash—like Scrooge McDuck a few pages back.

Starting from Scratch

Anyone with a bit of gumption can replicate Scrooge's feat, at least over a period of time. I once discussed the problem on a television talk show. A young woman in the audience stood up and explained how she was a casualty of a cutback in social work programs; she had supervised a day school for children of working mothers. Since the mothers were now forced to either quit their own jobs or make less convenient arrangements for their children, there was clearly a need for her services. Unfortunately, she seemed to think that only the government could employ her in the child care business, and she resented them depriving her of a livelihood. Since there was a need for child care, and since she liked her work, I suggested that she cut out the middleman, set up her own day care center, and send the government a thank-you note.

The woman lived in a ghetto with plenty of abandoned or underutilized buildings. I suggested she visit their landlords and find one willing to let her use it in return for a percentage of the gross income of her business.* It would be a deal that a landlord with a vacant building in need of rehabilitation couldn't refuse. The next step would be to get building supply contractors to donate the materials necessary to fix up the building in return for her promise to repay them if the business succeeded. Labor to restore the building was available from the unemployed black youths in the neighborhood, and men in public service groups could teach them how to do it.

In the meantime she could contact the parents of the children and let them know that she was in business. With fifty children under her care and each parent paying a low fee of five dollars per day, she could have grossed $1,250 per week. Even after repaying expenses, she would have doubled her old salary.

There's no telling what that young lady did, but it would have been to the advantage of the children, the parents, the community—and herself—if she joined the underground economy and simply went ahead. Armed with a disregard for the bureaucracy and a little bit of creativeness and gumption, she would have made the world richer by a school and by an example to lead the way for others.

There's a good chance the depression of the '80s will cut off her unemployment benefits, and that woman will have to take a shot at running her own school just to survive. If she does, the depression will have been a good thing for her; the catalyst that forced her to take action.

Is it a feasible scheme? The only thing to prevent its success would be, ironically, the very government that

---

* While it's true that in cities like New York landlords are often dummy corporations who would as soon burn a building for the insurance as anything else, there are also cities like Baltimore, which has an "urban homesteading" program allowing the purchase of buildings for one dollar.

cut off the funding to the welfare program. The permits from God-knows-how-many agencies to approve the renovation of the building, the legal fees, the time and trouble of acquiring the numerous licenses, the increased real estate taxes due once the building was productive, and, of course, her own income tax, self-employment tax, social security tax, and the bookkeeping nightmares to go with it would make it much harder to do and less profitable. In a free market society without agencies like the Securities and Exchange Commission, she might even have gone around to visit members of her community to raise money for the school through a small stock offering. But who knows?

It's necessary to assess your abilities, skills and desires to determine what you really want to do, can do, and should do. So often people find themselves in a dead-end job with no prospect of getting out. In fact, polls show a rousing 41 percent* of the people working today would change their jobs if they got a chance. Of course, they can get out any time they want to. They simply have to shake off their apathetic attitudes.

Many of the hobbies that you have today can readily be turned into productive businesses. They're probably hobbies of yours because you're both good at them and enjoy them. People usually are good at the things they enjoy. No wonder so many workers aren't good at their jobs; it's hard to enjoy a mindless job where you're trading eight hours of your life for just enough money to survive the other sixteen hours of the day.

Galt's Gulch

With a little bit of luck, reality will start to imitate art. In Ayn Rand's classic novel *Atlas Shrugged*, the producers

---

* The question asked by Gallup International was: "If you had the chance to start your working life over again, would you choose the same kind of work you are doing now or not?"

of the world became fed up with government's taxation and regulation, and they retreated to an inaccessible spot in the Colorado Rockies called Galt's Gulch. They knew that all they needed was a place where production, not theft, was the way of life.

People are productive and creative for their own selfish benefit, not because they feel an obligation to supply goods and services to the rest of the world. Rand transported her heroes to a community totally isolated from the outside world where they were able to do what they wished, and only what they wished. The hidden productive society quickly advanced to a level where it was able to successfully counterattack the forces destroying the outside world.

But it need never have counterattacked. All it really takes is for the world's productive people to tune in to the problem, turn on their minds to solving it, and drop out of the old system.

Don't worry about the system. It's got a life of its own, and you can't prevent it from hemorrhaging and bleeding to death. But you certainly don't have to roll over and die with it. Rather, by becoming wealthy yourself, you'll be in a position to help those who are less fortunate, if you care to. Looking out for number one is the most effective way you can solve the world's problems.

There's always going to be a demand for goods and services; you just can't be sure there will be one for those you're presently providing.

Positive Actions

- *Don't be afraid to discard your present job.*
- *Work to develop your present abilities and interests into marketable skills.*
- *Adopt an entrepreneurial attitude about everything.*

Chapter 10

Taxes and Tax Planning

If I deny the authority of the State when it presents its tax-bill, it will soon take and waste all my property, and so harass me and my children without end. This is hard. This makes it impossible for a man to live honestly, and at the same time comfortably, in outward respects.
Thoreau

I became a tax resister, not simply because of war, not simply because of wanting to emulate the tax-free status of so many big corporations, and certainly not because of a precise political position. I became a tax resister . . . because I got mad and because somewhere in everybody's life there probably is a line in the real world which you will not or cannot cross and which, often with the sudden sort of anger I felt, you balk at, stand on, and fight on.
Karl Hess

The state calls its own violence law, but that of the individual crime.
Max Stirner

The world always solves its problems some way; that's how man has survived and prospered through the millennia. Our sick economy is a problem, and like all other problems in the past it will be solved. You don't have to go off on a personal crusade to save the world. In fact, nobody does.

Even if we team up with a lot of other people, and even if we can agree on how things ought to be, we aren't going to be able to change the old order; it's ingrained. Most people have planned their lives around things the way they presently are. And most people don't like to change their plans.

149

Even if I could change the world, I probably wouldn't, for at least three reasons. First, I have no more right to impose my solutions on others than they have to impose their solutions on me. Second, it would take a lot of time, and I can think of many more pleasant things to do. Third, it's unnecessary. There's already a Galt's Gulch harboring a great many of today's producers; it's called the alternative or underground economy.

The Tax Problem

There is one big external obstacle to making the tale of Scrooge McDuck in the last chapter a reality for us: the government. If Scrooge McDuck had to join a union to paint the boat, get a license to sell fish, pay over 50 percent tax on his profits, and have his money bin rezoned to keep fish in it, what he accomplished in a single day would have taken years.

Taxes are the most serious government obstacle to economic success. Regulations generally describe only what you may not do, and that leaves a lot of leeway. Debt is something you can incur at your option. Inflation creates an environment that speculators can thrive in. But taxes mount a direct assault on your financial position.

First you pay income taxes. Then you pay taxes on everything you buy. If you still manage to save enough after all that to start a business, there are license fees and franchise taxes. Then profits are taxed, salaries are taxed, and inventory is taxed. It's no wonder that most people find it difficult to make ends meet, even before inflation.

The Nature of Taxes

According to Webster's, *theft* is "the taking away of another's property without his consent and with the intention of depriving him of it." The dictionary doesn't follow that definition with a parenthetical clause saying, "Unless you're the government; then it's not theft anymore." It doesn't matter why the theft is committed (to feed the starving poor, to create jobs, to bail out failing corporations, or to feed the war machine), or who does it (the Congress, a mugger on the street, or an armed band of terrorists that would like to become a legitimate government). The definition remains the same; only the semantics change.

Overt theft discourages production (Why produce something if it will only be stolen?), creates hatred and antagonism (the thief doesn't respect his victim and the victim desires to retaliate), and wastes resources (people spend time defending against further theft rather than producing things they really want). Taxation has the same effect.

Taxes are *not* necessary. Taxation is based upon the assumptions that (1) government should provide needed services, and (2) the only way the services can be financed is through compulsory exactions.

There is, however, no more necessity for government to supply roads, fire protection, and schools than for it to provide autos, restaurant chains, and television programming. And entirely apart from *what* should be provided, there are three ways any activity can be supported:

1. By user fees.
2. By voluntary, charitable contributions.
3. By coerced contributions (or theft).

Many people look upon taxes as in the third class.

No one person can solve the tax problem for society. Every person, however, *can* solve the problem for himself, and that, paradoxically, is the solution for society. Obviously the best thing to do about taxes is not to pay them, but there are smart ways to go about it and stupid ways to go about it; there are legal ways and illegal ways.

The 150 million taxpaying entities in the U.S. know that Big Brother is not watching them all of the time; they know the IRS has only 70,000 employees, and only 15,000 of them are actually in the field. But there is a *chance* that government might be watching, if not now, maybe next month or the month after that. That inculcates fear.

The IRS is able to maintain the myth of "voluntary compliance" only because taxes are withheld at the source and Americans fear the consequences of not paying. In reality, tax compliance is about as voluntary as the "contribution" you make to a mugger on the street holding a gun to your head. If you don't "voluntarily" comply with the "requests" of either the mugger or the IRS, you'll quickly find your property forcibly confiscated.

Taxes are serious business, both personally and financially; how you handle them will probably be (after your success at speculating) the major factor determining how much wealth you have at the end of the depression. It pays to analyze *all* of your options. If you don't like your tax situation, there are basically two legal things you can do about it: Use loopholes, and/or relocate. Or you can become a member of the alternative economy.

Loopholes

Loopholes are legislatively condoned opportunities to avoid taxes.

There are numerous books and newsletters that address themselves to this subject, and I list several good ones in Chapter 33. In particular, however, there are at least three areas of importance in the present context, especially since the tax laws were revised in 1981.

Pension Plans

If there's any way at all possible to establish or participate in a pension at your place of work by all means do so.

One of the greatest fringe benefits of being self-employed is the ability to create and structure the plan in ways that suit you—not a third-party employer—best. There are many varieties of corporate pension plans such as "Money Purchase," "Defined Benefit," "Profit Sharing," and "ESOP."

Pension plans are available to corporate employees. "Keoghs" and "IRAs" (Individual Retirement Accounts) are two very popular tax-sheltered savings vehicles. A Keogh (or HR-10) amounts to a pension for a self-employed person. Keogh plans allow the self-employed to shelter 15 percent of their income to a $15,000 maximum. An IRA allows an individual to shelter an additional $2,000 contribution without respect to income in addition to anything he may have in a pension or Keogh. IRAs are available to everyone, even if the person doesn't qualify for either a pension or Keogh.

It's simply stupid not to take full advantage of the maximum contribution to a pension, Keogh, or IRA. The money contributed is tax-deductible, and hence shows an immediate 50 percent return on investment; the interest and dividends earned in the plan accumulate tax free, and hence are effectively 100 percent greater; capital gains are also tax free, saving the 20 percent tax there.

One supposedly unfavorable consequence of the 1981 tax law is that it's now impossible to put precious metals and collectibles into a pension. Although this provision was added to promote the interests of cash-hungry banks, it's a boon in disguise, as many unsophisticated savers might have put those things into their plans if it was possible. Collectibles and metals have no place in approved plans, since neither earns a current return, and that obviates a substantial advantage of having a pension. Also, when funds are withdrawn, gains are taxed at ordinary rates; outside of a plan, appreciation on these things would be taxed at lower capital gains rates. For that reason a pension plan should contain only securities, and preferably those with a high current yield.

Even a non-working spouse can have an IRA. The advantages of working in an unincorporated business with your spouse are greater than ever; both can have full Keogh and IRA plans, but the party who's an "employee" is exempt from Social Security taxes since he (she) is a family member. That's more reason than ever to start your own business.

Gifts

The limit on the amount of gifts that can be made without any adverse tax consequences has been raised from $3,000 to $10,000. That means that if you have any children it might be wise to give that much to each one every year (or to a trust set up in their benefit), since the earnings on that money will be taxed at their (lower) bracket.

Tax Shelters

Since the maximum tax bracket has fallen from 70 percent to 50 percent, the relative advantage of shelters has also fallen, but shelters should be aggressively explored nonetheless. Even if their investment merit is questionable, tax advantages can load the odds in their favor. After all, the worst investment you can possibly make, and one that is absolutely guaranteed to be a total loss, is any check you write the government.

The ideal tax shelter is a good investment that has just been structured to take advantage of the revenue laws. Research and development projects can offer up to a 25 percent tax credit (equivalent to a 50 percent deduction), and can have all the advantages of a shelter combined with equity participation in a growth company. Oil and gas partnerships allow immediate write-off of most expenses, while returning 15 percent of the income generated tax-free because of the depletion allowance; the whole partnership can later be sold for low capital gains rates if it's properly structured. (To avoid a hassle with the IRS, you should of course get an authoritative opinion from your accountant or tax lawyer.) Real estate, of course, has been the classic situation of investment potential with tax benefits, but more on that in Chapter 17.

Estate taxes and the treatment of stock options were changed significantly in 1981; that's all the more reason to enlist the aid of tax advisers who are not only competent but aggressive.

Too many accountants and lawyers see themselves as unpaid representatives of the state, since clients can be replaced but a license to practice can't. If your tax planner doesn't take a totally one-sided view on the situation (i.e., your side) fire him and get one who does.

Relocation

Taxes vary greatly from one political jurisdiction to another within the United States. Nine states (Connecticut, Florida, Nevada, New Hampshire, South Dakota, Tennessee, Texas, Washington, and Wyoming) have no state income tax. Others have no sales tax (Alaska, Delaware, Montana, New Hampshire, Oregon) or estate tax. Other taxes, such as inventory tax, also vary greatly from jurisdiction to jurisdiction. If taxes in your area are high, consider relocating. And why stop at U.S. borders? Many tax-wise entrepreneurs are considering moving abroad.

The U.S. is unique among major countries in taxing its citizens on the basis of their nationality rather than their residence. For example, a Swedish citizen (who can be taxed up to 102 percent of his income in Sweden) can legally avoid all taxes simply by leaving Sweden and living in a low-tax country. An American citizen, however, is legally obligated to pay U.S. taxes even if he moves abroad and never sets foot in the U.S. again.

All is not lost, however. There has always been an exemption of about $25,000 on earned income for Americans living abroad, and in 1981 this was raised to $75,000. That means if you're able to locate your business abroad, the tax savings alone could pay for a house where it's cool in the summer, another where it's warm in the winter, and a new Mercedes to drive between them.

It is naturally much more difficult for the IRS to know what you are making if you are living and banking abroad, but if they find out you are evading taxes, you will be in big trouble if you ever set foot on U.S. soil again.

An alternative is to give up U.S. citizenship and become a citizen of another country. There are many nice places in the world with few if any taxes, and some—such as the Bahamas and Cayman Islands—are quite close to the U.S. This is a particularly appealing proposition for retirees and persons whose business is out of the country already. I discuss the merits and problems of moving to many other countries in my book *The International Man,* listed in Chapter 33 of this book.

A less radical alternative is simply to get *your assets* out of the country. The IRS has made it difficult but not impossible to legally avoid U.S. taxes through the use of offshore tax havens. The mechanics are complex, and you will need competent legal advice, but it can still be done. See the books on tax havens in Chapter 33.

The alternative economy offers a third option.

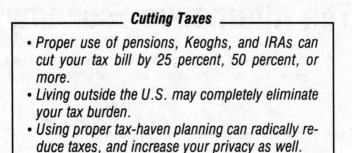

Cutting Taxes

- *Proper use of pensions, Keoghs, and IRAs can cut your tax bill by 25 percent, 50 percent, or more.*
- *Living outside the U.S. may completely eliminate your tax burden.*
- *Using proper tax-haven planning can radically reduce taxes, and increase your privacy as well.*

Chapter 11

The Alternative Economy

The only limit to the oppression of government is the power with which the people show themselves capable of opposing it.
Enrico Malatesta

Good men must not obey the laws too well.
Emerson

The more corrupt the state, the more numerous the laws.
Tacitus

Tax shelters, offshore tax havens, and such offer realistic refuge for many people. But for the person who is in the less-than-50-percent tax bracket (after deductions), the transaction costs of using them may be too high. As usual, government action hurts the little guy most. But people have a way of subverting the best efforts of the legislature, and one answer to the whole problem of taxation, regulation, and inflation for many is a rapidly growing phenomenon often called the "underground economy." A better term, however, is the "alternative economy." "Underground" is a vaguely pejorative word, and is inaccurate as well.

The alternative economy is simply the untaxed, unregulated free market in action; it's a bit like business in America was before 1913, when the Federal Reserve and the income tax were created. It is private individuals and groups providing goods and services that other people want without the added costs of taxes, licenses, and government controls. The alternative economy means that sellers make more and buyers pay less; everybody wins.

The alternative economy is sometimes legally questionable, but there's often been a conflict between things that are moral and things that are legal. The correlation between them frequently is only accidental. Unfortunately, the law sometimes confronts you with the dilemma of putting your interests or those of the government first. Here are a few examples of the alternative economy. Decide for yourself:

- A non-union plumber fixes a sink for cash, charges half the union rate, and does not report the income.
- A street vendor sells the leather pocketbooks and briefcases he makes for bargain prices, because he chooses not to pay fees, licenses, and taxes.
- A housewife sells a vase for twice what she paid and doesn't report the income.
- A farmer sells a portion of the fruits and vegetables he grows at a roadside stand for cash and fails to report the income.
- An appliance store owner gives irons, toasters, and microwave ovens as Christmas and birthday presents to friends, but records them in his books as having been shoplifted.
- A waiter systematically underreports his tips, knowing they are essentially untraceable.
- A trucker exceeds the fifty-five m.p.h. speed limit to get a cargo to its destination more profitably.
- A college student offers taxicab service in New York without first purchasing a medallion (license) from the city.
- A repairman fixes an accountant's TV in return for straightening out his books. Neither considers the transaction a taxable event.
- A restaurant owner turns off the tape on his cash register two hours before he closes so he can keep 100 percent of the income he takes in during that period.

• Uncle Scrooge trades his way to three cubic acres of fish by considering only the desires of those with whom he deals.

The alternative economy may include as much as 20 percent of all work now being done in the U.S. As the above examples illustrate, the kinds of unreported, unregulated, and untaxed transactions are so varied that practically every American will be a participant in the alternative economy at some time or other in his life. And it will probably grow. The International Labor Organization estimates that it has doubled in Britain over the last ten years, and it constitutes 25 percent of activity in France and 35 percent in Italy, where whole areas of some cities have been taken over by hidden factories specializing in shoes and clothing. They believe that 65 percent of Italian government workers have a second, undeclared job. As taxes, regulations, and inflation grow to European levels in the U.S., so will the size of our own alternative economy. Surprisingly, the Soviet Union may have the largest one of all; the more oppressive the state, the more creative the individual. The underground in the U.S.S.R., ironically, is the main reason the giant slave empire hasn't collapsed from massive starvation decades ago.

The alternative economy is certainly growing in the U.S. Many don't even realize that not paying taxes on the sale of old furniture, or on cash received for babysitting, or benefits received from barter may well be illegal. Many others don't care. A growing number of Americans are finding it plain economically impossible to survive without it.

Barter

Barter is one of the most common manifestations of the new economy. Barter is the direct exchange of goods or services without using money, one that has a way of restoring a bit of reality to economic transactions. When you give somebody paper money for his products, it's easy to forget that it stands for the hours of your life spent earning it.

Many people have forgotten that the checks they write every day are only warehouse receipts for a government currency. A "currency," in turn, is nothing but a receipt for "money" (which is any commodity, usually gold or silver, that people are willing to accept as a medium of exchange and a store of value). Money is just a way of expediting barter, but it has become so far removed from the marketplace that form has become confused with substance. A return to direct barter tends to restore value-for-value reality.

The legality of barter is iffy. On the one hand, the tax code permits the tax-free exchange of gifts, and in practice people continually do favors for one another that may or may not be considered taxable by the IRS. Some barter transactions, notably tax-free exchanges of real estate, are explicitly permitted by the tax code. You can, for instance, trade a house on which you have doubled your money for another without paying tax on the gain. But there is a real question of whether you legally owe any taxes if you swap a piano for twenty cases of home-canned vegetables. On the other hand, new tax rules explicitly make organized barter via formal barter clubs subject to taxation, although most of these rules have yet to be tested in court. Many forms of barter will fall into a gray tax area; the following example might well raise the eyebrows of the IRS.

The Way It Works

A dentist might need a new porch on his house; one of his patients, a carpenter, offers to build it for $5,000. In order to pay the $5,000, however, the dentist would have to earn at least $10,000, as he is in the 50 percent tax bracket and half of his income goes to the government.

At the same time, the carpenter might need braces for his children costing $5,000, but he too has to earn $10,000 to be left with that much.

Moreover, if the dentist bought the porch and the carpenter bought the braces, there would be additional income tax of 50 percent due on the $5,000 each received. (I'm disregarding expenses, and assuming it's an exchange of labor alone to keep the example simple. The principle remains, no matter how it's figured.) At the end of the taxable transaction, the men have the porch and the braces, but the government has raked off $15,000, leaving only $5,000, or 25 percent of the total that changed hands.

A barter deal would have worked out better. Both men get what they want, and the $15,000 denied the state may prevent it from hiring another building inspector to harass the carpenter or bureaucrat to license dentists, in the bargain. Instead, the money the barterers saved between them can go to buy something else their families need. Or at least a leveraged tax shelter to cut taxes on their cash income.

Barter, to be sure, is cumbersome. That's why money was invented; it's pretty hard matching up the appropriate dentist with the right carpenter at the opportune time. But as long as one is dealing with honorable people, an obligation owed can be repaid at some time in the future; it's worth some inconvenience to keep 75 percent from the taxman.

Barter can be the simple direct trading of valuable goods and services, but that's cumbersome and inconvenient. How do you trade a Cadillac for a year's supply of food? Indirect barter, using gold or silver coins, can facilitate the transaction. Rather than using check or cash, many barter deals involve gold and silver, the original money. You might say high taxes and inflation have caused money to be reinvented. It's ironic how things often come full circle. Men first traded by direct barter, and as civilization developed they used gold as money. Later, currency became a substitute for gold, and now checks and bookkeeping entries are a substitute for currency. Like artwork, the monetary system has gone through a primitive, a classical, a baroque, and finally a rococo period on its way to a renaissance. The free market is remonetizing gold; the alternative economy isn't waiting for the government to pass a law as the old order collapses.

Those who don't earn an income in dollars and don't save them aren't hurt by their inflation. Inflation only affects those who use inflated currency, and barter makes currency unnecessary. It's the free market's antidote to the poison of inflation. As government attempts to limit the number of $100 bills in circulation to prevent people from dealing in cash, it only encourages them to use gold coins instead.

Countering Regulation

The alternative economy solves regulatory problems the same way. If a migrant worker from Mexico or a black teenager from the ghetto wants to work, he may have to take less than the minimum wage, simply because his labor isn't worth any more. It may be hard to see how someone's labor couldn't be worth $3.50 an hour (or whatever the minimum wage may be as you read this), but $3.50 is just as arbitrary a figure as $35 or $103.50 an hour. By disregarding the regulation, the worker gets employment, the employer gets cheap labor, and both parties emerge better off.

In some parts of the country it's illegal to use plastic instead of copper pipe for plumbing; or to use margarine instead of butter in restaurants; or to charge more or less than fixed rates for a taxi ride; or to sell laetrile. The very existence of these regulations creates the opportunity for entrepreneurial profit. They create a void that will be filled by the best, brightest, and most daring, benefiting themselves and their neighbors.

While red tape and restrictive regulations befuddle and hamstring the Establishment, whose members feel they have much to lose by breaking them, entrepreneurs take advantage of that fact. Han Solo, the hero of *Star Wars*, thrived on subverting the evil Empire's regulations and taxes to make his living; adversity and suppression create opportunities for both profit and heroism.

The New Economy vs. the Depression

If the government tries to regulate its way out of this depression, as it did during the last one, the economy will collapse. But only the old economy and the people who've given up responsibility for their own decisions, their lives, and their businesses to the regulations above them.

As the old order of things comes unglued during the depression, the alternative economy will ride the wave of the future. That's not because its members have any special understanding of economics or libertarian ideology; it's just because they want to survive. Some people won't like it, or will have a "gut feeling" that it's wrong. Those people often present a case study in the psychology of envy. Even those who believe taxes should be lowered are often resentful when they see others doing what they aren't clever or courageous enough to do, i.e., not pay. Envy makes people want to deny others what they can't or don't have themselves.

The idea that anyone who pays less than his "fair share" of taxes is somehow stealing from everyone else naturally creates suspicion, hostility, and envy. People become either exploiters or the exploited. The solution is to eliminate taxes and regulation, not make sure everyone is equally burdened.

In warfare it's been said that psychological strength is three times as important as physical strength, and in your own battle for personal and financial survival it's even more true. People are basically moral beings; if they feel they should do something, by and large they will. That's the reason the government directs so much effort to convincing people that it's "right" or "public spirited" to do what they're told, and "wrong" and "selfish" to act in their own best interests. The conflict only serves to instill guilt and hypocrisy. Anyone who can make you feel bad about yourself has a great deal of control over you. And control is what the Establishment wants.

The Future of the Alternative Economy

The alternative economy will continue expanding as the existing economy deteriorates, inflation and taxes increase, and regulations become more oppressive. The government obviously loathes the alternative economy because it decreases the government's control over the population.

Big Business dislikes the alternative economy because it enables small entrepreneurs to compete successfully without complying with all of the government regulations to which Big Business is subject.

Labor unions dislike the alternative economy because freelance workers undercut union wages, and a self-employed person obviously doesn't need a union.

Social planners and moral authoritarians hate the alternative economy because it enables people to buy and sell things that they think are bad for them.

Almost everyone else, however, likes the alternative economy very much, since it eliminates taxes, circumvents government regulations and red tape, and helps diminish the impact of inflation.

The alternative economy is a dynamic market process which enables people to live their lives as they see fit. It assaults the old order not by attacking it but by ignoring it. The members of the alternative economy are the modern equivalent of small, smart prehistoric mammals who weaved and dodged about to survive, while gigantic dinosaurs tore up the countryside. The dinosaurs were much more impressive, but the little mammals eventually inherited the earth. Perhaps someday a paleo-economist will rename Big Government, Big Business, and Big Labor with scientific names ending in "saurus."

Regardless of whether your business is part of the alternative economy or the old one, there are smart and not-so-smart ways to run it. In the Greater Depression, a lot of the old rules aren't going to work. At the same time it will present the best business opportunities in thirty years. The next chapter will tell you the smart ways to capitalize on them.

Regaining Your Freedom

- *The alternative economy is the true "growth" industry of the 1980s.*
- *Barter for your needs whenever possible.*
- *Taxes, regulation, and inflation are bad for the economy but create opportunity for the entrepreneur.*

Chapter 12

Empire Building in the Greater Depression

Work and creativity are what built this country—not money.
Karl Hess

Every man is worth just so much as the things he busies himself with.
Marcus Aurelius

I got rich because I always made my own lucky breaks. I didn't let my mistakes floor me, by jingo. I set out right away to recoup my losses.
Scrooge McDuck

Many people who wanted to start their own businesses during the '70s were frozen out by a spastic economy and high interest rates. Not surprisingly, they feel that if it was hard in the '70s it will be impossible in the '80s. The opposite, however, is true.

Opportunities in Business

People's consumption patterns change radically in a depression, and a lot of once-productive businesses bite the dust. The fast-food business, for instance, was built on cheap energy and lots of leisure time, and that's changing rapidly. It's important to get into a growth industry, so that even if you make mistakes in management a rising tide will sweep you up with it; stay away

167

from companies that will wind up like the swimming pool contractors in Chapter 3.

Hundreds of thousands of existing businesses will be bankrupted in the next decade, and they will leave a void to be filled; they'll also leave assets to be acquired for bargain prices. That's the break that those who would like to get into business, and couldn't afford it during the '60s and '70s, will need. Most businessmen will be unable to deal with conditions in the economy, even if there's a real demand for their products. There are a number of reasons why.

How to Survive and How to Fail

When inflation is running at 20 percent, it's hard to watch anything that's not directly ahead and only a short distance away. Management will be forced to devote more time to financial markets than to taking care of business, and business will suffer. Most people don't think like economists, and can't see both the short-run immediate consequences and the long-term delayed ones of their actions. That's why most businessmen will be in trouble. To run a business successfully in the years ahead you've got to simultaneously get through the short run and prepare for the long run.

Inflation inevitably focuses attention on the short run. With financial markets swinging up and down unpredictably, the long term seems irrelevant; it's hard enough to predict what's going to happen tomorrow morning. Business becomes more a matter of putting out fires one day and trying to make a killing the next. Business management has a way of becoming crisis management.

Most businesses will eliminate research and development budgets because the payout will extend too far into the future to make it predictable or worthwhile—at least while they're trying to manage tomorrow's crisis.

With 20 percent interest rates, an investment in R and D has to double capital within three and a half years in order to make the risk worthwhile in the short run. But a business that doesn't do its homework today won't have what its customers want tomorrow.

Marketing and public relations are other areas likely to be cut. Marketing and PR build confidence and loyalty for a firm's products while they help create a demand for them. A lot of money that would go into these areas will instead flow into advertising to give instant results at the cash register. That's fine, of course, but both are needed. As strapped as a business may be, it must still budget for intangibles like marketing and PR if it hopes to survive the long run. Training programs for future workers will also be mistakenly overlooked by businessmen chasing high and "riskless" yields in short-term government paper.

Some businesses will count on inflation to bail them out of debt and mistakes. Gradually increasing inflation has helped poorly managed businesses over the last twenty years; prosperity made it easier to pass along uncontrolled costs. Many businesses will be caught at the low end of the increases in the CPI, however. Just because prices in general are rising at 20 percent doesn't mean a particular company's prices are; perhaps they're rising at only 10 percent while raw materials are going up at 30 percent. They average out to 20 percent, but that's meaningless to the company caught in the squeeze.

As the depression deepens, a lot of businessmen will find that their skill at making widgets is less important than their ability to dodge regulations, second-guess radical price changes, and get the highest return on cash. In stable times productive companies can thrive, but when things get out of control the balance shifts to those who are adept speculators, or those who can pull political strings.

In 1961, for example, the Small Business Administration provided $260 million in loans to small businesses. In 1980 the figure was over $3.5 billion. That infusion of capital, along with inflation and a false prosperity, suggests why the rate of small business failures fell steadily from a high of 64 per 1,000 in 1961—the beginning of the boom—to only 24 per 1,000 in 1978, when the long-term trend started turning. You've got to use one philosophy of business when a boom is building, another when a depression washes over the financial landscape.

If you knew we were going to have a deflation, you'd want to be completely out of debt to weather it. If you could be certain inflation was going to get much worse very soon, you'd want to be a heavy borrower. Unfortunately, we don't know the exact sequence of events. The principles in the chapter on borrowing hold true for businesses as well as individuals, but if you are in any doubt, the best solution is to adhere to Shakespeare's dictum: "Neither a borrower nor a lender be." Borrowers can be wiped out in the recurring "liquidity crises" or "credit crunches" that will continue until the whole financial system collapses. Lenders (and those who extend credit to customers) also stand to be wiped out by the "credit crunches" when those to whom they lend default. And in the long run, higher levels of inflation will certainly get them.

The smart way to run a business in the years ahead is on a cash basis (if at all possible): Don't extend credit, and be careful about using it. It's not going to be easy, but keeping things on a cash basis is the only way you can be sure of never becoming overextended yourself, or ever doing business with people who are.

That means you won't be able to expand the way some competitors might. By extending credit you generate more business, and by borrowing you can expand faster. But the credit you extend will likely be to potential bankrupts who need it, and the expansion you make will prove disastrous when the economy eventually crash-lands.

By staying completely liquid, you're not going to have to distract yourself second-guessing the money markets, and you can devote your attention to turning out a proper widget. You'll be building on a solid foundation; and by not making the mistakes of other businessmen, you'll survive. And that alone will put you head and shoulders above the crowds.

Although nominal interest rates will go erratically higher, which is one problem, real interest will bounce around even more radically. In Israel, for instance, real interest rates were negative (−13 percent) in the fourth quarter of 1979 and 38 percent in the first quarter of 1980, 0 percent in the second quarter and 29 percent in the third quarter of 1980. In Argentina it was possible to get a real 7 percent per month on ordinary bank deposits in 1980; in 1981, however, the local currency lost 65 percent of its value against the dollar, and import prices suddenly rose by that much. The American economy will grow to resemble that of Argentina and Israel, and bankruptcies skyrocket under those conditions—just as they have in those countries.

Candidates for bankruptcy court tend to borrow a great deal in an attempt to fend off a reckoning. Predict-ably higher inflation has rewarded them; but the erratic movements in interest rates typical of the final stages of a business cycle can bring it all down at once.

Buying Bankrupt Companies

When conditions force otherwise viable companies into liquidation, opportunities will appear for those with some daring management ability—and understanding of economics—to step in. Bankruptcies are messy affairs, and the desperate owners of businesses on the rocks will grasp at straws in hopes that someone can bail them out. It's your chance to get into business for little or no cost, and even less risk.

Lists of troubled businesses are available from Dun & Bradstreet, or from the docket of the local bankruptcy court. Go through them and see if any of the companies on them pique your interest. The next step is to visit the business and interview its owner; he'll be glad to talk to anyone offering a ray of hope at that point. It's quite possible that you may be able to bring something to the game needed to turn things around. Perhaps you have a persuasive way of collecting overdue accounts receivable; perhaps a small infusion of money you've saved can pull it through; perhaps you can act as a broker for a merger with another, stronger company in the same field.

Rather than wind up with a besmirched reputation and zero assets, the owner should be willing to offer a substantial portion—perhaps a majority interest—of his company for such services. There are hundreds of techniques for turning bad businesses into good businesses; it's only a matter of developing the skills and mental attitude needed to do it. If you can, everyone—the old owner, yourself, the employees, and the public—will all emerge better off.

It may be possible, for instance, to fire full-time employees and hire some of them back as independent contractors. That will tend to improve everyone's efficiency, and result in tax savings all the way around.

It may be a better idea to confront them with a choice of either losing their jobs or being compensated with a share of profits instead of a salary; it's a measure that provides incentive.

Or it may be possible to substantially reduce the staff and automate if you have sufficient capital and technical expertise. Machines don't get sick, need raises, or pay taxes—but many small, failing businesses are unaware of what's available or how to use it. That's why they're in straits.

Some of the techniques of playing the game are covered in books I've listed in Chapter 33. But mostly you'll need only a little capital and a lot of common sense, or "street smarts." You can get a free education by visiting a different troubled business each day in your spare time; soon ideas will start presenting themselves to you.

Conglomerates will arise from the ruins, built by entrepreneurs with courage, skill, and vision. They'll be the billionaires of the 1990s, revitalizing the traditions of Rockefeller, Carnegie, and Daddy Warbucks. Best of all, many have nothing today. It's all as it should be, and the story of business in the Greater Depression will have a happy ending because of them.

May the spirit of Scrooge McDuck be with you!

How to Build an Empire

- Don't mortgage your business's future for the present.
- The Greater Depression will present more and better business opportunities than during prosperous times.
- Your attitude toward and understanding of the Greater Depression are more valuable than technical expertise in the business you'll buy.

Consolidating for Safety and Profit

PART IV

Chapter 13

Buy Now, Beat the Rush

If we are wise, let us prepare for the worst.
George Washington

*Naturally before one thinks in terms of investment one has to
give consideration to the basic necessities of life.*
G. M. Loeb

*Who bids his gather'd substance gradual grow
Shall see not livid hunger's face of woe.
No bosom pang attends the home-laid store,
But fraught with loss the food without thy door.
'Tis good to take from hoards, and pain to need
What is far from thee: —give the precept heed.*
Hesiod

The consolidation phase of the strategy is intended to establish a floor under your standard of living, so no matter how bad the Greater Depression gets, you'll be secure and have a solid risk-free foundation that will allow you to speculate—and amass a fortune—in the years ahead.

The First Step

An investment program must have a sound foundation. It's not enough to just run out, buy some gold coins, and hope for the best. A plan must underlie any action.

A plan should get down to the most basic and simple elements. The name of the game is to maintain your standard of living. What are the most basic elements of a standard of living? The answer lies in a third-grade geography book: food, shelter, and clothing. The question is: How can you ensure that you will always have adequate supplies of those three things well into the future, even at times when they may be unaffordable or unavailable? The answer is to acquire them now when you know that they're available at prices you can afford. And to put away enough gold so that you'll always have something to trade for other things you want; dollars may not fill the bill.

If you can go to sleep every night knowing that regardless of what else happens the necessities are covered, it will liberate you psychologically as well as financially to engage in speculative high-potential enterprises. If you always have to worry about where the basics are coming from, it's much more difficult to have either the psychological attitude or the financial wherewithal to multiply your capital.

The keystone to your financial foundation, therefore, is a well-thought-out program of hoarding. This is of critical importance. The whole point of accumulating money is to ensure that you'll always have the things that you need in the future, but the money you accumulate may be worthless on any Monday morning when you wake up. Or the political process may simply take your money through a new tax assessment. In addition, many of the things that money can now buy may become unavailable owing to direct or indirect government action.

Rather than saving the money that you'll need to buy necessities in the future, why not cut out the middleman and save the things themselves?

Hoarding or Stockpiling

The word "hoarding" is loaded with psychological baggage and moral opprobrium. There's no reason why that should be the case. To hoard is really nothing more than to save with physical goods. The act of hoarding is simply the act of saving so things are available to you in the future. If at some time in the future when shortages occur you are the only person prudent enough to have hoarded, then you will be in a position to be a humanitarian and dispense part of what you've set aside to other people. By hoarding you make yourself independent of other people; you put yourself in a position in which you can only be an asset to society in general and your friends in particular, rather than a liability. Nevertheless, the word "stockpiling" is more acceptable to some people. Semantics is a funny thing. Stockpiling is considered socially acceptable (if a little unusual) in good times, but in bad times—the whole reason for doing it —it becomes "hoarding."

An intelligent program of hoarding is the first and most important financial activity that you can get into. Even Nobel Laureate Milton Friedman has observed that in an inflationary environment hoarding is the only sure way of maintaining wealth. There are at least six specific advantages to hoarding.

1. *It's risk free.* Every other financial transaction has an element of risk. A company you buy stock in can go bankrupt, your currency can be inflated, a commodity can go down in value, your house may prove unsalable, and your precious metals can be stolen. (Of course, the consumer goods you store can be stolen too, but not as easily.) But the things that you stockpile are those that you plan on using yourself sometime in the future. They are things that have value to you in and of themselves, and don't just represent value as money does. Since you can always use them in the future, and you will eventually have to buy them, they are a totally risk-free investment. You literally can't lose.

2. *Stockpiling avoids taxes.* If you bought a tube of toothpaste two years ago for a dollar, that same tube

today might cost $1.40; no taxes are due on the increase. On the other hand, if you'd bought the share of a small mining company two years ago for a dollar and today it was selling for $1.40, capital gains taxes would be due on the increase in dollar value if you sold it to buy the toothpaste. Your real gain therefore wouldn't be 40 percent but (depending on your tax bracket) more like 30 percent. In other words, the real reason you bought the share was so it could eventually increase your standard of living. But although the share went up in value just as much as the toothpaste, after taxes it didn't increase your standard of living as much.

Any goods that you stockpile and consume yourself are not subject to capital gains taxes. Since those taxes effectively decrease the return on an investment by up to 20 percent, avoiding them increases your return by the same amount.

3. *Stockpiling automatically keeps up with inflation.* Price increases aren't inflation, just the effects of inflation. You can't fight inflation itself, unless you are personally in a position to abolish both the government and the Federal Reserve. But by locking in the prices of things that you are eventually going to consume you can very effectively fight the effects of inflation. What does it matter if over the next few years the price of light bulbs, ketchup, or soap triples or quadruples or worse if you have all that you're going to need over that time frame? The very items you're hoarding will go up in price by the amount of inflation simply because their price increases are the very measure of inflation.

4. *Stockpiling can cut your unit costs.* We normally buy things in the minimum needed quantity. That's natural enough, since without a plan you simply want to fulfill an immediate need or desire. If, however, you hoard according to a plan, it's possible to reduce current costs tremendously by waiting till they're sold at specially discounted prices and then purchasing in quan-

tity, which allows even greater discounts. Rather than buying things piecemeal and haphazardly over a period of years at ever higher prices, it makes much more sense to buy in quantity at "sale" prices and put them away. As the hemorrhaging of the economy in the next few years continues, many businesses will be bankrupted or forced to unload inventory at distressed prices. That presents a great opportunity to buy "right" in preparation for much higher inflation. By doing so, you are in turn taking advantage of both deflation and inflation—and that's what strategic investing is all about.

5. *Stockpiling results in time savings.* How many times have you been forced to stop what you're doing to pick up a bar of soap, a can of tunafish, a tube of glue, or any of a thousand other day-to-day items? Add in the cost of driving to the store, the lost time looking for the item, purchasing it, and the general nuisance of not having something when you need it; those costs dwarf the item's high per-unit cost. Time is the most valuable single commodity you have. If you prefer to "waste" it watching television or sleeping, that's one thing. But time wasted in nuisance busywork chores is truly wasted.

Most of us have wished that needed items could be willed to appear magically in hand at the right moment. You can't make that happen in real life, but you can come as close to it as possible by assessing what you're likely to need over the next several years and storing it away close by. Walking down to the basement for a can of tunafish beats the heck out of driving to the store for it.

6. *Stockpiling heads off shortages.* As inflation gets totally out of control in the next few years, shortages will become a fact of life. They'll occur not only because inflation and the vagaries of the business cycle will bankrupt some businesses, and thereby take their products off the market, but also because inflation will make

it increasingly hard for retailers to inventory goods and distributors to distribute them.

Much more dangerous than inflation, though, is the specter of wage and price controls.

The government has long been in the habit of blaming everyone but itself for consumer price increases. Rather than controlling itself, the government prefers to control its subjects. In the past, that's often meant controls on wages and prices; perhaps in the future there will be controls on profit margins as well. Controls always cause shortages. As shortages erupt, you don't want to be left out in the cold.

If a light bulb in your house burns out today, you'd probably be willing to pay no more than a dollar, say, for its replacement because you know it's available at the corner store. But if the light bulb burns out two years from now when bulbs are not available at the corner store, rather than go without the light you'd probably be willing to pay two dollars or five or even ten to get one. You may think it's highly unlikely that light bulbs will disappear from the shelves; and even if they do, you may think it equally unlikely that you'd pay that much for one. But many thought it unlikely that the gas shortages of the '70s would occur. If you ran out of gas on a country road you might be willing to pay three, four, five, or ten dollars per gallon at that time. It's the same with almost every commodity.

This is precisely how hoarders have earned the dislike of the public—because they are in a position to sell to others at what seem like outrageous prices during times of shortage. Hoarders are alternately accused of driving the prices to those levels and of creating the shortage itself by virtue of their having hoarded. Both allegations are completely false, but people don't think logically when they're desperate. If somebody else has what they want, they create excuses to take it, and simple name-calling is one excuse.

Obviously, this aspect of stockpiling opens up tremendous possibilities for profit in the future, but by the time the shortages occur you might do just as well to keep knowledge of your possessions to yourself.

Disadvantages of Stockpiling

There are only two reasons I can think of why you shouldn't put a hoarding plan into effect. One is a lack of storage space; the other is a danger that the things that you accumulate could change in style, become outdated in technology, or spoil during storage. The solution in both cases revolves around the types of things you should stockpile. Naturally if we have a deflationary depression the values of your acquisitions could drop, but not as radically as those of conventional investments. And they would never default as would dollars in many banks in a deflation.

Where to Stockpile

A stockpiling program may present something of a logistics problem for those who live in small apartments. But if you lack storage space you'll simply have to be more selective about the type of items to put away. As an example, you would store less paper towels—a high-bulk non-critical low-unit-value item—rather than cut into the amount of high unit value and potentially critical medical supplies. Like anything else, it's necessary to work within the constraints of reality. But then, if we lived in the best of all possible worlds, I wouldn't have had to write this book and you wouldn't have to read it.

Storage space can be a problem, but there are a lot of places in the average apartment or house where goods can be put away for a rainy day, without getting in the way while the sun's still out. Under the bed. On the top shelf of a closet. In back of the couch. If you followed the liquidation plan, you should have gotten rid of lots of junk, and that in itself will generate some extra room. The problems of storage space are small and technical compared to the benefits that can be achieved. If you have no other alternative, consider storing things with trusted friends or relatives who have a large house or a farm in the country. They might be pleased to have the stuff there as an insurance policy, and in return offer you a retreat if the going gets tough.

Another alternative, although it's not quite as practical, is to rent storage space. Look in the Yellow Pages under the category "Moving and Storage" to find mini-warehouses.

The question of storage space relates to the problem of what to store, as do the other problems presented by changes in style, technology, and the deterioration of shelf life. Let's look at the problems of storing the three basic classes of necessities: food, shelter, and clothing.

What to Stockpile

Food. There's no immutable law written in stone that says food must automatically appear on the shelves of the Safeway on any given morning. A complex chain of events must occur in sequence from the time the farmer plants the seed in California or Nebraska to the time you put a spoonful of cornflakes in your mouth. If any of the elements of the sequence break down, you're not going to eat.

If the farmer can't get diesel fuel for his tractor, or the trucker for his rig, or you for your car, the food can't be grown and transported. A long strike, crop failure, civil commotion, non-sterile fruit flies, or a breakdown of the currency system can all keep food off your table. If you have a year's supply of food safely stored away, however, no matter what happens you'll be able to eat.

The implications of needing a food storage program

are so horrendous, yet so obvious, that most people don't like to talk about them. But the most obvious things are the ones that are overlooked, and the most unthinkable things are the ones that happen. Not too long ago people by the millions starved in Cambodia and Uganda. Others are undernourished today in Cuba. In Chile after Allende took over, hundreds of thousands of people were malnourished and starving. In Germany in 1923 (an advanced industrial economy) people went hungry, as they did again in that country after World War II. You'd never believe it to look at Germany or Chile today, unless you looked at Poland.

One report from Poland stated that in 1981 many Poles were preoccupied with "the struggle for biological survival." Poles have learned to protect themselves by hoarding. One teacher, for instance, was found to have a store containing 259 cans of meat, 307 jars of jam, 273 packets of soup, 123 packets of tea, 110 pounds of sugar, 65 pounds of flour, 214 bars of soap, 64 rolls of toilet paper, and 64 pounds of salt. He was quoted as saying he was preparing "for hard times."

Things change very quickly. Many people have become quite wealthy on the black market by preparing for the inevitable.

An increasingly popular way to accumulate food is via the prepackaged survival programs sold by companies that specialize in the field. If you do buy the so-called survivial food programs, I'd urge you to try samples first. The advantages of dehydrated or freeze-dried food are its light weight and indefinite shelf life. The disadvantages are high cost and what some consider unappetizing taste.

Food hoarding might include stocking up on your favorite alcoholic beverage. Even if all economic conditions stayed the same, which they won't, environmental conditions alone could drive wine prices way up. All it takes is a cold wet summer in Bordeaux, and grapes skyrocket. If you need an excuse to stock a wine cellar, here it is. Wine connoisseurs are just specialized food hoarders. Any problems you may have with keeping your stockpile intact are your responsibility.

The worst thing that could happen if you hoard a year's supply of food is that all the best things that could happen to the world do happen. Not to worry. You'll be able to use the money you won't have to spend to see more movies, buy more books, or take more vacations. If, on the other hand, worse comes to worst, you'll have food when nobody else does. It would be nice if everybody stocked up, but unfortunately that's wishful thinking. You can't possibly lose.

Shelter.   The first thing that comes to mind when the subject of shelter is brought up is obviously a place to live—a house or an apartment. I deal with that in Chapter 17. More to the point here are the things that you use from day to day that make the shelter itself livable. Call them tools if you will. These include all the necessities that are not food and not clothing. You'll want to hoard as many day-to-day consumables as your space can accommodate. Housewares like soap, paper towels, aluminum foil, plastic bags, light bulbs, and batteries. Personal supplies like toothpaste, razor blades, and cosmetics. Things for the car like tires, spark plugs, and fuses. And all types of miscellany, like paper, Scotch tape, and garden seeds.

In addition, there are some things that people always want, regardless of how good or bad things get, and are willing to pay almost any price for if they don't have them. Most are luxuries and are considered morally questionable by some people. Not to worry. You simply need not offer them to those who disapprove. These include liquor and drugs, candy and chewing gum, guns and ammunition, cigars and cigarettes.

You know best what you use from day to day: Take the project seriously and stock up.

Clothing.   The big problem in storing clothing is style. The money spent on a pair of bell-bottom trousers ten years ago could be money wasted, since you'll never wear them. Clothes you store should be basics that don't go out of style—things like underwear, socks, stockings, conservative shoes, jeans, business shirts, and almost any type of outdoor gear, i.e., the type of thing that Brooks Brothers and L. L. Bean have sold for decades. This isn't an argument to go out on a fashion splurge and use your investment/survival money to become a clothes horse. But why not pick up the things that you need and put them on the shelf now, not to be used until you would ordinarily go out and buy them anyway.

Figuring Your Stockpiling Plan

Because my advice is to make a plan and follow it, I've given you the rudiments for your hoarding plan. It's up to you to develop a personalized list of the items to include. No single plan can possibly fit all individuals; there are factors of personal philosophy, personal taste, home economics, material management, logistics, chemistry, and business management involved, to mention only a few. It's no simple task, and Chapter 33 has some resources you may wish to use.

Stockpiling is one of the most important single things that you can do—although I give the advice and devote this space in the book to it with some trepidation. Anyone who talks about such things is inevitably styled a prophet of doom. But in order for this program to work and be of profit to you, the world doesn't have to collapse. It just has to keep going the way it is at present. You're hedged against good times because you can always consume the things that you've bought, and you're hedged against bad times because you'll have *what* you need *when* you need it.

Some might say that this proposal is too unsophisticated to concern themselves with. Actually, it's only the most sophisticated people who can leapfrog their thoughts to the logical conclusion of present trends.

Stockpiling for Financial Security

- *There are six advantages and no disadvantages to stockpiling, or investing in consumer goods.*
- *Fortunes will be made on the black market by farsighted stockpilers.*
- *After you've stockpiled, everything else can be considered risk capital.*
- *Stockpiling is a basic and critical part of any investment plan.*

Chapter 14

Gold—and Silver

In the history of the world we find the record of savings really saved through buying gold, hoarding precious stones, and other forms of "hard wealth" privately secreted. In the future history of America most of us will, in my opinion, learn this lesson too late.
G. M. Loeb

My belief is that nothing short of national bankruptcy will ever stop this extravagance. Americans have been taught that the national treasury is an illimitable pool of money and they'll not be disabused of that delusion until they wake up some morning and find it quite empty.
H. L. Mencken

Gold is a barometer of the value of fiat currencies.
Jerome F. Smith

Gold is a critical part of your consolidation effort. As such, it must be seen as a *store of value, not a medium of speculation.*

People have only started to see gold as an investment in the last ten years. In the past, it's always been a medium of exchange and a store of value. People didn't accumulate gold because they thought it was going to make them wealthy; they held it because it was a convenient way to represent the wealth they already had.

That's not the way things have been recently, but that's only because the government had arbitrarily price-controlled the metal at $35 an ounce for decades while the price of almost everything else was allowed to rise in response to inflation. When the lid finally blew off the pressure cooker in 1971 and the U.S. government was forced to let the price of gold float free, it had to go up radically to regain its price relative to other goods and services. Anyone who understood elementary economics could see what was going to happen. At that time, gold was the ideal speculation—something with low risk and high upside that most people (who have no real understanding of economics) wouldn't find out about until the early birds needed somebody to sell to.

In other words, gold was a very safe bet in 1971, when it was price controlled at $35 and only a few shrewd speculators were buying it. But today, after going up ten or twenty times in only a decade or so, there is much more risk. The metal rewarded early buyers by quintupling from $35 in 1971 to a $200 peak in December 1974. The market backed off over the following two years, losing nearly half its value in dollars, and over half in real terms, to a low of $103 in August of 1976, when a second bull market started. But even in 1976 gold wasn't the low-risk proposition it was in 1971; the price could always drop back to the government's floor. Although a portion of its upside potential had clearly been realized, there was a lot more left.

A second bull market started in 1976, and took gold to a climax of $886 in January of 1980, an eightfold increase. Once again the market sold off as it had before, but even more dramatically, losing about 60 percent of its dollar value and 70 percent of its real value.

Because all of the fundamental problems that drove gold above $35 are still unsolved, and compounding, the price of the metal can be counted upon to cyclically keep trending up, charting a course like a roller coaster along the way as the economy becomes ever more chaotic and markets ever more emotional. The chart below can easily be interpolated out to another, even higher, peak.

Trends in motion tend to stay in motion until some grand climax, some major crisis, turns them around.

Chart I
Gold (Comex) New York

(Monthly High, Low and
Close of Nearest Futures)

Dollars
Per
Ounce

As the long-term bull market in gold reaches a grand climax, the price should go off this chart to perhaps $2,000 an ounce. Beyond that, figures may become academic as the dollar goes into hyperinflation.

That applies to gold as well. The major bull market that started in 1971 is still in existance and probably will continue until the present monetary system collapses and somehow restructures itself on a sound basis. But although your basic bias toward gold should stay very bullish, let me reiterate that its character as an invest-ment has changed radically since 1971. Gold is no longer the low-risk high-potential speculation it once was. Throughout the 1970s, gold was an *ideal* specula-tive medium. People could buy at almost any price with the assurance that they'd eventually be able to sell at higher prices. Gold at $400 or $500 or $600 or more an ounce is not the same investment as gold at $35 or even $200 an ounce. You have to realize that the huge for-tunes made during the 1970s were a once-in-a-genera-tion, or even a once-in-a-lifetime, opportunity. But any commodity which goes up fifteen or twenty times in value in the space of ten years can no longer be viewed as a low-risk high-potential speculation.

That's not to say that gold won't explode in price by the time the next bull market crests; in fact, it probably will. But it's getting very late in the game, and at some point soon the downside risk will greatly exceed the upside potential. The market will have matured, and all the potential for gains (in real terms) will have vanished. At that point the metal will keep pace with the debase-ment of the currency over the long haul (which is enough) but the gains in real terms will certainly be gone. Gold at $35 is one thing, at $400 another, and at $3,000 yet another.

Predictably, most of the dealers selling gold today use its tremendous performance record as a reason to buy it, but that same performance record is the best reason not to buy it. At least not to buy it as a speculation.

Changing Your Thinking About Gold

If you see gold as a speculative vehicle, then you should treat it as any other widely traded commodity and use the methods outlined in Chapter 28. The only caveat is that gold is much more politically controlled and politically sensitive than the other commodities and as a result can be quite unpredictable in the short run. Of course, political sensitivity also makes it much more predictable in the long run, and that's the way to play the market. The easiest way to do that is to change your perception of gold and view it as *a store of value.*

Eventually gold will return to its role as money, and it's wise to make sure that you have as much as possible when that time comes. Although gains still lie ahead for the gold market as people in the future panic into it from fear and greed, that kind of market is innately volatile. Rather than wrenching your emotions when those price movements occur, and trying to second-guess the market for trading profits, buy gold because it's prudent. As the financial world starts hemorrhaging, gold should be held for safety and insurance, not capital gains. Gold provides a safety net to catch you in the event of total collapse.

How to Buy Gold

Accordingly, it's best to accumulate the metal steadily, at regular intervals, over time. Your major purpose is savings, not speculation, and it's essential to use a plan that is sure to prevent your emotions getting out of control when the market heats up. Let others buy gold for emotional reasons; that's a losing game.

There are two workable methods of accumulating: *unit averaging* and *dollar averaging.* To unit-average, put in a standing order with a gold dealer to purchase a Krugerrand (or ⅒ Krugerrand, or 10 of them, depending on your finances) every week (or month). That assures that your gold holdings increase steadily over time, which is the object. Although this is the most obvious method, it's not the best; dollar averaging is both more convenient and potentially more profitable.

Unit Averaging vs. Dollar Averaging

Buying a fixed number of ounces (or grams) of gold at fixed intervals is called unit averaging. Buying a fixed dollar amount is called dollar averaging. If you're in the market for the long pull, dollar averaging is far superior. It's not a new concept, and has long been touted as an advantage of mutual funds (purchased by dollar amount) over individual stocks (purchased by the unit). As with stocks by the share, people usually think of buying gold by the ounce, not the dollar amount.

There are two major advantages to using this method in your accumulation program: reward and convenience.

Reward. Dollar cost averaging ensures you'll buy more gold when it's low, less gold when it's high. Unit cost averaging does the opposite. It's simple mathematics.

Table I illustrates the point. If one person bought a fixed number of ounces (unit averaging), and another bought a fixed dollar amount (dollar averaging), each quarter since 1970 the second person would have achieved a much lower average cost. The actual dollar amount, or number of ounces, is irrelevant as long as both amounts remain constant over the entire time.

In practical application, the results should be even better, as there's a natural tendency for most people to buy when prices are exploding and gold is in the evening news. That, of course, is the worst thing to do, the exact opposite of the technique I suggest in later chapters. If nothing else, a dollar-cost-averaging plan ensures discipline in purchase. Dollar averaging is, in addition, more convenient.

The essence of a gold accumulation plan should be consistency. You should continue to buy regardless of market conditions, by setting aside a fixed percentage of your income each week or month to put in gold. If you use the unit-averaging method and decide to buy one-

Table I   GOLD PURCHASE COMPARISON
Cost Averaging vs. Unit Purchase Averaging
1970 through 1981

Year and Quarter	Average Quarterly Gold Price Per Ounce	Unit Method: Cumulative Average Price Per Ounce Purchased	Cost Method: Cumulative Average Price Per Ounce Purchased
1970 1	$ 35.01	$ 35.01	$ 35.01
2	35.73	35.37	35.37
3	35.30	35.35	35.34
4	37.47	35.88	35.85
1971 1	38.46	36.39	36.35
2	39.87	36.97	36.89
3	41.89	37.67	37.53
4	42.94	38.33	38.13
1972 1	47.45	39.35	38.98
2	55.25	40.94	40.16
3	66.06	43.22	41.65
4	63.89	44.94	42.89
1973 1	74.57	47.22	44.34
2	104.19	51.29	46.24
3	110.01	55.21	48.10
4	100.58	58.04	49.72
1974 1	149.21	63.40	51.75
2	163.20	68.95	53.79
3	149.67	73.20	55.67
4	174.84	78.28	57.63
1975 1	178.02	83.03	59.55
2	167.16	86.85	61.34
3	157.42	89.92	63.02
4	141.51	92.07	64.51
1976 1	131.71	93.66	65.85
2	126.86	94.93	67.09
3	113.94	95.64	68.13
4	126.81	96.75	69.27

Table I GOLD PURCHASE COMPARISON (continued)

Year and Quarter		Average Quarterly Gold Price Per Ounce	Unit Method: Cumulative Average Price Per Ounce Purchased	Cost Method: Cumulative Average Price Per Ounce Purchased
1977	1	138.94	98.21	70.49
	2	145.52	99.78	71.72
	3	145.95	101.27	72.92
	4	160.50	103.12	74.19
1978	1	178.33	105.40	75.52
	2	178.45	107.55	76.83
	3	202.62	110.27	78.21
	4	213.75	113.14	79.61
1979	1	238.33	116.52	81.07
	2	258.62	120.26	82.56
	3	316.93	125.31	84.16
	4	415.46	132.56	85.87
1980	1	632.18	144.76	87.72
	2	544.92	154.27	89.51
	3	648.95	165.78	91.34
	4	627.54	176.27	93.15
1981	1	518.47	183.87	94.88
	2	478.15	190.27	96.56
	3	421.41	195.19	98.17
	4	420.74	199.89	99.77

tenth of an ounce a week, you may be able to afford gold at $400 an ounce but may have to scrap your plan at $800. Once you lose the discipline of the plan, it may be hard to regain. But by dollar averaging it's possible to predict that what you buy will always be within your means. The dollar-averaging approach is by far the superior method.

There are two ways you can dollar-average with gold:

buying different sizes of gold coins and buying into a gold mutual fund.

Gold Coins. There are hundreds of types of gold coins widely available today, but most of them have some value as collectors' items. It's for exactly that reason you don't want most of them. Most numismatic coins are grossly overpriced today.

What you do want are bullion-type coins, currently being struck by a number of countries and private mints around the world. The table below contains the commonly available bullion-type coins in decreasing order of gold content.

Table II GOLD COINS

Coin	Mint	Gold Content (Ounces)
50 Peso	Mexico	1.2056
Krugerrand	South Africa	1.000
Maple Leaf	Canada	1.000
One Ounce	Mexico	1.000
100 Corona	Austria	.9802
100 Korona	Hungary	.9802
½ Krugerrand	South Africa	.5000
Half Ounce	Mexico	.5000
20 Peso	Mexico	.4823
4 Ducat	Austria	.4438
¼ Krugerrand	South Africa	.2500
Quarter Ounce	Mexico	.2500
10 Peso	Mexico	.24115
5 Peso	Mexico	.1206
1 Ducat	Austria	.1110
⅒ Krugerrand	South Africa	.1000
2½ Peso	Mexico	.0603
2 Peso	Mexico	.0482

The best choice among these coins is the Krugerrand, as it is the most widely recognized coin available. As such, it tends to command a slightly higher premium than the others.

A standing arrangement can be worked out with a gold dealer to purchase whatever number of whichever coins add up the closest to the dollar amount you've decided to invest. The following gold dealers all have good reputations:

Lucien L. Birkler & Company
1100 17th Street NW
Washington, D.C. 20036
(202) 833-3770

Numisco
1423 West Fullerton Avenue
Chicago, Illinois 60614
(800) 621-1339 (Toll-free)
(312) 528-8800

U.S. Paper Exchange
2401 Lowry Avenue
Minneapolis, Minnesota 55418
(612) 781-5001
(800) 328-2480 (Toll-free)
Attn. Jane Kettleson

Blanchard & Company
8422 Oak Street
New Orleans, Louisiana 70118
(800) 535-8588 (Toll-free)
(504) 865-9919

Investment Rarities, Inc.
One Appletree Square
Minneapolis, Minnesota 55420
(800) 328-1860 (Toll-free)
(612) 853-0700

Monex
4910 Birch Street
Newport Beach, California 92660
(800) 854-3361 (Toll-free)
(800) 432-7013 (California only) (Toll-free)
(714) 752-1400

Panamex
P.O. Box 137, Villa du Bochet 20
1815 Clarens/Montreux,
Switzerland

Gold Mutual Funds.   A gold mutual fund allows you to gradually accumulate a position in the metal by purchasing shares in a trust set up to buy gold.

Most of the major U.S. brokers offer plans that allow accumulations of gold on a dollar-averaging basis, and a call will deliver sales literature to you.

Merrill Lynch Gold Sharebuilders Plan
Merrill Lynch, Inc.
P.O. Box 399, Bowling Green Station
New York, N.Y. 10274
(800) 221-1840 (Toll-free)
or in New York (800) 522-1880
or contact your local Merrill Lynch office

Citibank Gold Purchase Plan
Citibank Gold Center
399 Park Avenue
New York, N.Y. 10043
(800) 223-1080 (Toll-free)
or in New York (212) 559-6041

Deak's Gold Certificate Program
Deak & Co. (Washington)
1800 K Street NW
Washington, D.C. 20006
(800) 424-1186 (Toll-free)
or in Washington, D.C. (202) 872-1233

Few people, however, are aware of a similar plan available in Europe offered by a Swiss company, Goldplan, A.G., which may be a better alternative.

Goldplan, A.G.
Volkmarstrasse 10
P.O. Box 213-44
8033 Zurich, Switzerland.

The plan has two advantages over those offered by the American brokerage firms: it's out of the U.S. and it's private. Gold held by a foreign bank or company is beyond the control of the U.S. government. If the government decides Americans must turn in their gold, the U.S. brokers will be forced to comply, even if that means compromising their clients' interests. A foreign company is in a position to disregard U.S. law. That leaves the choice up to you. And because foreign companies don't require Social Security numbers or make their client lists available to government agencies, this gives greater privacy.

I'm not, incidentally, counseling that you break the law should the law not suit you, even though that may be the intelligent, productive, and ethical thing to do. But I am suggesting you leave your options open. For that reason, all your gold acquisitions should be made in a private way. There are several books on privacy listed in Chapter 33. If you buy gold using money orders or other untraceable instruments, you're still well within the law now. After all, if the government does something stupid, you want to be the one who determines what will happen to your gold, not them.

Predicting Gold Prices

The ideal time to buy gold is when the market is quiet; it's a lot easier then to make up one's mind in a thoughtful manner. Rational decisions are hard to make in a market that's running rampant up or down, with frenzied buyers and sellers stumbling over one another, jamming telephone lines to their brokers. It isn't always fun trying to determine whether you've been wiped out or made a fortune on any given day. Which is another reason to buy gold gradually, according to a plan, because the 1980s will have plenty of chaotic days. The best thing to do in markets like that is to stay out until the dust settles.

It's harder to be objective about gold than about any other commodity. Many buy the metal for ideological reasons as much as for financial considerations. The ideological gold buyer believes he is doing his part to affirm capitalism and fiscal responsibility. His act defies the Washington socialists, affronts *The New York Times,* and raises the blood pressure of Federal Reserve Board members. He considers it an act to punish those who don't understand that a government can't inflate without consequences.

For many gold buyers, therefore, gold isn't just an investment; it's a political statement. That feeling is *exactly* why libertarians and fiscal conservatives always get caught long in gold bear markets. They feel that betting the gold price will decline—even thinking it— shows a break of faith in American ideals. They don't understand that "investment" and "ideology" are two different things. They don't understand that gold isn't a religious relic, it's a commodity.

In light of recent history, what means can be used for predicting the price behavior of gold over the next few years? There is a recurring pattern; the recent top at $886 was quite predictable. There have been similar patterns in sugar, coffee, cocoa, copper, wheat—all the commodities. The sequence goes something like this:

1. A long, moderately rising period of accumulation.
2. An event which causes a runaway bull market.

3. A collapse.
4. A rally near, but not as high as, the original high. Then comes another, more serious collapse. After the final collapse, a commodity will usually remain bearish for one to three years. Accumulation must again occur before another bull market can get under way.

If you look at the prices of gold since 1971, you'll see that it behaves like any other commodity, although each commodity market moves for reasons peculiar to itself. Wheat can move because of Soviet politics, orange juice because of frost, and lumber because of interest rates. Gold is a barometer of financial crisis, economic sickness, and political stupidity. But it's still a market like any other.

Gold prices hit a major top in December of 1974 and January of 1980, each time marking an end of a bull market. Naturally, people rushed into gold—hundreds of thousands of them for the first time, figuring it was a smart move. Of course, by the time "everyone" knows that an investment is the smart move, the bottom is about to fall out, and that is exactly what happened. Just when the public was most involved, the top came—on January 3, 1980, when gold hit $886.40. And it was all downhill from there. Prices fluctuated as bargain hunters, late entrants, and early buyers with profits bought and sold in a frenzied market, but the emotion of fear was starting to overcome greed. And when reason started to replace emotion, the end was near.

Being Comfortable with Gold

There are still a fair number of people at large who won't buy gold themselves, or propagandize against others doing so, because they think it's somehow un-American. They see gold as a socially repugnant investment, a long-term bet that the social order will collapse. They seem to think gold owners have an interest in making sure things get as bad as possible in order to underwrite their investment success. It's probably a good idea to deal with those fatuous arguments, because if you're going to own gold, you have to be comfortable with it on all levels.

Is Gold Unproductive?

Since gold has no intrinsic value in some people's eyes, they think the money put into gold could be used more productively in another investment. From a strictly economic point of view, buying gold is no different from buying copper or food or a house or a car or a work of art. If enough people buy the products of those industries, the industries will become more profitable and expand by building new plants and hiring new workers. Some people may think an expansion of the gold industry is bad, because they dislike gold. But then again others (such as environmentalists) may think an expansion of the copper industry is bad, while others (such as zero-population-growth enthusiasts) may not want to see more food grown. Zoning boards may disapprove of more construction, and safety crusaders dread an expansion in the number of autos.

Buying a work of art doesn't seem to meet with the disapprobation that buying gold does, although people do it, in fair measure, for the same reason—to beat inflation. The one act employs artists, the other gold miners. The art gives pleasure by hanging on the wall, the gold by sitting in a safe. It's all subjective value judgment, and allegations that putting money into gold or anything else is "unproductive" don't prove anything but the preferences of the speaker.

Is Gold Un-American?

Nationalistically inclined goldphobes like to say that buying gold sends "our" dollars abroad into the hands of untrustworthy foreigners who will plot to use them against us or for some evil purpose. The U.S. produces less than 900,000 ounces per year—just over 2 percent of the world total—and in 1980 gold contributed $1.53 billion to America's $25.342 billion trade deficit. I don't know about your share of "our" dollars, but I own mine. The fact that they're printed in Washington doesn't transform them into communal property. Even if I could lay partial claim to some because as an American I'm part of the "our," I'd probably refuse because it would imply some liability for their declining value.

In fact, an intelligent nationalist should argue that it's patriotic to buy all the gold (and everything else possible) abroad because the foreigners will eventually get stuck holding that much worthless paper while we will have real wealth in exchange.

A variation of this argument is that buying gold, unlike making a deposit in a savings account, allows the money to lie dormant. The argument is fatuous, because the world grows in wealth by production and saving, not consumption and spending. If you keep your gold in a safe, that only increases the unit value of all the other gold in the world. You've only deferred your own consumption, but haven't changed anyone else's pattern of behavior. But then you might wonder what the gold dealer or gold miner does with the dollars you used to buy the gold.

Is Gold Racist?

Another argument intended to shame the gold buyer is the allegation that he supports the repressive regimes in South Africa and Russia—the world's number 1 and number 2 gold producers—by buying the stuff. It's just as easy to argue that gold purchases help keep both the black miners in South Africa and the slave laborers in the U.S.S.R. from starving to death, and as such is a humanitarian gesture. Anyway, if the Soviets didn't have gold to pay for the food that's shipped to them, the U.S. government would probably give the food to them for free.

In the last analysis, it doesn't really matter what you do with your dollars once you earn them. If you'd like, you can burn them, or toss your gold in the ocean, and the world wouldn't be one iota poorer. (In the case of the gold, it would be a bit poorer, since gold, unlike the dollars, *is* real wealth, as well as representing it.) The dollars are just a bookkeeping measure to show what goods or services you've created, and they are what made the world richer.

In short, it's more important to spend time thinking about the safest way to store gold after you've bought it than the academic reasons why you shouldn't buy it.

Storing Gold and Other Things Privately

The question often arises where to store one's gold (or, for that matter, other valuables). Although it may sound a bit flip, the best answer is "In the safest place you can think of."

That usually means a bank safe deposit box to an American, and a secure plot in the garden for a Frenchman. European peasants like to keep gold and other valuables nearby not because they think they'll be more secure from theft than in a bank vault but because that method is more private and secure from the government. It might be wise to consider their reasoning before you put all your gold in one place.

It's hard for a thief to break into a bank's vault and then into your box, but it's no problem at all for a government agency to do just that under cover of law. Gold could become "politically sensitive" in the future. Therefore, your holdings should be both purchased and stored in a secure manner. Purchases should ideally be by money order, cashier's check, or cash; just keep the receipts for tax purposes.

It's happened before, and possession of gold (or silver) could be illegalized again. If it is, the government might require the inspection of everyone's safe deposit box so agents could check for the presence of the newly controlled substance. Anything is possible. I don't know, and neither, probably, does the government; but there's no point in painting yourself into a corner.

There are, in addition, other things that you may want to store securely, but not in a place that's readily available to the government.

Tax and financial records are some of them. When dealing with the IRS, it's best, of course, to stay completely aboveboard. But you never know when some Byzantine twist of the tax code could overturn the entire financial foundation of your life and you might be presented with a tax lien; a "jeopardy assessment" could be levied upon your assets, perhaps for some mistaken or trivial reason. At that point your local safe deposit box could be sealed by the IRS, and if it's opened the contents could further complicate matters. It's best that you be in control of the information available to the government.

A readily available safe deposit box can complicate your estate planning as well. Most banks make an effort to determine if any of their boxholders have died, which includes daily reading of the obituary columns. Should a boxholder die, the usual policy is to seal the box and prevent any co-signatories from entering it until an agent of the IRS can be present to determine what assets might be sequestered there for estate tax purposes.

There are probably some other areas where an intrusion by the government could upset your plans, or at least inconvenience you. But the point I want to make is that having gold and other valuables in a bank safe deposit box only insulates them from conventional thieves; it substantially increases your risk from governmental action, because those sensitive possessions are stored in a controlled central place along with hundreds of others in the same position. There seem to be several logical alternatives:

1. *A bank box outside your city or state.* The box will still be subject to the fiat of government affecting all boxholders, but they won't realistically be able to go after yours in particular.

2. *A bank box in a foreign country.* The most likely choices are Canada, Switzerland, and the Bahamas. Here you've totally insulated yourself from the U.S. government, and you have very little to fear from the foreign governments, since you're not one of *their* citizens. In addition, there are no reporting requirements for foreign safe deposit boxes, unlike foreign bank accounts. The disadvantage is solely the inconvenience of travel to the box, but that is balanced by the geographical and political diversification you'll gain for a portion of your assets. Simply walk into a big bank the next time you're abroad and take action.

3. *Non-bank depositories in the U.S.* These can have a number of advantages over a bank. Since these depositories are not banks, they're not subject to bank regulations and reporting requirements, including disclosure of your identity. Also, in the event of some unpredictable political action, the private vaults may be overlooked, at least for a while, giving you time to act. The banks, as unofficial minions of the state, would respond immediately. The only one I can recommend is

the Security Center, which is associated with the James U. Blanchard Company. The center is housed in the former Federal Reserve Bank of New Orleans Building and seems as physically secure as any bank. There are several other advantages, including the ready availability of all-risk insurance, 24-hour, seven-day-a-week service, and a bonded custodian who can make deposits or withdrawals to your box should you authorize him to. Costs appear to be about 50 percent above standard bank rates, but it's probably worth it.

J. U. Blanchard and Co.
4425 West Napoleon Avenue
New Orleans, Louisiana 70001
(504) 456-9034

But there's always another alternative.

4. *A hole in the ground.* It may be primitive, but it's secure, private, and has worked for thousands of years. A small safe set into concrete in the foundation of the house might be an excellent alternative.

Just as it's a good idea to keep the purchase of some assets private, it's important to keep their location private. If you want to keep the existence of *any* box private, it's essential to (1) not pay the box rental fee by check and (2) not tax-deduct the fee on your income tax return. Paying by check is, of course, easier, and taking the legal tax deduction cuts your real costs by up to 50 percent; but it could be penny wise and pound foolish, especially with a small box costing as little as fifteen dollars per year. Anything in either your checking account or tax return is a matter of public record.

The Bottom Line

Since money was invented, gold has always been the preferred financial asset. It's the only financial asset that is not simultaneously someone else's liability; as such, it can't be inflated out of existence or defaulted on. It's convenient, consistent, durable, divisible, and can't be created or destroyed by fiat.

Gold is, in short, the ultimate insurance policy against financial crisis. View it that way. At least *10 percent* of your net wealth should be in gold coins in your own possession. Additional purchases should be made outside the U.S. If you want income from gold or wish to use it as a speculation, turn to the securities listed in Chapters 24 and 26. As for gold itself, buy it, put it away, and forget about it. It's your vehicle for all long-term savings until at least the end of the decade.

In addition, one other investment, silver, can be considered as part of your sound investment foundation.

The Golden Rules

- *Regard gold only as a store of value; it's no longer a low-risk medium of speculation.*
- *Accumulate gold by dollar cost averaging.*
- *Keep 10 percent of your net wealth with you in gold coins.*
- *Buy and store your gold privately, and consider a foreign depository for a portion of it.*

And Now for Silver

Throughout history three metals have been used as money: gold, silver, and copper. All share the five qualities of a good money—durability, divisibility, portability, consistency, and intrinsic value—but in different proportions. All three metals can be bought for the same reasons as well—each is a long-term store of value, a medium of exchange, and an interesting speculation, at least periodically.

Gold has always been, and probably always will be, used primarily as money. Copper will probably remain an industrial metal. Silver falls neatly in between them both in price, the way it's used, and where it fits into your investment portfolio. It can be viewed both as a way to save—like gold—and a way to speculate—like copper.

A very bullish fundamental case has been built for silver over the years, and I lay it out in detail in *Crisis Investing*. In a nutshell, the available supply of silver will tend to diminish, since most easily available supplies have probably already been discovered and mined, and a great deal of the supplies hoarded over the past centuries have already been distributed. Meanwhile, technology is discovering hundreds of new uses for the metal each year. Over the long term, that is bound to put upward pressure on prices, handsomely rewarding both those who want to conserve capital and those who wish to speculate.

Silver belongs in every portfolio for both those reasons, and also for a third: barter. It's hard to make change for a Krugerrand, but a silver dime, quarter, or half-dollar is just the right size for most everyday transactions. Further, if the U.S. dollar ever becomes unacceptable because of hyperinflation, war, or some other catastrophe, most Americans are familiar with silver coins and would be willing to accept them in trade.

You should, therefore, hold silver both in the form of pre-1965 U.S. coins kept in your own possession for the purpose of "insurance," as well as bullion. The bullion portion of your silver position can be used almost interchangeably with gold for the reasons covered earlier. You'll want to hold most silver in bullion, since the coins typically sell for a premium of 10 to 30 percent above their intrinsic silver value—at least while the metal is at the low end of its trading range.

You'll do well to accumulate silver the same way you

would gold, although as the following chart shows it can
be much more volatile than gold.

Silver is a textbook example of something that is a
superb speculation, but only if you buy at the right
price. What might that be? The metal is eight dollars as
this book goes to press, and that presents excellent
value. Buy silver for cash from any of the companies
listed for gold in this chapter, or in the futures market
as you would copper. Which you choose depends on
whether you're treating the metal as a store of value or a
speculation at the time. There's every reason to believe

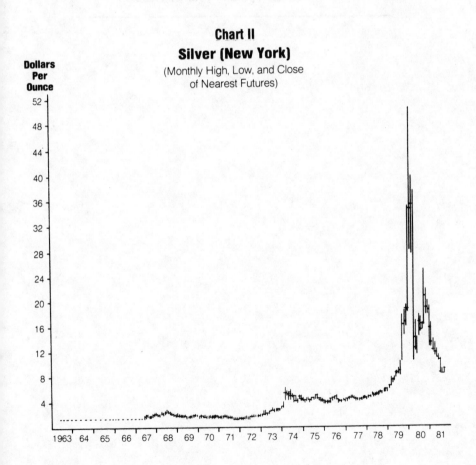

Chart II
Silver (New York)
(Monthly High, Low, and Close
of Nearest Futures)

Dollars
Per
Ounce

that in the speculative manias of the '80s silver will reach, and far exceed, its previous highs. But with a lot of drama along the way to wipe out amateur speculators.

Silver

- *View silver as both a store of value and as a speculation.*
- *Accumulate pre-1965 silver coins the same way you would gold.*
- *Keep between 3 percent and 20 percent of your net worth in silver coins in your possession.*

Chapter 15

Swiss Francs and
Swiss Banks

The state is a force incarnate. Worse, it is the silly parading of force. It never seeks to prevail by persuasion. Whenever it thrusts its finger into anything it does so in the most unfriendly way. Its essence is command and compulsion.
M. A. Bakunin

Because none of the fundamentals behind gold and silver has changed radically since 1971, I won't repeat in detail the arguments *Crisis Investing* makes for them or for the Swiss franc either. It's enough to say that the franc has been inflated less than the dollar in the past, and that is likely to continue. Further, because of that, Switzerland is much more likely to have a deflationary depression than is the U.S.; the franc could become much more valuable, quite quickly, as billions of them are wiped out in a credit collapse.

It's a prudent diversification to have a portion of your assets in some foreign country, apart from the investment potential. The greatest risks confronting you are not investment risks; they are political risks. Just as it's wise to diversify among different investments to ensure that no matter what happens you'll always have a "grubstake" left, it's even more important to diversify among different countries. Whether you like it or not, your government considers you and your property a "national resource" to be used as needed. So it's wise to have some assets where the government can't reach them.

The simplest solution, of course, is just to open a foreign bank account and start moving cash into it. But that presents a problem, in that the government requires you to report the existence of all such accounts. (There are minor exceptions, including accounts of under $1,000.) That means that if (*when* is a safer word, actually) the government imposes foreign exchange controls, you'll be required to repatriate the funds—and that, of course, will be the very time it's most important to have them abroad. The problem is similar to that presented by gold in most ways. Only you can provide the answer, and you must accept the consequences of taking—or not taking —action.

Should you care to explore the services available through a Swiss bank, the following institutions have good reputations and are easy to deal with:

Bank Indiana Suisse
Avenue Gare 50
1001 Lausanne, Switzerland
Attention: Mr. F. C. Mishrahi

Foreign Commerce Bank
Bellariastrasse 82
8038 Zurich, Switzerland
Attention: Andre Rufer

Cambio und Valorenbank
Utoquai 55
8008 Zurich, Switzerland
Attention: Werner Schwartz

Bank fur Kredit und Aussen Handel
Talestrasse 82
8010 Zurich, Switzerland
Attention: Ernst Pernet

Ueberseebank, A.G.
Limmatquai 2
8024 Zurich, Switzerland
Attention: Kurt Kamber

There is, incidentally, a route between the horns of the dilemma: the Swiss franc annuity.

Portfolio Management

Switzerland has been managing investment portfolios for an international clientele for decades, and Swiss financial institutions rank among the most sophisticated in the world. While Swiss banks offer most financial services, there are, in addition, non-banking institutions which specialize in investment advisory services, portfolio management, and similar activities. These specialized financial institutions in Switzerland resemble U.S. stock brokerage firms, and are often able to offer more personal service than the banks. They may be a better alternative for most Americans.

I am familiar with one such firm in Lugano, and you may want to write to them to get more information:

COFET, S.A.
Compagnie Financiere des Europlacements
Via S. Balestra 27
6900 Lugano, Switzerland
Attention: H. R. Brandenberger (Director)

Swiss Franc Annuities

An annuity is a contract that guarantees a stipulated return of both principal and interest over a period of years. Because of that, annuities have been terrible investments over the last thirty years.

On the face of it, the thought of buying an annuity is silly, but there can be real advantages to getting one in Swiss francs regardless of your age. The annuity you want should be structured to give an excellent measure of privacy, safety, and investment potential in a convenient package while it solves the political diversification problem. There are at least five major advantages to having one:

1. A legally binding contract with a foreign insurer should insulate you from foreign exchange controls. The

government can always require you to repatriate funds in a foreign bank account, but they can't make a Swiss insurance company violate its contract with you.

2. Annuities are not reportable assets under current law, so you can quite legally keep your business private, again unlike a foreign bank account.

3. The annuity pays interest about twice that available from a bank.

4. There's no Swiss withholding tax on the interest an annuity pays, which further increases its effective yield.

5. Like most annuities, it shelters your interest income from U.S. taxes, until you take a distribution.

The time to buy, of course, is when the Swiss franc is low relative to the dollar, and, as of press time, the franc is starting to come out of a major bear market.

The following companies can supply full information:

Assurex, S.A.
P.O. Box 209-44
8033 Zurich, Switzerland

Troy Associates Ltd.
Case Postale 157-D
1211 Geneva, 12, Switzerland
Attn. M. G. Marsh

Swiss Francs

- *There's nothing a domestic broker or bank can do that a Swiss bank can't do more privately.*
- *Political risk is the greatest single danger confronting you, and proper offshore planning is necessary to neutralize it.*
- *The Swiss franc is more likely to go through a 1933-style deflation than a 1923 German-style hyperinflation.*

Speculating for Maximum Profit

PART V

Chapter 16

Going on the Offensive

At his best, Jay Gould was always compelled to face the chance of failure. Commodore Vanderbilt, though he often had the Street in the palm of his hand, was often driven into a corner where he had to do battle for his life, and so it has been with every great speculator.
Henry Clews

It is only by risking our persons from one hour to another that we live at all.
William James

A wise man was he who counselled that speculation should have free course, and look fearlessly toward all the thirty-two points of the compass, whithersoever and howsoever it listed.
Thomas Carlyle

The program of liquidation, creation, and consolidation laid out earlier can financially and psychologically liberate anyone to pursue bigger and better things. If you've followed it, you're beyond past mistakes and ready to earn more, and you have a floor under your standard of living so that even if you make a serious mistake in speculation it won't alter your lifestyle.

The first three parts of the strategy were defensive. Now it's time to go on the offense, something many investors seem to be afraid to do.

The 1980s will be the decade of the speculator. Successful speculators should emerge from the 1980s wealthy beyond their wildest dreams. Fortunately, it's a profession open to all. No formal education, credentials, or licenses are required. All training is on the job, and best of all, the apprenticeship is "earn while you learn." It's an appealing job opportunity, but unfortunately one that carries a stigma.

I've been talking about a lot of suspiciously asocial concepts in this book: financial crash, depression, hyperinflation, the alternative economy, hoarding. They're all buzz words that arouse vivid images and strong emotions. Perhaps the most powerful word of all, however, is "speculator." It sounds so irresponsible, opportunistic, and dangerous.

Politicians and the media throw the word speculator about so abusively, I suspect few people have ever dared to ask what one really is. In the popular mind a speculator is someone associated with shortages, price hikes, wars, natural disasters, and other calamities. A speculator is simply someone who sees, or anticipates, distortions in the marketplace and positions himself to take advantage of them. He can do that because he understands their causes, and their effects.

Bear in mind, *no speculator causes any of this*. He merely profits from it. Or he may lose from it. But anyone who understands economics and politics, and what's likely to happen when the government mixes its inflation, taxes, and regulation together in a witch's brew, can be a successful speculator.

The Speculator as Hero

Speculation will be the foundation of dynasties in the turbulent years ahead. The original Baron Rothschild knew how to profit from the politically created chaos of the French Revolution era. He became rich and famous by following his own advice to "buy when blood is running in the streets."

That doesn't mean the speculator is predatory; paradoxically, he's a humanitarian. When people are desperate to sell their possessions, he appears with cash—the very thing they want most. When they change their minds and clamor to buy those things back from him during good times, he once again graciously accedes to the desires of the majority. The speculator, like any other worker, tries to give his employers what they want. Value is subjective, and the price at which something voluntarily trades hands is exactly what it's worth at the time; the speculator simply gives value for value. If he wasn't there to buy, perhaps no one would be, and sellers would really be in trouble.

There is nothing more immoral about being a speculator than there is about being a soldier or a doctor. People in each profession provide a service. The services of a speculator are needed only during times of panic or mania; those of a soldier only during times of war; those of a doctor only when the body is ill. Each is an honorable trade, although it would be nice if we didn't need any of them. But that's not the way the world is structured at the moment, and there's no point in weighing yourself down with grief (because things aren't perfect), guilt (because somebody says your pro-survival acts are "wrong"), or shame (because you continue speculating even if you believe him).

A speculator doesn't pass moral judgment on the way things are. A socialist sees government intervention as "good," a libertarian sees it as "bad," but a speculator doesn't clutter his mind with those opinions. He tries to maintain a scientific "value free" approach, and doesn't mix investment with ideology.

An unregulated market is fairly efficient. There are gradual adjustments in price, responding to supply and demand, but rarely any wild gyrations.

In a stable free-market society, speculators would be chronically unemployed because there would be no government intervention to cause the distortions needed to create profitable opportunities. That means the 1980s have both some good news and some bad news for everyone. The bad news is that, in an inflationary, heavily taxed and regulated society such as ours, one has to become a speculator out of self-defense. The good news, however, is that the same governmental intervention creates plenty of opportunities to speculate successfully. There's nothing wrong with taking advantage of those opportunities. Price controls, manipulated interest rates, strikes, war rumors, subsidies, and hundreds of other politically related actions all pull the market in predictable directions.

The classic examples of a government-guaranteed speculation are gold and silver. The state price-controlled silver at $1.29 an ounce until 1965, and gold at $35 an ounce until 1971. After having been artificially suppressed for so long, the metals were a sure bet to explode upward in price. Speculators made fortunes with no risk. It's ironic, because government, despite the fact it has all the guns, a great deal of moral suasion, and an undying hatred for speculators, created exactly the opportunities they needed. If the metals hadn't been price controlled, they would gradually have drifted up with inflation, and there wouldn't have been any predictable distortion to capitalize on.

Somehow, speculators have gotten the image of careless gamblers charging about in wild, frenzied activity. It's a totally inaccurate image, at least where successful speculators are concerned. Good speculations are always low-risk speculations. Far from taking risks, speculators only go in for "sure things." They are rational and unemotional if they're successful; the irrational and emotional who like to gamble and take chances don't last long playing the game, and they soon become ex-speculators.

The Successful Speculator

Most people won't succeed in speculating. How can they predict the effects of inflation if they don't understand its causes? They think inflation must be the fault of the butcher, the baker, the gasoline maker, or, ironically, the speculator. That misconception is reinforced wherever possible by the government. As a result, most people plan their lives and investments around Establishment economic projections.

It's partly for that reason that successful speculators give little weight to economic projections emanating from the government, financial institutions, or the media. All those groups live in a static environment they think they can control; they don't understand the dynamics of markets. They all think economics is a matter of mathematics, statistics, arcane formulas, graduate-level symbols, and computer programs. But economics has absolutely nothing to do with any of that; it's simply the study of the way the world works, of how people go about getting what they want out of life.

Math and statistics are helpful in figuring out how things have been in the past, but in themselves they've got no predictive value whatever. The most "sophisticated" computer models available really do no more than just project previous trends into the future. They do it with more fanfare than a ruler and a calculator, but with no more accuracy. Even the raw data used in these complicated projections aren't to be trusted.

The government can't even be sure how large its own money supply is. (Is M-1A or M-3 or M-5 the better gauge? Should the value of things like stocks and bonds be counted? How about real estate and mortgages? Or money market funds? Or Eurodollars? All can be turned into cash equivalents in short order and can skew figures dramatically.) It doesn't know or consider the true extent of production in the alternative economy, nor can it predict developments in technology, natural disasters, the chances of war and political turmoil, or simply the development of a mania or panic. And even if it could predict what was going to happen, it can't be relied on to interpret results with any accuracy.

It's critical you learn to act as your own economist. Most of those calling themselves economists are really just social engineers and frustrated politicos in masquerade. They're generally the same crew who thought they could "fine tune" the economy over the last several decades, and they just don't have a good record of describing the way the world works—even if the public still listens to their opinions. But that's all they are, opinions.

If you don't clutter your mind with the misconceptions held by Establishment economists, there's no reason your own projections shouldn't be more accurate than those of Chase Econometrics or the Brookings Institution. You have a unique set of experiences and knowledge, and your viewpoint is as valid as anyone else's. The successful speculator never allows others' opinions to determine his action. It's just as important to be yourself in the markets as in life. Can you imagine the likes of Rothschild, Vanderbilt, or Baruch acting on the opinions of the minor clerks who predicted interest rates and economic trends of their day? Not likely.

The Necessity of Speculation

A wealthy Englishman once sought a private interview with Nathan Rothschild and expressed his great happiness at having finally amassed a fortune worth one million pounds. All he wanted to do was preserve it intact. "How," he asked, "can I be sure to have exactly that much the day I die?"

Rothschild reached into his desk drawer, took out a small pistol, and told his guest, "There's only one way; use this right now."

Most people might think that is just a funny little story, but it's an apt description of the way the world works. There are scores of millions relying upon a bank account, an insurance company, an employer, or a pension fund to provide for them in the future; they want to believe their money will compound safely. These people believe they can't afford to speculate, that they need "income" and security. Those things don't exist in the real financial world. Investing for safety and income were naive ideas in the best of times, but in today's environment the thought is tragic and pathetic, especially for those who rely on hidebound, conventional money managers. There's no such thing as a safe and secure investment with a stable yield. Everything is a speculation on something.

Nothing goes on forever. If the Medici family of Italy in the fourteenth century had set aside the equivalent of $100,000—equal at the time to a globe of gold nine inches in diameter—and had been able to make that capital grow at only 5 percent compounded over the next 600 years, its value in 1980 would be about $1,000,000,000,000,000 (one quadrillion) or 3,000 times the existing monetary stock of the U.S.

If the Indians who sold New York had only invested the $26 in beads and trinkets they were given at an assured 5 percent, they'd have enough to buy back the whole of Manhattan today. Even if they'd wanted to, though, they couldn't have, because there's never been an assured 5 percent.

Investing for income is the kiss of financial death. Why haven't any of the great millionaires of the past taken advantage of the simple gimmick of compound interest to eventually take over the world? Or why haven't they used it to simply remain intact? It isn't because they haven't tried, I'm sure. It's because no investment will give you a *true* 5 percent for even the length of a lifetime. In fact, there's probably nothing that can be relied upon to yield even 3 percent over more than forty or fifty years. You might comment, "What difference does that make? I'm not going to be here that long." But it does make a difference, because it shows the futility of trying to stay ahead in any type of "secure" investment. Everything is a speculation, whether people know it or not; those who settle for a low but "secure" return are penny wise and pound foolish in the most profound sense.

When you settle for a "conservative" return, even the slightest miscalculation, bad luck, or government fiat can wipe you out. Taxes will always erode your capital, directly or indirectly. Inflation, for the foreseeable future, is sure to both get worse and fluctuate wildly as it does. Banks and insurance companies—the very institutions that have always gotten away with offering low yields because they were so stable—will fail as they always have. The government itself will eventually be replaced and currency will become worthless. And there's no way to truly protect against the risks of war, theft, fraud, and natural disaster. Investing for income —especially in today's climate, when cracks can be seen in the foundations of society itself—is the height of stupidity.

If you invest for income, you're handing over responsibility for your future to others. You don't know what they're doing with your money, you can't know how intelligently they're going to conduct themselves in the future, and you don't even really know how sound their capital position is. That's a bad enough set of fundamentals for a madcap gamble, but in return for a simple yield it's absurd.

What, then, to do? What is the method to overcome this madness? The only answer I know of is to lay the type of foundation described in the first half of this book, and then gather up your cash and your courage and learn the art of speculation.

The rest of this book gives specific applications of the rules of successful speculation. Below are some general rules, in summary.

The Practice of Speculation

There's no certain way to gauge the proper time to enter a market, but there are certain rules that will likely be just as good in the future as they have in the past because they're based on human nature, and that hasn't changed much over thousands of years.

I've listed five signals that should be present before you enter a market. You may never find a situation where they're all there, but the more that are, the more the odds are tilted in your favor. The five rules are equally applicable whether you're buying or selling (with obvious adjustments), but I've skewed them toward the buyer. Since the long-term bias in the years ahead is going to be toward higher prices, most of the time you're going to be buying more aggressively than you'll be selling.

1. A Climactic Bottom

People tend to get carried away with greed after an investment has treated them well, and by fear when the market's been bad. The same herd instinct that causes a crowd to gather when someone stares up in the sky, or causes a stampede if someone yells "Fire!" in a crowded theater, causes markets to overrun themselves at both major tops and bottoms. Price moves typically become very radical and unpredictable at the point where a market is searching for either a top or bottom after a panic. If you can keep your head (easier said than done), those conditions present—or at least foreshadow—the ideal time to buy or sell.

"Blood in the streets" selling climaxes aren't the only time to buy, and manic blow-offs aren't the only time to sell, but they're certainly the best times. Climactic bottoms, in particular, are often followed by a period of exhaustion which can give you a chance to appraise the market coolly.

2. A Period of Accumulation

After a climactic bottom, a market becomes exhausted. With prices low, a lot of money has either been wiped out or has left the market. Like an athlete after defeat, the marketplace takes a while to recuperate.

It takes a sharp—and lucky—trader to catch a market that turns on a dime and heads the other way. It's more prudent to let it plateau, stabilize, and establish a new equilibrium level before buying. The plateau is often characterized by a "low volume" of trading.

3. Relatively Low Volume

Low volume, with few buyers or sellers, means few people are really interested in what's going on; a good speculator looks where nobody else does, to afford a better chance of finding bargains. When there's a high volume of trading, it's a sign that a lot of people are paying close attention, and that can lead to radical swings for purely psychological reasons. Successful speculators never allow themselves to be rushed or panicked, and a low-volume market offers leisure to make up one's mind.

4. Historically Low Prices

Nothing is eternal in the markets. What seems like a "high" price one year may turn out to be a "low" price the next; it's all very relative. Speculators who get the bargains are patient.

The bottom of a bear market comes but once every two or three or five years, and smart buyers sit tight until the odds are loaded in their favor. Only amateurs, pathological losers, and bank trust departments are in the market all the time.

Commodities can be considered "cheap" when they are selling for less than production costs and close to historical lows in real (after inflation) terms while there's a prospect of higher inflation.

Stocks can be considered "cheap" when they are selling for high dividends, low price/earnings ratios, below book value, and are off at least 50 percent from their previous highs.

There are plenty of exceptions around all the time, and I list some newsletters in Chapter 33 to aid you in pinpointing them. But successful speculators play a waiting game; blood isn't in the streets every day.

5. Pessimism in the Market

It's only when stories start circulating about how much lower a stock or commodity could plummet that you can be sure a bottom is near. By the time the pessimistic stories take hold, most speculators will have already unloaded, while no one else will want to buy for fear of further losses. After a long bear market, the stock or commodity has established a "poor track record" and is perceived as a "bad investment," with no future. That is, of course, usually the best time to buy.

Buying when your broker, neighbor, and the taxi driver are all telling you why they sold is hard on the nerves, but rewarding. If it were easy, everyone would be a professional speculator—and that obviously wouldn't do.

It's not easy to lay down hard and fast rules for successful speculation. There are plenty of them I could repeat here, but it's more important to adopt a mental attitude that will allow you to pick them up for yourself. Three books, none of which has anything to do with investing, illustrate the kind of approach to life, the way of thinking, that can only lead to investment success. You will likely find it helpful to become a Nexialist, a Renaissance Mechanic, and an Adventurer on the way to becoming a Speculator.

The Nexialist

A. E. Van Vogt's science fiction novel *The Voyage of the Space Beagle* tells of an officer with no fixed assignment aboard an intergalactic exploratory ship. Nobody knew what he did. He didn't know enough about physics to be a physicist, about chemistry to be a chemist, about astronavigation, or frankly anything else. He did, however, have a broad knowledge of matters totally unrelated to anything the spaceship was expected to deal with: archeology, philosophy, and psychology. He knew a little bit about everything, a Renaissance man. Van Vogt called him a nexialist, a word coined from "nexus." Suffice it to say, the nexialist saves the day for the expedition because as a generalist he is able to see relationships, solve problems, and find opportunities that others are blind to.

The speculator is a financial nexialist. He doesn't attempt to specialize in stocks, real estate, gold, or anything in particular, because that can only limit his opportunities and lead to tunnel vision. Look at the forest; let everyone else watch the trees. If gazing at the economic forest sounds a bit philosophical to you, that's because it is. In broad terms, economics is a division of philosophy.

The Renaissance Mechanic

It's necessary to become your own economist to become a whole human being. It was a point that Robert Pirsig made in the book *Zen and the Art of Motorcycle Main-*

tenance. Consider the humble motorcycle mechanic who might look to all the world like a greasy long-haired high school dropout. In reality, however, a good motorcycle mechanic must become a true Renaissance man simply in order to be a good mechanic.

When a mechanic torques down a bolt, he's got to know how much pressure to apply or he will strip the thread; if he wants to do the job well he's got to learn a bit about metallurgy. But the science of metallurgy doesn't exist in a vacuum, so he's led into chemistry. Chemistry will take him to physics, physics to astrophysics, astrophysics to astronomy, astronomy to philosophy, philosophy to economics, economics to sociology, to English literature, to Oriental literature, to Zen Buddhism; the entire world opens up to a man who is willing to pursue only the simplest action to its most logical conclusion. Knowledge is indivisible; all parts lead to other parts and eventually go full circle and return to themselves.

It's entirely within your purview to become a competent economist, just as it's quite within the ability of that motorcycle mechanic to grasp Zen Buddhism if only he truly wants to learn how to properly tighten the bolt. There's no voodoo or mysticism or mystery to it. Becoming your own economist, financier, or investment adviser is just another small part of exploring the mystery of life itself. To be truly successful at any of those things, you must eventually walk the motorcycle mechanic's path. It's easier to invest in auto stocks if you know a little bit about engineering, or in defense stocks if you know a bit about military tactics, or electric utility stocks if you understand a bit about physics.

The idea is not to clutter your mind up with a lot of meaningless trivia but rather to see the big picture. And it doesn't have to be an academic exercise. The process is fun. More to the point, since you're reading this book, the process can make you wealthy in a very short period of time.

The Adventurer

Money itself is like a lover. If you must possess it and clutch it at all times for fear it will get away, then you never really have it. But if you are able to let it go psychologically, once lost it will always return. The ability to earn money and keep it is all a matter of psychology.

A hero in one of my favorite books, *Illuminatus!* by Robert Anton Wilson, first became a multimillionaire practicing law. He'd always wanted money, but it didn't make him happy, because his wealth owned him rather than vice versa. As heroes are wont to do, he took drastic action and gave away his entire fortune except for a hundred-dollar bill and a first-class one-way ticket to Zaire. He suspected—he knew—that the money would come back to him even if he had to start over again from scratch in the jungle, and of course he was right.

Later in the book we find him a hundred times richer than he was before he gave the money away. He set himself up a trial by fire. He realized that the only wealth that anyone really has is that which is within his own mind and spirit. Money inevitably comes as a result of your inner wealth—if money is what you want.

Experienced speculators know the markets are just, and people always get what they deserve in the long run.

My Recommendation, Your Money

I'll take responsibility for my recommendations, but you have to take responsibility for what you do with them. Hiring some investment advisor to do your thinking for you may seem like the principle of specialization and division of labor in action, but it's meaningless to delegate responsibility for lost money. And only you will suffer the consequences should you blindly follow advice that doesn't pan out.

In the 1960s Marshall McLuhan said: "The medium is the message." He, of course, meant that the way things are communicated is just as important as the things themselves. The corollary in this business is: "The method is the message."

A Word to the Wise

I've had mixed thoughts about including a "model portfolio" in this book, or naming particular stocks and commodities. On the one hand, it's a good idea, since it gives solid form to what might otherwise seem to be nebulous general recommendations. It's a bad idea, however, insofar as it encourages people to slavishly follow advice, perhaps without understanding fully all the reasons why it was given. That, of course, is the exact opposite of what I'd like to accomplish.

The purpose of this book is to make the world more understandable to its readers, not less so. For that reason, whenever any author tells his readers to do something "because I say so" he's doing them a grievous disservice—even when the advice is profitable. By not explaining things, or by explaining them in an obfuscating way, he's not only mystifying the subject but creating a "black box" syndrome (i.e., I don't know how it works, but since it does I won't try to take it apart to find out). Sometimes readers tend to treat model portfolios that way, and they buy the recommended securities just because they're listed, without knowing any more.

The function of someone in my position is to act as a filtering mechanism, as a screen. The name of my game is to sort out what appear to be the greatest dangers and opportunities and tell you why that's the case. But I suggest you not skip over the reasoning in order to get to the bottom line, because that builds very sloppy mental habits and dulls the wit. The people who pick up the chips during this depression can't afford that luxury if they hope to afford anything else.

Despite my fixed feelings about a model portfolio I'm bowing to convention and including one.

The Model Portfolio

The various programs below are intended to be reasonable guidelines, simply to keep things in perspective, and are quite arbitrary in some ways. For the under-$5,000 portfolio, for instance, I was tempted to advise simply buying as much tunafish as you can put in available storage space and rereading the "Creating" section of the book; $5,000 is no longer very much money.

One of the advantages to more money is you need tie up a smaller proportion of it in static things, like the hoarding program.

Silver coins offer most of gold's advantages, plus more upside potential, while being more familiar to most Americans. The fundamentals of silver, at least as this is written, are the same as they were when I wrote *Crisis Investing*, and I suggest you review that chapter in that book.

Money funds are no more than a temporary parking place for cash, to provide liquidity and a reserve to take advantage of new opportunities.

Swiss francs belong in everyone's portfolio because they're a political diversification. Larger portfolios should have some of their gold abroad as well.

Real estate doesn't belong in any portfolios, certainly not beyond purchase of your own home. But those with larger portfolios may want to consider a few options recommended in the next chapter. And the time to buy will once again come.

Stocks belong in everybody's portfolio. Smaller amounts should be purchased with no-load mutual funds, and the penny mining stocks should be bought by everyone, although in different amounts. The division between the other stocks is at your option.

The convertible bonds I discuss later in the book can be used interchangeably with many stocks and a few commodities—especially silver. It's a matter of judgment when best to use them.

Table I   TOTAL PORTFOLIO VALUE

Investment	Under $5,000	$25,000	$100,000	$1,000,000
Hoarding Program	25%	10%	5%	2%
Gold Coins	10%	10%	10%	15%
Silver Coins	20%	10%	5%	3%
Money Funds	10%	20%	20%	20%
Swiss Francs	10%	10%	10%	10%
Stocks:	25%	40%	40%	40%
Blue Chips				
Utilities				
Penny Mines	50%*	35%*	20%*	10%*
Gambling				
S.A. Golds				
Bonds, Converts	*	*	*	*
Commodities	0	0	10%	10%
Real Estate	0	0	?	?

* Percentage of stock portfolio.

Chapter 17

Real Estate

If a man own land, the land owns him.
Ralph Waldo Emerson

You can forget about the idea that real estate always goes up in value. It doesn't.
John A. Pugsley

Investment does not exist.
Franz Pick

By the end of the 1980s, a new class of millionaires will have been made in real estate. But before investigating how the new fortunes will be made, it's wise to look at how some old ones will be lost, to make sure you're a member of the right group.

In *Crisis Investing*, I predicted a devastating real estate crash. The facts I presented there haven't changed, and there's no need to review them here; if they are dim in your memory, reread Chapter Seven of that book. You simply must face reality about real estate: The crash has a long way to go.

During the 1970s, a house seemed like the panacea for all financial ills—a combination tax shelter, savings account, retirement plan, investment portfolio, and can't-lose-get-rich-quick scheme all in one. As the market built to a fever pitch in the late 1970s, the name of the game was "Buy now, before it's too late." Of course, by the time that cry went out it was already far too late. That game is now over, and a new one called "Sell now, if you still can" has already begun.

I can't be sure what the date is as you're reading these

words—perhaps in the spring of 1982, possibly the summer of 1983, or maybe this book has only come to your attention as late as 1984. If that's the case, some of the other investments I detail here may have already realized their potential, but the real estate market may still be in free fall to a climactic bottom.

U.S. real estate in the mid-1980s has the potential for becoming the greatest financial collapse in history, and there's an excellent chance it will realize its potential. But that doesn't need to worry you—unless you own some and hold on to it. To the contrary, bull markets are always born from the ashes of bear markets, and chances are you'll have opportunities to buy real estate at bargain basement prices by the mid-1980s.

The Time to Have Sold

When an economy is prosperous and stable, there is always demand for real estate; real estate prices are a function of prosperity and stability. That's why a town house in Manhattan sells for more than one in the Bronx, why farmland in Alberta goes for more than its equivalent in Zaire, and why an apartment in Switzerland sells for triple the price of an identical version only a mile across the French border.

As the depression deepens, it will be reflected in lower real estate values. The real estate game in the 1980s will be totally different from that of the 1970s.

Homeowners who had gotten used to the idea of trading up to a bigger and better house every few years will be forced to stay put by declining real wages—that is, if they don't lose their jobs and aren't forced to sell their homes.

Businessmen who have gotten used to expansion and compound growth will have to think in terms of closing plants and stores, not building new ones. The properties of contracting and bankrupt businesses will go on the market.

Speculators used to holding properties in hopes of unloading to a greater fool—an excellent strategy throughout the '70s—will become discouraged and then fearful. The carrying costs, the perceived risk, and the forfeited opportunities elsewhere will cause a wave of sales. Few will be in a position to buy in a weakened economy, because they forgot, or never knew, what Baron Rothschild said when asked why he was so wealthy. He said, "I always sold too soon."

Even if you believe real estate fairly valued at 1982 levels, it's still not the type of thing you want to be in as the economy enters the Greater Depression, characterized by people running from one hot market to the next in hopes of outracing inflation. Real estate was the first to have crested, but now that the cheap borrowed money that drove it to unaffordable levels is gone, the bubble must burst.

I don't expect property to recover quickly, because it's such an illiquid investment. In the best of times it can take months to sell, but in a chaotic environment it can be a drug on the market, hardly the type of ball a broken field runner wants to carry. It's hard to sell unless there's a boom on, and it's always expensive to sell. Commissions, fees, and transfer taxes can easily eat up 10 percent of the gross.

When I wrote the *Crisis* book in 1979, a speculative boom was in progress. That crazy peak, in which people exchanged tales of housing values at cocktail parties, has passed, and prices have already dropped substantially since then in most parts of the country. But just because the top has passed doesn't mean that the bottom has come.

In retrospect, most people can see that the public mania for real estate signaled the ideal time to sell. But they're so used to thinking that real estate can only go up many can't wait to jump back in. It's nothing new. Millions were burned jumping back into stocks in 1930, thinking the '29 crash was just a healthy correction. But that's why most people never make any money in the financial markets. If the time to sell was 1979, when everyone was optimistic and buying, the time to buy won't come until everyone is pessimistic and trying to sell. Your strategy, therefore, is to stay out of real estate and increase your wealth in other areas, so that when the crowd is selling en masse you can go bargain hunting with plenty of change in your jeans. The house of your dreams—or perhaps two or three of them—will once again be affordable when the equivalent of 1933 in the stock market finally arrives. And you may not even need a mortgage to buy them.

But first, let's get residential real estate in particular into perspective.

What Is a House?

The ingredient most critical to success in the real estate market is perception. You can see real estate one of two ways: as an investment or as a consumer good. The word "investment" has been bandied about so much in recent years by people selling things that it has lost any meaning it might once have had. Today everything is supposed to be an investment, but most such investments are only uninformed speculations. Examine the three alternatives:

A *speculation* is something you purchase to resell at a profit.

An *investment* is, more properly, something that creates new wealth; it's a capital good.

A *consumer good* is anything you purchase to use and enjoy.

Houses were never investments, and the day of the

house as a speculation is over; they were only good speculations before everyone thought of them that way. Houses are consumer goods.

In other words, a house *is* wealth, but it doesn't *produce* wealth as would, say, a factory. The house you live in doesn't create new wealth, it simply increases your standard of living. That's why it's a consumer good, like a car, a wardrobe, or, for that matter, a toothbrush. It just has a longer useful life.

Houses like those being built today may last thirty years; a car might last five years, a wardrobe two years, and a toothbrush three months. You use them during that time and then discard them. Sure, you can make them last longer, but only with great care and maintenance and improvement costs.

That's what the concept of depreciation is all about; things wear out and start falling apart after a while. The concept that a house should automatically appreciate (grow more valuable) in real terms while it is depreciating is a contradiction in terms. Furnaces break, plumbing leaks, wood warps, roofs sag, and electrical wires fray. To be sure, there are special situations, but on the whole consumer goods become less valuable as they age. The fact that houses have been going up in price for years proves nothing but the fact that the currency is being debased.

There's no denying they have been great speculations, but that shouldn't come as a shock. As inflation gets worse, people will start to perceive their cars the same way; it has already happened. Used Mercedeses are represented as "investments" by naive salesmen selling to gullible buyers. But it's all an illusion. If you lived in Argentina, everything you own would "double" every year, but you'd have no more real wealth. It's time to start seeing through the illusion. Start thinking more like an Argentinian when it comes to prices, because the dollar will eventually wind up like the Argentine peso.

The price of houses today, however, shouldn't concern smart speculators, because smart speculators wouldn't own one—at least not as a speculation. Because it's now only a consumer good. If you want a house, if it gives you pleasure, *and* you can afford it, buy it and hope for the best; but don't count on it for an old age pension as most of your neighbors have done. Perfectly sensible people who wouldn't think of buying $40,000 automobiles or $1,000 suits have bought $250,000 houses on their $30,000 salaries. Somehow they can see the expensive suit or car as living above their means, but not the house, because they've talked themselves into believing they're investors. Such is the stuff of economic collapse for a society, and bankruptcy for the people who indulge in it.

If you see your house as a consumer good and if you can afford to have such a large amount of money tied up in one consumer article, by all means enjoy yourself. But realize it may be no more prudent than having a proportionately large amount of money tied up in an expensive car or an expensive wardrobe.

If those thoughts make you feel a bit uncomfortable, it might be wiser to reduce your standard of living—liquidate and consolidate—now if you care to have one vastly higher in the future. If you see your house as an enormous financial asset, you'd do better to sell it, take the profits, and rent.

Renting Your Way to Financial Freedom

You really can't afford to purchase a home today unless you can afford to pay cash for it. That's because a mortgage loan is not self-liquidating. When a business borrows to buy a machine it expects the machine to pay for itself, to produce enough new wealth to repay the principal and interest and show a profit besides. The loan is

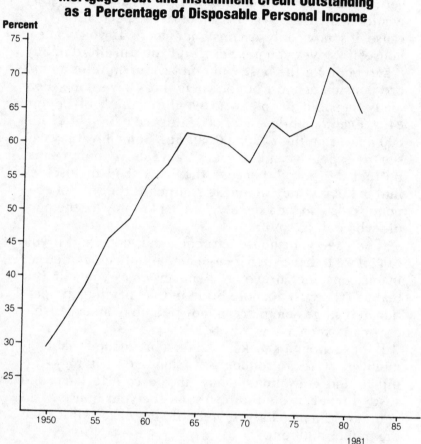

Chart I

Mortgage Debt and Installment Credit Outstanding as a Percentage of Disposable Personal Income

The huge amount of credit outstanding has allowed Americans to live above their means and is the essential reason why real estate has appreciated so much over the last 30 years.

guaranteed by three things: first by the earning power of the asset; second by the market value of the asset; and third by the credit of the borrower.

The rental value of a house is its "earning power," and few houses can now rent for enough to cover even half of the principal, interest, taxes, insurance, and, often, condo fees their owners must pay. That's one reason why the market value of houses could collapse. Massive unemployment of overextended house buyers who won't be able to pay their mortgage loans is another. All three points now signal that a lot of home loans aren't going to be liquidated.

Houses are financial assets, and in the long run their earning power determines their market value. Bonds fluctuate with interest rates, and housing fluctuates with rental returns. With 15 to 20 percent interest rates available on liquid investments, while housing shows 10 percent negative returns, prices could drop to less than half 1982 levels. It's for that reason housing could prove the financial graveyard of the average American.

Renting today, therefore, is not only prudent, but an excellent value besides.

During the last serious recession in 1974, before the last leg of the real estate boom, buying was wiser than renting. There's a time for each, and your strategy should take into account the cyclical nature of the market. The figures below were compiled for a typical four-and-a-half-room co-op in Manhattan, but could just as easily be for a home in the suburbs. The figures are equally applicable. Rents have lagged way behind the costs of ownership. The logic is simple: When rents are low relative to the cost of owning, rent. When rents are a substantial percentage of the cost of owning, buy.

If maintenance costs (or condominium fees) were included in the figures, the results would be even more dramatic.

There are those who counsel that when you rent, all you're left with is a stack of rent receipts. That would be true if renting didn't cost comparatively little today. In addition to their receipts, renters today have a stack of cash they haven't had to pay out. For the next several years, the renter will be in the catbird seat, since he will have neither the huge carrying costs nor the liability that goes with ownership.

The average house in many parts of the country now

Table I   RENTING: A BARGAIN RELATIVE TO BUYING

Year	Average Monthly Rent	Average Price	Monthly Payment 100% Financing, 30-Year, at Market Rates	Rent as % of Total Cost of Owning
1974	$ 500	$ 57,376	$ 460	120%
1975	$ 625	$ 60,750	$ 495	126%
1976	$ 750	$ 68,400	$ 554	135%
1977	$ 875	$ 81,000	$ 653	134%
1978	$1,000	$135,000	$1,144	87%
1979	$1,225	$180,000	$1,694	72%
1980	$1,450	$225,000	$2,461	59%
1981	$2,000	$255,000	$3,429	58%

costs about $100,000. Invested in a money market fund, that $100,000 could yield $15,000 a year in 1981, enough to rent the same house for about $500 per month (or $6,000 per year) and have $9,000 per year left over to pay taxes on the interest, increase your standard of living, and supplement your investment portfolio. Most importantly, the $100,000 is liquid in your own hands rather than tied up in an asset which may drop radically in value.

Renting makes economic sense; the $12,000 going into the renter's pocket in the above example is actually transferred from the landlord. A lot of landlords who thought they were shrewd investors during the '70s will be forced to unload because of the negative current yields they're absorbing. And on a $100,000 house, the negative yield is typically well over 10 percent—especially after counting taxes and maintenance costs.

The real estate market doesn't exist in a vacuum; many other attractive alternatives are competing for investors' dollars. And that is a primary reason why long-term mortgages, the main prop under housing prices, will soon disappear.

The End of the Mortgage

The price of housing and the cost of mortgage money are closely related, like opposite ends of a seesaw. Residential rental homes used to yield 12 percent in gross cash flow to landlords in the days mortgages cost only 6 percent. Now houses yield only 6 percent (i.e., $6,000 of gross rent on a $100,000 house), while mortgages cost up to 18 percent. The price of housing exploded upward because a huge pool of mortgage money created a demand for it. A higher demand for houses meant higher prices. At the same time, a greater demand for the money to buy the houses meant higher interest rates.

Higher house prices have decreased their rental yields, while at the same time higher interest rates increased the cost of carrying houses. Houses that appreciate at only 5 percent per year (as they did in 1981) are big losers if inflation is 12 percent and they're financed at 18 percent.

The easy availability of mortgage money is the only reason houses have outpaced inflation as investments. Since the last depression, housing has been the government's special pet; and fear of collapsing the construction industry has induced them to make huge amounts of credit available.

Before the last depression, houses were generally purchased with 50 percent down and the balance due on a balloon basis over no more than five years. The thirty-year fixed-rate mortgage has only appeared since the end of World War II. The amount of money in mortgages has exploded at an annual rate of over 16 percent for the last forty years—going from only $17 billion outstanding in 1944 to well over $600 billion today. The following chart shows what that's done to prices.

Chart II
Single Family House Price Index

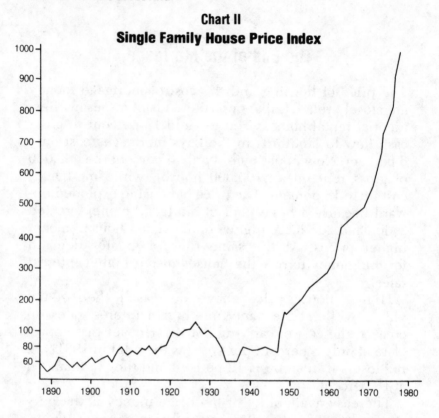

When that mortgage money (it's called "margin debt" in the stock market) is withdrawn, prices will collapse.

That's why the present downturn isn't just a healthy correction of the market on its way to even greater heights, as in previous years. The lack of mortgage money and the expense of what is available are the pinpricks to break the real estate bubble.

Throughout the '50s, '60s, and early '70s, loans were made to aspiring homeowners on the basis of their incomes and ability to pay the mortgage. Houses were "affordable" up to about 1976, before they began escalating almost geometrically in price at the very same time interest rates started their move from 8 percent to

18 percent. The more unaffordable housing became, the more people had to borrow to buy it. The following table and chart show why people will soon be unable to buy it, even if loans were available.

Table II   THE COST OF HOUSING, 1970–1981

Year	Median Price of New Single-Family House	Monthly Mortgage Payment	Average Mortgage Interest Rate (Effective Rate)	Median Annual Family Income	Mortgage Payments as % of Monthly Income
1970	$23,400	$150	8.38	$9,918	18.1%
1971	$25,200	$152	7.69	$10,338	17.6%
1972	$27,600	$165	7.53	$11,173	17.7%
1973	$32,500	$200	7.97	$12,113	19.8%
1974	$35,900	$239	8.96	$12,902	22.2%
1975	$39,300	$264	9.13	$13,719	23.1%
1976	$44,200	$296	9.07	$14,958	23.7%
1977	$48,800	$328	9.02	$16,009	24.6%
1978	$55,700	$403	9.59	$17,640	27.4%
1979	$62,900	$489	10.85	$19,684	29.6%
1980	$64,600	$569	12.84	$21,650	31.5%
1981	$69,800	$875	16.00	$23,000	45.6%

Although the price of houses has gone up almost three times since 1970, the cost of buying a house has gone up almost six times. In real terms, counting increased incomes, the net cost of buying a house has gone up two and a half times.

According to the Department of Housing and Urban Development, in 1970 half the families in the U.S. could afford a medium-priced new house. By 1980, less than 13 percent could. By 1981, the figure had fallen to 5 percent. And most of these families could "afford" the house only if they could get a high-priced mortgage.

Of course, that assumes mortgages were available. Real estate prices are built on a pyramid of long-term

Chart III
Median Prices

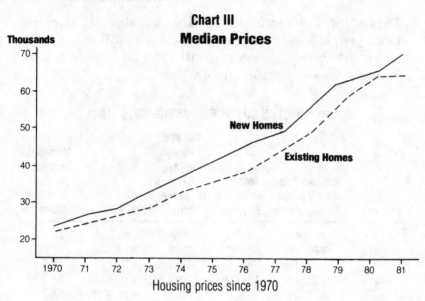

Housing prices since 1970

mortgage money, and it's totally impossible for most people to buy or sell a house today without creative financing.

Paradoxically, inflation, the very thing that people are counting on to present them with profits, is going to instead present them with huge losses, since inflation will destroy the mortgage markets. And without borrowed money, nobody can buy and nobody can sell a house. Money will flow wholesale out of lending institutions in the 1980s as the inflationary depression deepens; people will stop saving, and banks will have no money to lend.

Of course, there will be some mortgage money available (everything, after all, is available at a price), but it's going to be at interest rates that will make houses unaffordable. Even today's 16-plus percent rates are squeezing out huge sectors of the buying public that could afford houses at 10 or 12 or 14 percent rates. The table below shows how the cost of money has driven the average house totally out of reach. If the cost of money stays high, the price of houses will have to fall drastically if people are once again to afford them.

Table III	Monthly Payment for Thirty-Year $100,000 Mortgage
8%	$733.76
10%	$877.57
12%	$1,028.61
14%	$1,184.87
16%	$1,344.76
18%	$1,507.09
20%	$1,671.02

If it was hard to buy a house in 1981 with payments spread over thirty years at 18 percent, it will be very hard indeed over three to five years at 20 percent. And that's what "creative financing" is all about.

Creative Financing

"Creative financing" is the equivalent of baling wire and chewing gum and the only thing still holding the market together.

Owner financing is one such creative technique.

Until recently, a person with $10,000 cash could buy a $100,000 house because some lending institution would come up with the other $90,000. Without financing, all a person with $10,000 can buy is a $10,000 house. Without long-term mortgages, if the seller wants $100,-000 he'll only be able to get it from someone with that much cash. That means that the effective demand for $100,000 houses (i.e., people who can pay $100,000) is going to fall dramatically. And since prices are based on supply and demand, prices will fall. What's propped them up since 1979 is so-called creative financing. The seller in the above example might take the $10,000 cash, but with a note for another $90,000. To all appearances the house has traded hands for $100,000; but when that seller goes out to buy, he has only $10,000 cash in his own hand. He's now in the same position as the person who bought his house. Perhaps he can get away with the same maneuver himself with the next guy; but if any one person breaks the daisy chain, then no one can make his payments, and the illusion that houses are "worth" what they are sold for will be shattered.

The creation of credit through various types of real estate mortgages has been the essence of the housing market for several years.

Billions of dollars of borrowed money flowing into housing skyrocketed prices and presented early buyers with huge unrealized gains. That, in turn, had other effects. Although owners have no more real wealth, they feel—and act—richer.

One way homeowners have been able to act richer has been to borrow the equity out of their home through second mortgages (deeds of trust). That borrowing is probably the main factor that kept the economy from going into a deflationary depression in 1979, 1980, or 1981. But it guarantees an even bigger disaster for both borrowers and lenders in the mid-1980s. Irresponsible banks have used the device to lead their customers and themselves to perdition. One bank I know encouraged people to take out a second mortgage and use the proceeds for "a well-earned vacation."

Second, third, and fourth mortgages (in California in 1981 one house was foreclosed with nine mortgages) have allowed homeowners to keep up their lifestyles in the face of declining real incomes. It's been estimated (by the consulting firm of Townsend-Greenspan in 1981) that present homeowners paid about $1.6 trillion for single-family houses now worth about $2.6 trillion.

Nobody knows how much of that trillion dollars of appreciation has been borrowed out of them in the last few years, but we'll probably find out in the next few, because most of the junior mortgages created in the '79 to '81 period required the payment of interest alone with a final balloon payment for the principal coming due at maturity; 1982 through '85 are the magic years when most of that principal has to be rolled over. In face of a disastrous market, many sellers who "took back paper" will be unwilling to allow the unhappy homeowners to roll over their notes. And homeowners won't have the cash to pay them off. The result could be a wave of housing repossessions and forced bankruptcies. That, of course, will be the time to go house hunting.

A group of bankrupts could pass the same piece of property back and forth, offering each other more money in turn for it until both are millionaires. One because he has title to property that has "sold" for that much, and the other because he has a note for $1,000,000 given him by his friend secured by the same property. In point of fact—in the real world—the house is worth no more than the cash someone can muster to pay for it. It's been estimated that from 50 to 80 percent of all sales made in 1981 involved some form of owner financing. Yet owner financing is only the most popular form of maintaining the illusion of high home prices.

Wraparound Mortgages

The wraparound mortgage, whereby the previous mortgage is assumed by the new buyer and then supplemented by owner financing, is another variation on this theme. From the buyer-seller point of view, it's a real solution, but in most cases the amount of the transferred mortgage is insignificant relative to the purchase price of the house. The institutions balk at wraparounds because being held to a twenty-five-year 9 percent mortgage is a guaranteed loss of 6 to 7 percent per year before costs—even if interest rates don't go higher.

Most wraparounds violate what's known as the "due on sale" provision in mortgages and are only possible because various states have passed laws to abrogate those provisions of mortgage contracts. Of course, those same laws make it even more likely the banks holding the mortgages will fail.

Variable-Rate Mortgages (VRMs)

Another solution to the problem, the most realistic one, is the variable-rate mortgage. If the interest rate fluctuates every six months, the lender is somewhat protected against inflation. The danger of the buyer's default increases, however, with every jump in the interest rate. Most people who are getting into mortgages today in hope the rate will go down, or that their incomes will rise faster than their payments, will certainly be disappointed on the first count and, with the rising unemployment and decreasing living standards of this depression, probably on the second count as well.

The variable-rate mortgage shifts the risk of higher interest rates from the lender to the borrower, which is great for the lender. But if a large financial institution is unable to bear the risk, it's hard to see how the average homeowner can hope to. The VRM is likely to get many a buyer in over his head if rates go higher. From the speculator's point of view, the VRM is the least desirable type of financing.

Shared Appreciation Mortgages (SAMs)

The latest hope to save the real estate market from perdition is the profit-sharing loan. An institution will offer a mortgage at perhaps one-third less than the going interest rate in return for one-third of the profit. This gimmick does make houses more affordable, but at a cost. The below-market interest rate charged by the lender means it is forced to absorb a certain current loss in hope of a possible gain at some indefinite time in the future. In other words, lenders who make this type of loan are so sure that real estate is going up that they're willing to absorb negative cash flow to gamble on it. Just as they have in the stock market, however, the institutions probably will prove to be Wrong-Way Corrigans here, too. If the profits fail to materialize, they're going to be in a lot of trouble. In most cases the lender can't even realize the profit (if any) until the homeowner sells, something few with this type of loan will do. Why should a homeowner give up a third of his profits in order to refinance (if that's possible) at higher rates?

This type of loan is a good alternative if you can get one. See if the lender's stock is publicly traded, because it's a great long-term short-sale candidate.

These and other gimmicks are being tried, often in combination with one another. But they are all cosmetic solutions. Inflation is the problem, because it destroys long-term capital markets. And the real estate market is built on a foundation of long-term borrowed money, a foundation that inflation is rapidly washing away.

The Bottom Line: How to Buy, Own, or Sell a House

Is a real estate crash inevitable? If actions have consequences and causes effects, then the expanding crisis in real estate is predictable and inevitable.

Real estate prices have dropped significantly in real terms since the top in 1979, but it's just the beginning. Real estate will be the 1929 stock market lookalike by the time the final bottom comes.

If, after analyzing your present or intended house in the light of all that, you still believe you can afford it and want to buy, the question is: How? There are two options: cash or charge. Even if you stay out of the market for the next few years, as I recommend, there will be a time to buy again. There's a right way and a wrong way to buy. If you have a house, the mirror image of these rules applies in selling it.

Cash. One thing about the real estate market isn't likely to change, and that's the disadvantage presented by paying cash. It is the worst possible way to acquire or own a house. If you view your house as a long-lived throwaway item, as I suggest, you should be able to pay cash and feel you can write off the value of your house as you would rent. But just because you have the *ability* to do it doesn't mean you should in fact do it. When you own a house for cash, you bear all the consequences of its falling in price and you suffer the consequences of having your money tied up in an illiquid asset. From a financial point of view—setting aside the warm glow of psychological comfort it may give—owning a house for cash is insane.

The mortgage company can't repossess it when you own it. But if you would have trouble meeting mortgage payments, you'll probably have trouble paying the utility bills and the tax assessments anyway. Rest assured that both will continue to climb in the years ahead. You can't live in a house without utilities; and if you don't pay your taxes, you may be distressed to find out who really owns the house to start with.

Real estate taxes are, in effect, rent you pay to the state. "Ownership" of a house really gives you rights only to any increase (or decrease) in its value; but real title rests with the government, and if you don't make what amounts to leasehold payments in the form of real estate tax, they'll repossess it as surely as a bank will if

you default on your mortgage. And since the state's
claim to taxes is senior even to a bank's claim to principal and interest, paying off a mortgage does nothing but
increase your real total exposure. While the bank holds
a mortgage what happens to a house is partly its problem; once you pay it off, the utility, tax, and resale market value problems are all yours. The world is full of
paradoxes.

If you now have substantial equity in your house, the
smartest thing that you can do tomorrow morning is start
calling savings and loans trying to find one dumb
enough to give you the biggest and longest-term fixed-
interest-rate mortgage that you can get.

I know a lot of people are afraid to do that because
they fear they might be tempted to dissipate or consume
the money that would generate and they would wind up
with an unsupportable monthly payment. But if you
want to profit from what's inevitably going to happen in
the next few years, you're going to have to take some
responsibility for yourself, and that includes trusting
yourself with however much money the bank will give
you, while they'll still give it to you.

Put the money in a money market fund investing in
government securities if you can't figure out something
better to do. But by all means act now, because soon
banks will no longer offer fixed-rate long-term mortgages, and the option will no longer be available to you.
The worst thing that can happen is that you'll keep the
money liquid and pay the mortgage off later. And the
money you borrow is 100 percent deductible against
your income, which cuts its cost in half, if you are in a
50 percent tax bracket.

By the same token, when you sell, you shouldn't take
back paper. More on that in a moment.

Charge. There is one, and only one, way to own real
estate: with the longest-term fixed-rate mortgage pos-

sible. Despite the likelihood that the property will collapse in real terms, and most likely in dollar terms as well, having a long-term fixed-rate mortgage could bail you out. The reason is simply that the mortgage will eventually be inflated out of existence and be totally worthless, whereas the property it encumbers will still have real value, albeit a diminished value relative to other things. The long-term fate of the dollar is $99^{44}/_{100}$ percent certain. (I arbitrarily assign a $^{56}/_{100}$ percent chance to some "deus ex machina" device—such as the arrival of friendly aliens who bequeath us an unbelievably advanced technology to solve all our problems!)

How It May End

Within a few years—even months—the Greater Depression of the 1980s will cause a major financial cataclysm, and the only question is *how* your mortgage will be wiped out. There are four possibilities which I've listed in order of likelihood:

1. Runaway inflation.
2. Uncontrolled deflation.
3. Debt moratorium followed by runaway inflation.
4. Soft landing.

1. Runaway Inflation

The story comes to mind of the man who fell asleep for ten years and first thing upon waking called his stockbroker to see what his portfolio looked like. The broker said, "IBM $10,000 a share; Xerox $8,000; GM $7,000 . . ." The man was ecstatic until the operator cut him off to say, "Please deposit $100,000 for the next three minutes." To keep the numbers in proportion, you may someday be living in a $10 million house.

Runaway inflation, for the reasons given in the first few chapters, is the most likely possibility as the government creates the hundreds of billions of dollars necessary to bail out failing banks, corporations, and local governments. Inflation will dynamically expand in an upward-sloping sine wave to 20 percent, then dip, then go up to 40 percent, and so on. The unbelievable amount of debt in the country will be totally wiped out, to the delight of those debtors who were able to service their debts through the credit crunches along the way.

In case of this eventuality, an 18 percent mortgage will look like a bargain, especially considering it's only costing its holder 9 percent after taxes. The arithmetic is simple. If you borrow $100,000 at an effective 9 percent while it's being inflated at 20 percent, you're left with a net 11 percent profit on borrowed principal each year. Better yet, it's a tax-free profit. In other words, borrowing will prove even wiser in the future than it has in the past.

If inflation goes much higher, as I suspect it will, real estate will continue to fall in real terms simply because there will be less mortgage money than ever available, and real estate is built on a pyramid of borrowed money. At some point—probably around the mid-1980s—the liquidation will slow as inflation drives the price of other consumer goods into line with the value of houses, which should be about half their early 1982 prices *in real terms*.

Real property will always retain some value, despite the chaotic social conditions a hyperinflation would cause. The mortgagee would be left with his asset (the house), but his liability (the mortgage) would be wiped out. The house may have lost 75 percent of its peak 1979 real value, but it won't have cost him anything but his down payment and some psychological trauma while he watched its value disintegrate, because his mortgage will have lost value at least as fast. Inflation eventually will bail out homeowners with unaffordable mortgages, just as they always hoped, but in a rather perverse way. Under this scenario, those who had the biggest mortgages would be the biggest winners. Unfortunately, though, your mortgage is someone else's wasting asset, so everyone can't win. Those who have cash in their houses will do better than they would have if the money had been in the bank; unfortunately, that isn't saying much.

But hyperinflation is the long run. Along the way there will be a series of deflationary credit crunches; and, as a result, many may be forced to sell their houses and give up their mortgages before the hyperinflation can bail them out. And there could be a full-scale deflation before the hyperinflation.

2. Deflation

If the U.S. experiences a deflation, or credit collapse, real estate will meet the same fate it did in 1929—total disaster. Dollars will become more valuable overnight. That, combined with accompanying massive unemployment and business failures, will cause a wave of mortgage defaults. Those who overreached themselves and took out big mortgages in anticipation of further inflation will be unable to continue meeting those easy monthly payments. After they lose their jobs they'll be lucky to stay out of bankruptcy court (or else anxious to get in, depending on their character). The banks and savings and loans will fail as loans default.

In the long run, this is actually the best thing that could happen—the optimal realistic scenario, something close to Scenario 1 in Chapter 1.

Many people would lose their homes, true. But many others who could not previously afford them would be able to buy them from repossessing banks for pennies on the dollar. The drastic contraction of the money sup-

ply combined with wholesale forced selling would collapse prices to a tiny fraction of present numbers. Those
living above their means would be chastised, but their
desire to regain a house would provide a fair incentive
to straighten out. And in the meantime they'd find
plenty of rentals at correspondingly low prices. None of
the houses would collapse, just the financial structure
built up around them.

In this scenario, you're better off owning cash than a
house dropping in price. As I explained in Chapter 4,
this scenario is quite possible under a more or less free
market–oriented President. Of course, if it happened,
he'd probably change his tune quickly and "do something" rather than allow the market to liquidate. Certainly the man who'd be elected when the incumbent
was booted out of office as the "second Hoover" would.

Until the government does step in, the worst situation
would be to have a big mortgage. But realistically, I
wouldn't worry about it too much. A free market–style
uncontrolled deflation is not "politically possible." So
rather than the brief readjustment that that would bring,
the government will probably step in with loads of regulations to prevent a liquidation and with lots more debased currency to "get the country moving again."

If a deflation starts to occur, it's quite likely that the
government will call for a moratorium on debt.

3. Debt Moratorium

If a deflation gets under way, millions of homeowners
will be unable to make their payments, and the government will almost certainly be called upon to "do something." That something will almost certainly be to call a
moratorium on debt repayment. In that case the banks
will be left in the worst possible predicament. Not only
will all their loans be in default, but because all their
depositors will know it there will be wholesale with-

drawals. The government will directly or indirectly be compelled to infuse scores of billions of dollars to fill the gap while calling a bank holiday to keep depositors from withdrawing more funds.

The winners in this scenario again would be the mortgagees, as they wouldn't have to pay their loans while money is tight, during the deflation, but only after the moratorium is dropped, when inflation may be running at over 30 percent and payments would be academic. From the point of view of the debtor, this is actually better than moving right into hyperinflation, because he wouldn't even have to pay his debt while it's being inflated out of existence.

This scenario is a fair probability while any President like Reagan is in office. His attempt at disinflation could snowball into a deflationary collapse; any financial accident could send the house of cards crashing down. The President, being first a politician, would probably feel obligated to "take action" in order to "show leadership." As a practical matter, at that point the only thing he could do would be to call a moratorium and reinflate. This would be an even worse disaster for society than a simple runaway inflation, because government regulations would prevent people from adjusting to it.

But there is another logical, if unlikely, possibility—a "soft landing."

4. Soft Landing

I suppose anything is possible, but I wouldn't recommend that you plan your life around this scenario. It presupposes that inflation and interest rates that have been moving upward for thirty years will somehow level off and the distortions caused by inflation, debt, taxes, and regulations will never need to be liquidated. It couldn't happen in the simple economic example I gave in Chapter 3, and it's even less likely to happen in the vastly more complex real world. But even if the going gets as tough as I expect, this is still the option most people will count on.

Why Real Estate Can Go Higher

Every real estate booster feels he has a few aces in the hole that he expects will bail him out, regardless of what happens. There are at least five fatuous ones I've heard. They include the higher prices in other cities, rich foreigners, the fact that the local area (wherever it is) is "special," and that there's a lot of "pent-up" demand waiting in the wings. There's also one meaningful reason why real estate could become a good buy by the mid-'80s. But let's dispense with the wishful thinking of erstwhile promoters first.

American Land a Bargain?

The well-traveled American might remark that real estate in the U.S. is still cheap compared to that in some other parts of the world, like Tokyo and Zurich. And it hasn't appreciated as fast here as in some other areas, like parts of Spain and Ireland. The reasons would require a book to explain, but the boom in real estate has been really worldwide, just as inflation is worldwide. The house that costs $250,000 here would probably cost about $400,000 in Zurich, $125,000 in the Bahamas, $75,000 in Portugal, and $15,000 in Zimbabwe. Whether the house in Zurich is "dear" and the one in Salisbury is "cheap" is pretty hard to determine objectively.

I can conceive of the $400,000 house in Zurich doubling in value in a couple of years if Italy or France goes Communist and everyone hides in Switzerland.

And it's easy to see the house in Salisbury tripling to $45,000 if stability finally comes to Zimbabwe. But I'm hard put to see why that could happen here at the moment, at the top of the longest speculative boom in history.

Still, "value" is as hard to determine in land as it is in the stock market. Another argument holds that foreigners see unique value in U.S. property.

Foreign Buyers?

It's true that wealthy Arabs and Europeans, among others, are doing a lot of buying in America. The main reason for it, however, is not that they think they're getting such a great deal—they aren't price shoppers to begin with—but because they're looking to diversify their assets to a more stable country. America is the final major bastion of what's left of capitalism in the world, and foreigners with money know that and want a stake in it. The trend will probably grow, but it's just a small drop in a very big bucket, even though it's gotten a lot of publicity in localities like New York City and Miami. If you want a floodtide of foreign money to raise your sinking real estate ship, I suggest you perhaps look to Switzerland, Andorra, the Bahamas, or Costa Rica, among other very small markets that stand to be relatively big beneficiaries from this trend.

Some would say, however, that just as there are preferred areas of the world, there are preferred areas of the U.S. as well.

Depression-Proof Areas of the Country?

Even when there's agreement that the market in general may be in trouble, the residents of any given region usually feel their area is "different" and will continue onward and upward. The explanation usually goes something like this: "Yes, but [pick a city, any city] is different because . . ." San Francisco: "Everyone wants to live here"; the Sun Belt: "This is the Sun Belt"; New York: "This is the capital of the world"; Washington: "This is the seat of government."

That one seemed like the most compelling argument, so I decided to use Washington as a test case. The majority of its citizens work directly or indirectly for the federal government, or cater to those who do, and the U.S. government is possibly the world's greatest growth industry—if its expenditures are any indication. Of course, it's not really an "industry" at all, because it produces few things of real value, but that doesn't make much difference, because it's in a position to make sure the rest of the country pays for its services. Not only is Washington's largest employer a growth industry, but it's contra-cyclical besides. In other words, the worse things get for the economy, the bigger the government will grow.

New deals and frontiers, great societies, and chickens for every pot are all hatched there, especially when the going gets tough and the hue and cry goes up for somebody to "do something." So without a doubt Washington will be in a better position to take care of its own than, say, Detroit.

But it will be affected. Washingtonians use leverage in buying real estate and are in debt like everyone else. Interest rates on mortgages are about the same in the nation's capital as everywhere else, and no more available. Property is as illiquid as in Peoria. Washingtonians pay taxes just like everyone else. Real estate has an even worse negative cash flow there than most places because prices are higher. Worst of all, the very belief that nothing bad can happen to D.C. real estate has reinforced the kind of "sure thing" tenor to the market that is most pronounced in places that the residents think are different.

Yes, Virginia: Washington—and every other "special" area—is still part of the United States, just as it was during the 1930s, when the real estate market was flat on its back even though the government was growing like Topsy. And just as it was in 1974, when you could inspect hundreds of new town houses standing empty, with their builders trying desperately, and unsuccessfully, to unload them for what now seem giveaway prices. The 1974 setback will prove trivial compared to the 1980s.

There are no special areas of the country, unless it's those like the Midwest and the Northeast that have already been hard hit. A smart stock, commodity, or real estate speculator likes to buy when things are cheap; and when the bottom does come, those might actually be the best parts of the country in which to go bargain hunting. More on this below, when I cover where to buy as well as how to buy when the bottom *does* come, and real estate once again becomes a good place to invest.

Pent-Up Demand?

The final argument, and one that is often heard, is that there is a huge pent-up demand for housing in this country (mainly from post–World War II baby boomers who don't already own one or more of the things), and that demand will one day be unleashed upon the limited number of houses now standing. I suppose there's some truth to that, but, on the other hand, everybody wants a Cadillac and a Chris-Craft as well; and it's not argued that that will skyrocket their prices, although it would be just as logical. "Demand" is an economic concept. It's a function of people's wealth, not their desires, or even their numbers. Houses are manufactured goods, and they can be cranked out by the millions, just like boats and cars. In fact, they are. That's what "housing start" figures are all about, and anyone who looks at them and adds them up over the last ten years might come to an interesting conclusion: The number of new houses sold was at least equal to the net increase in population. In other words, there was a new housing unit constructed for every new American, one for one.

Table IV MORE NEW HOUSES THAN NEW PEOPLE

	Residential Housing Unit Construction (in Thousands)	U.S. Resident Population (in Thousands)
1971	1,953	207,100
1972	2,239	208,800
1973	1,830	210,400
1974	1,088	211,900
1975	949	213,600
1976	1,303	215,200
1977	1,692	216,900
1978	1,802	218,500
1979	1,553	220,600
1980	1,186	221,700
Total Increase	15,595	14,600

That is not the stuff of housing shortages, but of housing gluts. The situation is analogous to the boom in schoolroom construction during the '60s, which led to hundreds of underutilized or boarded-up schools throughout the country.

The housing glut will become evident as the standard of living drops. Lots of "swinging singles" and "young professionals" who are now stylishly living alone in two- and three-bedroom dwellings are going to be forced to move in with friends or relatives. Where there was a "demand" for three spiffy town houses, there will suddenly be a demand for only one, and the other two will either come onto the market for sale or become unrented albatrosses around the neck of an overextended landlord before going onto the market a little later.

The demographics in this area are not widely appre-

Chart IV

Millions   **Housing Starts**

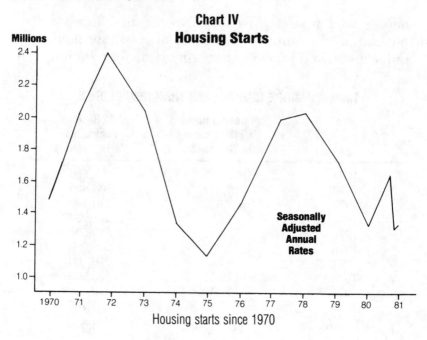

Seasonally
Adjusted
Annual
Rates

Housing starts since 1970

ciated. In 1970, single persons were responsible for less than 1 percent of home purchases. By 1980, they accounted for 24 percent (Investors Mortgage Co. of Boston figures). In 1970, more than 90 percent of houses were bought by people over age thirty-five. In 1980, 68 percent were bought by people *under* thirty-five. In other words, the generation that real estate economists are counting on to keep the boom going has already bought. And because they've tended to marry late, they've already bought more than their share of houses. When some of the single people who've been buying recently do marry, they'll have an extra house to rent or sell. There's now a large inventory of houses in that category.

Even the families who own houses today have a different make-up than those of the stable '50s and '60s. In

1970, 94 percent of homebuyers had children; in 1980, only 22 percent did. In 1970, probably only 10 to 15 percent of families had two breadwinners; in 1980, the figure was closer to 60 percent. What those figures mean is that wives are now working in force, and whether or not they want to, they have to, just to keep the family's head above water. The wife used to be a "backup system" for a family. If the husband lost his job or became disabled, she could always step into the breach. But today she's already working, and now if *either* of them loses the job the couple is in deep trouble.

The important thing to remember is that real estate is a financial market like any other. There are times when it is smart to buy, and times when it's smart to sell; right now is still a time to sell.

There will come, however, another time to buy. Bear markets don't go on forever. If nothing else, government action will eventually turn it around. It's convenient for the speculator, because governmental intervention will both give him the cue he needs to buy and almost guarantee him profits when he does.

Government Action

Eventually, the real estate market will bottom. It's perfectly true what promoters have been saying for decades: People will always need someplace to live, and they're not making any more land. But the natural forces of the marketplace probably won't be the only things to turn it around; the state will undoubtedly take action in the future, as in the past.

Throughout the 1970s, government agencies like the Veterans Administration and the Federal Housing Administration intervened to make mortgages "affordable" for increasing numbers of people. Other agencies, such as Ginny Mae (GNMA) and Fannie Mae (FNMA), provided an aftermarket for the illiquid instruments as a courtesy to the financial institutions that granted them.

As government deficits and inflation both explode in the 1980s, it's uncertain exactly how the government will react to the real estate collapse. Certainly just making more credit available won't be as easy as it was in the past. But just as it's foolhardy to underestimate government's stupidity, it's equally dangerous to underestimate its ingenuity when the support of the voters is at stake, as it certainly will be. The government is bound to try to buoy up prices at some point. As the market craters, millions of homeowners will have their equity wiped out, and many will be unable even to meet their monthly payments. They will scream at the government to "do something," and, certainly after the Reagan Administration has joined the ranks of the departed, it will. The VA and FHA might get a mandate to make more and larger morgages available to bull the market up. Or, perhaps, the Fed or Treasury will offer some type of cash aid or tax benefits to banks and thrifts to enable them to grant mortgages on "affordable" terms. They'll need aid desperately to keep from failing anyway. The vaunted "All Savers" certificates available since October of 1981 are a step in that direction.

It's probably "politically impossible" for the government to let the housing market languish for too long. Unemployment in the construction industry alone, entirely apart from the plight of homeowners, will probably prompt some type of bailout action. Because of inertia, the aid will probably come when the market has reached a natural bottom of its own accord, and at that point a new infusion of credit could send it skyrocketing. Once real estate is depressed enough (in real terms) it will once again become an inflation hedge. If the government ever does come out with some type of gimmick to support the market, that would be your cue to move into the market as aggressively as you can.

Rules for Sale Now and Future Repurchase

When you feel the bottom has come there are some keys to buying right.

1. *Try to stick to properties under 100,000 1982 dollars.* The risk is lower, the upside higher, and the return from rentals better. When expectations were high and the standard of living was rising, the smart speculator went "up market." During a depression, or coming out of one, it's best to stick with the basics.

2. *Borrow as much as you can.* Take advantage of the fact that interest payments are tax-deductible and inflation will work in your favor over the long run. Even if you do get over your head, it will likely be when everyone else does, and then there'll probably be a debt moratorium.

It's for that reason, of course, you shouldn't take back paper when you sell. If the market collapses before the loan is paid off, the buyer could just "walk away" from the house and leave you hanging, quite possibly with unpaid taxes on a poorly maintained house. In addition, should the buyer discover any hidden flaws in the house, he may use them as an excuse to withhold payments, claiming fraud. And you may get caught in the possible moratorium. If you sell, sell for cash. Don't delude yourself by getting what the house is "worth" and giving it all back in subsidized financing.

3. *Be patient.* There are plenty of low-risk, high-potential ways to increase your capital until it's right to move. Adopt an objective, even a cavalier, approach, since the markets always present new opportunities. When real estate hits a panic bottom as all markets eventually do, you'll be able to buy for "no money down" by taking distressed property from frightened sellers. The key is to leverage into any market at the bottom, not near

the top, as did the people who'll be forced to sell to you on your terms. But always keep some cash liquid so you can weather temporary downturns.

4. *Buy properties in "changing" areas.* Areas that are being upgraded offer the quickest returns. Perhaps the center cities will offer great opportunities by 1985, since it will be hard for them to sink much lower by that point. There's no hurry. Cities are where crime, welfare, and unemployment are most likely to combine to a critical mass. There'll always be a need for cities, and prices will always be higher in them when times are good. But most are disasters in the making. There will be plenty of time to go bargain hunting after the present social structure self-destructs. By contrast, buying a property in an area "everybody" knows is growing is like buying a stock with a high price/earnings ratio. You're not going to get any bargain.

Rural areas are a much better idea. First of all, small towns and the countryside tend to be more stable, and safer. And it's no longer a question of living like a mountain man. Satellite communications, computers, and new technologies for generating power and otherwise becoming self-sufficient can give the countryside all the comforts of home. More and more people will realize that, and they will buoy this market relative to the others.

The suburbs, however, are in many ways the worst of both worlds. I wouldn't be surprised to see suburbanites who are now having trouble paying the electricity bill turning their manicured lawns into gardens to grow food when they can't afford to buy the stuff.

If you're going to play this game at all, play it according to the rules in Chapter 16. Successful speculators don't run with the herd.

5. *Consider real estate outside the U.S.* There are a number of countries that should even profit from the problems the rest of the world is facing. Geographical

diversification is, increasingly, just as important as investment diversification. And money expatriated now and invested in illiquid real estate will almost certainly thwart the coming foreign exchange controls.

They can't make you repatriate the property, and in the meantime you can depreciate it, write off local taxes, and deduct interest just as you can on U.S. property.

6. *Go for the tax breaks.* If you're going to buy an existing building, consider one located in a designated "historic district" if possible, or get the property you like certified as a historic structure in its own right. The 1981 tax changes provide a 25 percent tax credit for rehabilitation expenses and accelerated depreciation on the whole structure.

It's true that real estate is one of the few remaining tax shelters available, and a lot of real estate has been purchased almost exclusively for its merit as a tax shelter. But the whim and caprice of Congress is an ephemeral base on which to build your financial future. In 1981 alone, more than 3,000 pieces of tax legislation were introduced; and from this point on, most of it is likely to hurt, not help, real estate, in view of the $100 billion deficit the government will be running. There are already serious proposals to limit mortgage interest deductions to $5,000 or $1,000 per year.

The effect of Reagan's cutting the maximum tax bracket to 50 percent from 70 percent alone should hurt real estate, paradoxically, because it reduces the value of deductions to high-bracket taxpayers.

The Grateful, Patient Speculator

Most people still believe that the softness of the market since 1980 is just another "healthy correction" in the thirty-year post–World War II bull market. Don't let them confuse the issue. They'll be the same ones who

Chart V

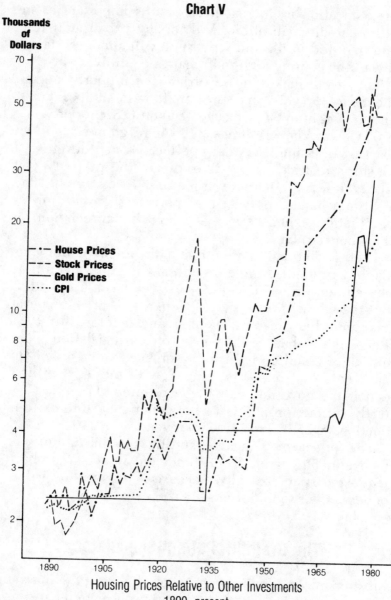

Housing Prices Relative to Other Investments
1890–present

Chart VI

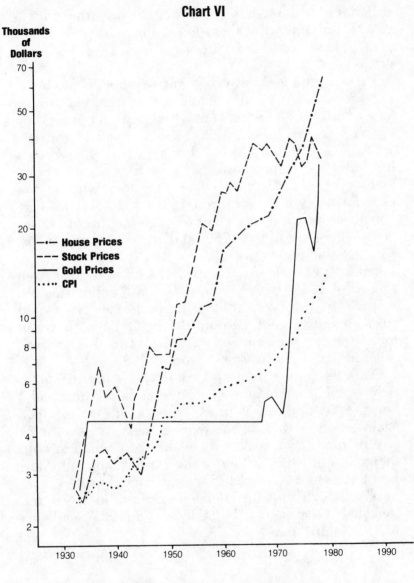

Thousands
of
Dollars

House Prices
Stock Prices
Gold Prices
CPI

Housing Price Relative to Other Investments
1933–present

will think real estate's dead forever after the bottom comes. Be grateful to them for acting as stewards over your property until you can buy it from them for lower prices.

The preceding charts give some perspective on housing prices. Chart V follows gold, stocks, houses, and the CPI from 1890 to the present. Houses didn't even keep up with the CPI from 1890 to their peak in the late 1920s. Despite that, during the last depression houses lost half their value, even though mortgages were generally granted for only five years, and then with 50 percent down payments required. In the 1920s, stocks were bought on the kind of "margin" on which most houses were purchased in the 1960s and 1970s, and stocks lost 85 percent of their value.

Chart VI plots housing against the other indices from a base of 1933, the bottom of the last depression. In relative terms, houses have outperformed gold and stocks by 80 percent, and outrun the CPI by a factor of four. Housing appears almost as overpriced relative to other indices today as stocks were in 1929.

Don't be conned by those who say it's unpatriotic to believe the price of houses is going to fall dramatically, because the opposite is true. Not only will homes once again be affordable for the average man; new fortunes will be made by those who are shrewd enough to hold their fire until the bottom of the market falls out. Markets fluctuate; real estate's day has gone, but it will return, although probably not before the mid-1980s and from half today's real dollar levels. Smart speculators will wait until then.

─────── *Being Savvy about Real Estate* ───────

- *Real estate prices probably won't bottom until 1984.*
- *Houses aren't investments, they're places to live.*
- *Rent, don't buy, if you can.*
- *Long-term fixed-rate mortgages may disappear entirely. Get one if you can on any property you do buy.*
- *The signal for the bottom of the real estate market, and a new boom, will be the creation of new government mortgages to make housing "affordable."*

Chapter 18

Stocks: Speculating
in the Market

*Speculation brings into play the best intelligence as to the
future of values. . . . The consequences of speculation are
thus financially beneficial to the country at large.*
Henry Clews

*Invest in America's future! But be careful. . . . After thirty-
five years in Wall Street, I have learned at least one lesson.
Opportunity is always here.*
G. M. Loeb

A whole new class of millionaires will be made in the
stock market in the 1980s. I was very bearish on most
stocks when *Crisis Investing* was written in 1979; now,
despite the fact that the fundamentals underpinning
American business in 1982 are far worse than they were
then, I've changed my opinion.

Relative to inflation and short-term interest rates—
both at double the 1979 levels—stocks are a worse buy
today than ever. The money markets and government
monetary policy are approaching the smash-up stage,
hardly the environment for prudent investing. Corporate earnings in real terms are accountants' fantasies,
and the potential for a collapse in even nominal terms
remains. Corporate pension liabilities have widened because of the collapse of the bond markets in 1979, 1980,
and 1981. The attitude of the public in general and labor
in particular toward business remains antagonistic, the

Reagan revolution notwithstanding. And the fuse on the international situation has gotten much, much shorter.

The Bull Market of the Century

The vagaries of publication schedules make it impossible to predict when this book reaches you, but if it's anytime after mid-1982, the stock market will probably have experienced most of its long-awaited crash. There's little point, therefore, in dwelling on the dangers of the market; most of them already have been realized. Let's concentrate on the profits ahead. The bottom line, despite the continuing collapse of the economy during the years ahead, is that *the stock market will boom by the mid-1980s.*

The fundamentals that security analysts usually look at will remain bad, but fundamentals increasingly have nothing to do with the market. What will really move the market in the years ahead will be psychology, the flow of funds, and the real prices of stocks as compared to other investments.

Psychology

In more stable economic times it was possible to see where a company was going, and concepts like "earnings" and "assets" had some meaning. At this point, however, it's mostly a matter of how people *perceive* these illusive concepts; that's why one stock can sell at a price/earnings multiple of 2 to 1, while a similar one can go for 200 to 1. Is a glass of water half empty, or half full?

Inflation always breeds speculation, and as inflation gets worse the time frame for speculation gets shorter. People no longer consider themselves "long-term investors." Even the words become meaningless. They are now "short-term traders." Inflation will increasingly cause chaotic markets that boom and bust in quick alternation as people rush from one hot prospect to another in a mad effort to outpace the depreciation of the dollar. In countries with terminal inflation, like Argentina and Israel, everybody who has any spare cash at all is a stock player. It's not only because everybody is forced to speculate, but because—as in America—capital gains are given tax preferences, and money made in the market is worth a lot more than salary or interest income.

In this type of hectic environment, the most liquid mediums tend to be the preferred ones, and funds will flow into stocks because stocks are an ideal speculative medium. But there are other reasons.

Flow of Funds

Another reason people will want to be in the stock market is because they won't want to be in the alternatives. A flight from currency seems almost certain to occur, and there's a good chance foreign exchange controls will be imposed at about the same time. Both should benefit securities greatly.

By the mid-1980s, as inflation goes to 30 percent and above, Americans will finally realize en masse that not only has the dollar been an unfortunate investment in the past but the worst possible place to keep assets for the future. But in 1982, most of the country's net wealth is still held in dollars, and most of those dollars are in the following areas.

Cash. This means bank accounts, savings and loan deposits, cash-value insurance policies, money market funds, and, of course, currency hoards from the alternative economy. Lots of those dollars will already have been wiped out by bankruptcies and defaults, as we discussed in Chapter 8. The realization will spread that even with the high-risk premiums available, after-tax interest can't possibly keep up with inflation. People will pile out.

Bonds.   The long-term bond market will cease to exist, for the same reasons it vanished in Argentina, Italy, Scandinavia, and many other countries. Bonds will be seen for what they are: trading vehicles, not long-term conservative parking places for capital. By the mid-1980s, it will be impossible to float a bond for a price any prudent businessman would be willing to pay, and the market will simply dry up for new issues.

The Eurodollar Market.   Eurodollars are U.S. dollars owned by foreigners. There are approximately $1 trillion of them. No one knows exactly how large this pool of dollars is or where all the assets are invested, but since—unlike Americans—foreigners don't have to hold dollars, it's unlikely they will when the danger of default is combined with very high inflation. The Eurodollar market could shrink dramatically for the first time in decades. The money now in Eurodollars will flow elsewhere.

Mortgages.   The mortgage market has all the disadvantages of the bond market, and is less liquid. And it's secured solely by real estate, another disaster area. The money that would have gone here, and a good part of the capital already here, will flow elsewhere.

A great deal of the money in each of these media will vanish; but in each case, those who withdraw cash from those markets in time will have to put it somewhere, and the main beneficiaries will be gold, commodities, and stocks. Of those three, stocks will be the big winner.

Why Stocks?

The stock market is dwarfed in size by the cash, bond, Eurodollar, and mortgage markets; and the money flowing out of them doesn't think in terms of gold and commodities as much as it does other securities. Many investors will drop one form of paper and move promptly into another. Like cash, bonds, Eurodollars, and mortgages, stocks offer a current cash yield—unlike real estate. Because they are underpriced compared to other inflation-boomed investments, because they are liquid, because they don't depend on the existence of borrowed money, and because they are so familiar to people, stocks could do very well indeed. Despite the economic collapse all around them, stocks could explode upward simply because that's where a lot of the money, leaving dollars, will go.

If this scenario sounds unlikely, remember it wouldn't be the first time. The German stock market lost on the order of 95 percent of its real value from 1914 to 1923, and then moved up by a factor of ten—in real terms—in November 1923, the worst month of that country's famous runaway inflation. But let's hope that's too drastic an example.

Italy provides a more recent and moderate comparison. The U.S. economy is being Italianized; high inflation, high taxes, a ponderous bureaucracy, strong unions —there are many similarities.

The Italian market lost 70 percent of its lira value from the peak in 1960 to a trough seventeen years later in 1977. Seventy percent in *lira terms*. Meanwhile, the lira was being inflated so fast that consumer prices quadrupled in the same time. *The Italian market thus lost 92 percent of its real value from top to bottom.* The year 1977 was the bottom, incidentally. Italian stocks exploded upward over the next four years.

Chart I

Capital International Index

Italy

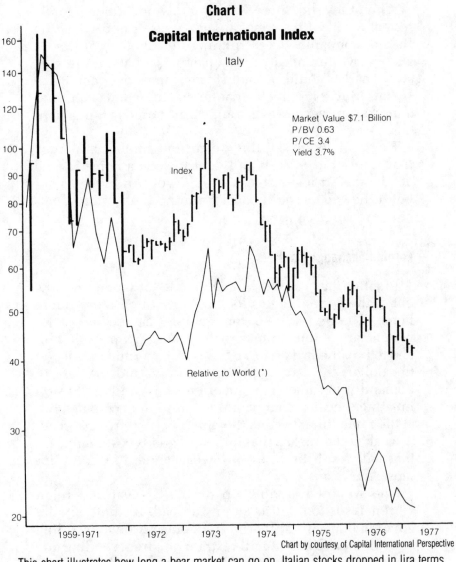

Market Value $7.1 Billion
P/BV 0.63
P/CE 3.4
Yield 3.7%

Index

Relative to World (*)

1959-1971   1972   1973   1974   1975   1976   1977

Chart by courtesy of Capital International Perspective

This chart illustrates how long a bear market can go on. Italian stocks dropped in lira terms —and even more radically relative to other world stock markets—for eighteen years.

When they did, there was certainly no "fundamental" reason for it. At the time, about a quarter of the leading Italian companies were running deficits (and still are), and everything negative that can be said about the U.S. stock market could be said several times over about the Italian. But sometimes a confluence of events can send a market up *despite* what appear to be poor fundamentals.

From this point on, the greater the amount of money that comes out of cash and debt to seek a home in real goods, the stronger stocks should get. An even bigger boost, however, could come from the imposition of foreign exchange controls.

Foreign Exchange Controls

Inflation has caused huge amounts of money to flow out of the United States looking for a safer, more stable home. The Swiss franc, for example, has been a major beneficiary of this. Francs rose because people sold dollars to buy them. The more the U.S. government inflated the dollar, the larger grew its supply, and the less in demand it became. The government is unlikely to stop inflating, because that would collapse the economy, but at the same time it wants the dollar to stay strong abroad. A weak dollar means that imported goods cost more, and that will result in an even lower standard of living for most Americans.

One way of propping up the dollar against foreign currencies is to limit its supply abroad. It's unlikely the government will do that by reducing its own spending abroad; more likely it will restrain *you* from sending any of your dollars overseas. There are several forms the controls could take:

1. Prohibition of foreign bank accounts.
2. Taxation or other restrictions on foreign travel. (The reasoning would be that every dollar spent

abroad by American tourists weakens the dollar; it "should" be spent here to create more profits in the United States.)
3. Prohibition of the import of gold—perhaps combined with some form of domestic confiscation (compensated, no doubt, in fiat dollars). Confiscation would be tough to sell, and to enforce, but a prohibition on new imports could be part of an economic boycott against South Africa or the U.S.S.R., the two major gold producers.

After the imposition of foreign exchange controls, a great deal of capital now flowing into gold and foreign bank accounts will almost inevitably go into stocks. Stocks will be the only available non-dollar investment.

At the same time, ironically, a flood of foreign capital may be trying to enter the U.S. Things will be bad here, but they'll be worse in most other places. (But not every place, by any means. There will always be isolated areas that, because of their freedom and stability, will inadvertently profit from the problems of their neighbors. This is covered in my book *The International Man.*) America, as the last major bastion of what's left of capitalism (it's all relative), could be inundated by foreign capital from Europe and the Middle East. And a great deal is going to flow into stocks for lack of a better alternative. And stocks actually won't be such a bad place to be, if only because by then they'll be cheaper than they've been in over forty years—in real terms.

Stocks as Value

It's important to understand how stocks relate to other investment alternatives in the minds of most investors. According to most traditional criteria of value, stocks are overpriced by a factor of at least two or three. But it no longer really matters. So what if stocks are 300 percent "overpriced" if all the alternatives are 1000 percent overpriced? In that case, stocks are cheap—compared to the competition. Looking at it that way, stocks *are* fundamentally underpriced—while at the same time they are also fundamentally overpriced, as I argue in *Crisis Investing*.

The question of value—what's cheap and what's dear —relates closely to time as well as to other investments. A good speculator buys when things are cheap, and the following chart offers a clue in that regard.

It's in many ways illusory to watch the dollar prices of stocks, since you're interested in growing *wealth*, not just dollars. If you invest in the Brazilian stock market, you might be able to "double" your money every year, even though you were losing ground in real terms.

The chart below puts the stock market in perspective. During the 1929 to 1933 stock market crash, equities lost

Chart II

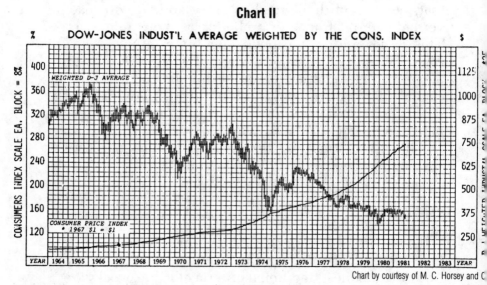

Chart by courtesy of M. C. Horsey and C

Nothing goes down forever. This chart of the DJIA in real dollars looks like that of the Italian marke from 1960 to 1977. It's getting close to the turnaround point.

87 percent of their dollar value as they tumbled from a nominal 392 to 41. In real terms (1913 dollars) they fell from 216 to 30, only 70 percent as much, because the dollar was becoming more valuable. It was a deflationary depression.

Since the 1966 peak of the great post–World War II bull market, the Dow has dropped almost 70 percent of its value in real terms, although in dollars it's only declined a few percent. That chart, or figures similar to it, has been used for over ten years to prove that stocks are cheap. And, of course, it's been true; they have been cheap, compared to where they were in 1966, for the last fifteen years. *Now, in 1982, stocks have lost as much in real terms as they did from 1929 to 1933.* It's approaching the time to buy.

All markets bottom eventually, and the bottom of the U.S. market should appear simultaneously with the financial smash-up of the early 1980s. Be prepared. It's going to be a wild and crazy roller coaster ride; Wall Street is probably going to remind people of the barroom scene from *Star Wars* more than anything else. But a new bull market will be reborn in the depths of the Greater Depression and the grandest financial calamity of the century. In order to capitalize on it, you need a strategy.

Taking Stock

- *Money will flow into stocks because of a flight from currency, foreign exchange controls, and foreign investments.*
- *Stocks are as cheap a buy now, in real terms, as they were in 1933.*
- *Prepare to buy with both hands.*

Chapter 19

Stocks: Strategies for Buying

If you want to accumulate capital—speculate, don't invest.
G. M. Loeb

When asked about it, Bernard Baruch is reported to have said, "Young man, if you want to make money in the stock market, buy stocks when they are low, and sell them when they are high." A lot of people, few of whom are half as smart as Baruch, decry the statement as so painfully obvious as to be worthless. To the contrary, it is the starting point for any valid theory of stock market speculation, and the most overlooked. The key, of course, is figuring out when stocks are "low" and when they're "high." To do that, you need a frame of reference and a method. You need a strategy.

A Strategy

There are about 40,000 publicly traded companies in the U.S. Even if you were to work eight hours a day, five days a week picking among them, you'd have only three minutes a year to devote to each issue. All you'd likely accomplish would be to get lost in the forest for all the trees.

In security analysis, there are many paths up the mountain. There are many ways to pick stocks and decide which way the market's going to go. The novice, who knows nothing but that it's possible to make money in the markets, will normally rely on the touting of his broker or the opinion of some newspaper reporter or the pontification of a newsletter-writing guru to make up his mind for him. Even if any of them gave consistently good advice, though, it would be unwise to take it.

It's not that I don't believe in taking good advice (if you know for a fact that's what it is). Specialization and division of labor can be as helpful in the market as anywhere else. But the only way to win the game is to play it yourself. The adviser who had a "hot hand" for years may devastate his clients if the tenor of the market changes; it's easy to be a genius in a bull market. The key to surviving the Greater Depression is to gain understanding and to take some personal responsibility. Nobody who relies on an oracle, or a magic black box, stands a chance.

It's a much better policy to get a grip on the basic methods of analyzing stocks, and choose one that is suited to both the conditions and, most importantly, your own psychology, abilities, and world view. The more you have a grip on, the wider the range of tactics you can use in the battle for investment survival. It's hard to say how many hundreds of books have been written about investing in stocks, but most of them offer assurances that the author's method is the way, the truth, and the light. Possibly. Every method, every investment philosophy, has its day in the sun. But the market environment is always changing, and by the time you hear about a particular way of picking stocks or market trends, the very conditions which made it valid have probably vanished.

Seven Paths Up the Mountain

To pick a good strategy yourself, it's helpful to understand some of the basic strategies used by "sophisticated" professional advisers. I have picked out seven approaches to playing the market. Each can be successful in the right environment, and since there's a lot of overlap among them, some methods, or their features, will be much more useful than others in the turbulent environment ahead. Choosing the proper approach is the essence of strategic investing in the stock market.

1. *Fundamental security analysis.* The fundamentalist believes that in the long run the price of a stock will reflect the health of the company that issues it. The classic fundamentalist likes to sort through the thousands of securities available, picking those he feels the market has undervalued, generally using statistical screens of some type. For instance, if the average price/earnings ratio of all stocks is 10, with a range from 2 times earnings to 100 times earnings, he'll choose those with P/E ratios between perhaps 2 and 5 to 1. If the average company is selling for twice its book value, with a range from perhaps 25 percent of book to 50 times book, he'll select those selling for between 25 percent and 100 percent of book. If dividend yields average 6 percent, with a range from 15 percent to 0 percent, he'll perhaps choose only those companies yielding from 9 to 15 percent.

The fundamentalist uses these screens to find what he believes is real underlying value, working on the assumption that the market will eventually come to appreciate the "facts."

Fundamental security analysts don't insinuate their subjective opinions on the economy or industry growth prospects into their conclusions. They want strictly the facts, oftentimes the more obscure the better. They're accountants at heart, correlating balance sheet and income statement data with the price of the stock. They tend to be fully invested at all times, but only in those stocks representing the best statistical value.

In the long run, a consistent fundamentalist will significantly outperform the market in general, but if the market crashes he's still going to lose money—just less than everyone else.

It was a good method throughout the '40s and '50s, but worked poorly during the speculative excesses of the '60s, when people just didn't care about dull things like value when quick fortunes were to be made. And since the '70s, a company's published statistics have lost meaning. With high inflation, concepts such as "earnings" and "book value" have become fictions of accounting. The method has value, but fundamentalists are living in the past.

2. *Growth stock analysis.* This is a variation on the theme of fundamentalism. GSA gives some credence to "value," but emphasizes the trend of earnings growth and the quality of a company's management. GSA analysts tend to buy only those stocks with consistent long-term records of increasing earnings (and dividends), feeling that past performance is the best indicator of future performance. For that reason, growth analysts will usually visit a company to size up its management, to assess its plans and general business acumen. They figure good managers and workers are behind past successes, and they believe, quite logically, that they're the best guarantee of success in the future. They figure a management team with a good track record of efficiently producing a sound basic product will make it through good times and bad. They tend to hold stocks as long as per-share earnings grow at a suitable rate. They don't care what price a company's stock sells for, as long as its prospects are good. They stay away from trends, fads, unproven concepts, new issues, and the like.

In the long run growth stock analysts are right on all counts, and should continue to outperform the market significantly—but they too will be hurt by down markets. A depression can totally negate the best track record; a company might have good earnings only because good times have made its growth possible. Growth stock analysts tend to be congenitally optimistic, and sometimes that's at odds with reality.

Growth analysts will find themselves confused by the chaotic environment of the 1980s. They've always bet on the long run, and the long run is quickly ceasing to exist.

3. *Economic analysis.* These folks believe that the stock market is the barometer of a country's overall health, and recommend buying or selling according to whether they see prosperity or hard times. The method has merit, of course. The markets in Hong Kong, Singapore, and Tokyo were great places to be (if you bought early and just waited) as the economies of those countries expanded throughout the '60s and '70s. The markets in Jamaica and Italy were devastated for the same reasons.

The economic analyst tries to predict interest rates, government monetary policy, the effect of taxes, the rate of unemployment, productivity, and the like to determine which way the market is going to go. Unlike the FA and GSA, the EA doesn't attempt to pick stocks, but rather the direction of the market as a whole. All the factors he considers are important, and in a rational free market world they'd have a good deal more predictive value than they will in the 1980s, when the financial markets will take on a life of their own with little relation to the underlying realities.

4. *Contrarian analysis.* The contrarian likes to do the opposite of "everybody" else, acting on the theory that even if "everybody" isn't absolutely wrong (which, in fact, they often are), then certainly there aren't any big profits to be made running with the herd.

This also is a sound approach to the market. If everyone is piling into a stock because he thinks it's a good deal, all that buying will drive its price to a level where, paradoxically, it becomes a bad deal. The contrarian, by doing the opposite of what most people do, usually winds up selling when stocks are high and everyone else is buying, and buying when they're low and pessimism is greatest.

It's not as easy a theory to put into practice as it might seem, at least not if you have emotions; although markets are emotional, they don't reward emotional action. Contrarians watch the same indicators as fundamental stock analysts, but also keep an eye on things like the volume of trading (giving a clue to how interested people are in a stock) and the amount of institutional ownership (if institutions—which have most of the money —already have major positions, they can't buy more, but only sell; if they don't own a stock, they can only buy it).

The danger, of course, is that a pure contrarian can have trouble hitting a home run (he would have sold Xerox, Polaroid, and IBM back in the early '50s just because they were popular). And at the same time, he sometimes buys disasters; he might have bought W. T. Grant or Franklin National Bank in 1974, for instance. But that's not an indictment; every method has its drawbacks.

It's a good idea to adopt the psychological skepticism of a contrarian in the 1980s. The public will cyclically go from apathy to fear to greed as the economy and the markets rollercoaster and this approach will—at a minimum—keep you from participating in a mania or a panic. It should reward followers with handsome profits.

There are two other primarily psychological methods that aim to involve you in both manias and panics, though. And that's fine too.

5. *The greater fool theory.* This states, in a nutshell, that it doesn't really matter what you pay for a stock because if the market goes wild there will always be a greater fool to buy it for more money a little later on.

The theory is held in low regard by conventional analysts, but is quite valid if you can correctly gauge the psychology of the market, and be sure to buy before a feeding frenzy overtakes the public.

The essence of this method is picking stocks that have a good story to be told about them, the type that is calculated to incite greed on the part of the credulous. It's helpful, of course, if there's substance to the story, but not essential. It's also helpful if the stock (or stock group) in question has a low capitalization and a thinly traded market. That's because when (and if) buyers decide they want some, a billion dollars trying to flow into a stock worth only a total of a million will have about 1,000 times the effect it would have trying to flow into a stock already valued at a billion. There are other characteristics, and I cover them a little later in Chapter 24 on penny stocks.

A less radical variation of this approach is flow of funds analysis. Here the analyst, using published figures, calculates the amount of money tied up in different media and gauges where there is "too much" or "too little." On that basis, he anticipates where the money will flow next, and acts to beat the last-minute rush. Flow of funds analysis is simply the greater fool theory applied to major institutionally traded stocks. That makes it sound a bit more legitimate.

In an unreal environment, stories, beliefs, illusions, and fantasies are much more real than the fundamentalist's facts and figures. The '80s are going to be truly unreal. There are two variations to the method. The speculator can wait until a trend gets in motion before he hops aboard, or he can get his bets on the table early and just await the arrival of greater fools. The first case will involve less waiting, but the second will produce larger profits. Greater fools will appear by the millions as they scurry about looking for some way to outrace inflation and taxes.

The mirror image of this method of playing manias

will allow you to take advantage of the crashes that always follow.

6. *The blood in the streets theory.* The original Baron Rothschild is reputed to have made his fortune by buying when a war, pogrom, revolution, or other politically caused unpleasantness depressed prices to bargain levels.

If the object of investing is to buy cheap and sell dear, then it's wise to wait until things are truly cheap, when fear and panic rule the marketplace. Paradoxically, that environment is ideal for the speculator to display his best humanitarian instincts. By making cash available to sellers when they need it, he's providing a valuable public service. Later on, when people inevitably change their minds and are clamoring for shares at any price, he'll once again bow to the wishes of the marketplace and magnanimously distribute stock certificates to them in exchange for their currency.

The 1980s will offer catastrophic cyclical collapses in many stocks and offer the speculator ample opportunity to go bargain hunting, while looking to all the world like an altruist.

7. *Technical analysis.* The technician (or chartist) believes that all information—fundamental, psychological, and other—known about a stock is already reflected in its price history as shown on a chart, and on other more arcane indicators such as the ratio of advances to declines, the trend of moving averages, and the percentages of odd-lot buyers and short sellers, to name just three. Over the years a whole liturgy of magical symbols has grown up that technicians use to divine the future price action of a stock. The movement of a stock's price forms things like "pennants," "head and shoulders tops," "triple bottoms," and many, many others that are read like tea leaves or sheep entrails by adepts at the art.

There's no proof that technical analysis has ever made any money for anyone, but that's not to say that studying the charts of stocks isn't most helpful. The pictures display very clearly and quickly whether an issue has perhaps moved up ten or fifty times in the recent past—a sure danger signal—or whether the price has stayed the same for years while fundamentals may have been improving. It's most helpful to have a graphic representation to see if something is relatively cheap or dear.

Which Path?

The first rule of successful speculating is to make a plan; the second is to follow the plan. But there's no reason why you shouldn't have several plans, each to be used under the proper circumstances.

A bit later on I will analyze several groups of stocks that hold great promise during the years to come. Each group lends itself to a different method, or different elements of various methods. Mix them and match them, as it were, whenever appropriate. The recommendations I make should remain valid for at least a few years, but more important is the method used to make them. Each group teaches a much wider lesson.

The utilities show up the flaws of growth stock analysis, a perverse way to profitably use fundamental analysis, and the value of contrarian thinking.

The uranium stocks offer a blood-in-the-streets opportunity. "Everyone" is sure the nuclear power industry is dead, and nobody believes that uranium mines will ever be worth working again. Of course, they believed that about gold mines ten years ago.

The South African golds are a case study in economic and fundamental analysis. They should prove rewarding, but not for the reasons most people think. They are actually more a conservative growth stock at this point than a leveraged speculation—like the penny stocks.

The penny stocks offer a nice melange of fundamentalism and the greater fool theory. As a group, they show

the highest potential and the lowest risk of any speculations I'm aware of, and since they offer a 50 to 1 upside
potential, a home run here will make up for a lot of
mistakes elsewhere.

The gambling stocks can be viewed as a new class of
growth stocks. They underline the importance of being
a "nexialist" in order to be a successful speculator in the
years ahead. The old "Nifty Fifty," now better described
as the "Fallen Fifty," and the Dow Jones Thirty Industrials are a study in how growth stocks can become contrarian opportunities.

I've looked at all of them with my own perspective
and with charts that illustrate the points from a technician's stance.

Remember, however, it's the method of arriving at the
conclusions that's worth study, not the conclusions
themselves. It's like a high school chemistry class,
where the grade wasn't given for the answer per se but
for the mehod of achieving the answer.

Stocks are touted by over 600 different investment
advisers and thousands of brokers. Recommendations
are cheap. I think these will turn out well, but you'll
have to take responsibility for the results—both good
and bad.

To tilt the odds a bit further in your favor, however, it
bears looking at not only which stocks to buy but which
ones *not* to buy. In fact, it's probably of greater importance.

Picking a Path

- *It's much more important to know how to pick
  stocks than to follow so-called expert advice and
  recommendations blindly.*
- *Each of the seven methods of stock selection can
  be useful, but in different ways, and at different
  times, with different stock groups.*

Chapter 20

Stocks: Picking Winners

*Market valuations of most securities change in a single pe-
riod of a very few months by an amount equivalent to many
years of dividends or interest coupons. Therefore such
changes in value are much more worthwhile seeking than is
straight investment return.*
G. M. Loeb

At the turn of the century Charles A. Dow said, "The
great mistake made by the public is paying attention to
prices instead of values," a statement so cryptic, yet obvious, that it could easily pass for a Zen koan.

What is value and how does it relate to stock prices?
Perhaps the best place to start is simply avoiding overpriced issues. Avoid mistakes, and the law of large numbers will present plenty of profit.

There are at least seven major criteria you should
apply against any stock you're considering purchasing:

1. Widely Circulated Bearish News

Buy when news is bad, sell when it's good. Good
news is often the first thing to draw attention to a stock.
A lot of enthusiasm and hot stories floating around about
a company's prosperous future indicate whether people
are more inclined to buy or sell. Of course, the stories
may be right in any given instance, but the price of the
stock will probably already reflect the best that could
happen to the company. It's one reason to be very suspicious of recommendations from big brokerage firms;
they typically only tell "salable" stories. Successful

speculators usually buy before the good news is out. Of course, that good news could just signal the beginning of a "greater fool" mania. Statistics such as price/earnings ratios, dividend yields, book values, and the like help determine which it is.

2. Low Price/Earnings Ratio

A low price/earnings ratio usually indicates an underpriced stock; high P/E stocks are never bargains.

People are usually willing to pay a high multiple of earnings for a stock if they think those earnings are going to increase radically. The higher the P/E the greater are people's expectations for higher stock prices, and P/E ratios are an accurate statistical barometer of the state of the market. This is especially meaningful if the present ratio is much higher than it's been on average in the past. That shows that enthusiasm is not only high but has grown in recent months or years.

3. High Dividend Yield

High yields are a hallmark of depressed stock prices; although a low yield doesn't mean a stock is overpriced, it can be a caution sign. Stocks don't exist in a vacuum. They have to compete with other financial instruments such as bonds, CDs, and T-bills for total overall return. The lower the dividend the less current reward the investor gets. And especially after the market has had a big run-up, 18 percent in the hand can be much more appealing than 1 percent and the hope that someone will appear a year hence and pay you at least 17 percent more for your stock.

Low-dividend stocks are also better short candidates, because when you short you are borrowing the stock in question and then selling it, so you must reimburse whatever dividend it pays to the person from whom you borrowed it. That can be a substantial drain while you're waiting for it to go down.

4. High Book Value

Everything else being equal, a stock with a high book value presents less risk than one with a low book value.

Book value represents what each share of stock would be worth if the company were liquidated and the assets distributed. It's an increasingly meaningless figure today because of the way inflation distorts accounting figures. Some companies carry properties on the books at acquisition costs when their market value may be ten times that. Oil and mining companies are outstanding examples of this. Others, with obsolescent plants (or devastated investment portfolios, such as most banks and insurance companies), could find the market value of their assets is much less than that being carried on the books.

Although companies can easily sell for only a fraction of book value (such as Ford, which as of January 1982 went for only 30 percent of its net worth), companies selling for a multiple of book have a lot further to fall, everything else being equal. A high book value represents at least some tangible reality; a low book value is usually an indication you're dealing with a "concept," something which often proves ephemeral in down markets.

5. Mediocre Price Performance

If you want to buy low and sell high, then the stocks to buy are the ones that have "fallen out of bed" in a short period of time. Stay away from stocks with a "good track record." Some companies' stock has multiplied by a factor of fifty from the bottom of 1974 to the peak in

1981. Few of them had fifty times the assets or could produce fifty times the earnings, though. What has usually changed is the public's perception. It happens again and again in the market.

A substantial run-up, after a stock has multiplied three or five or ten or more times, always makes people think it's a good investment and has a fine track record. It's certainly a time when the brokers feel they have a good story to tell. You're in the market to make money, however, not to act as a drama critic.

6. Low Institutional Holdings

Up to about the mid-1960s, stocks were owned mostly by private individuals, not institutions. There were long periods of accumulation or distribution, because movement was the composite of millions of people who were all watching their own portfolios. Now, however, institutions account for 70 to 75 percent of the market, and things are much more volatile. Most money managers for pension funds, mutual funds, insurance companies, and other institutions know each other personally and know what each is doing. They often have the same backgrounds and went to the same schools. They all read the same reports, all talk to the same researchers at the same brokerage firms. And they're all under the same constraints to invest like prudent men. With so much in common, is it any wonder they follow a herd psychology and seek safety in numbers by buying the same stocks?

You don't want to own stocks that are too heavily bought by institutions, because the price has usually been driven to unreasonable levels by all the buying. And once they own them, the only thing they can do is sell them. When they do, they usually act together, just as they did when they bought.

When you're long, you'll want stocks with very little

institutional ownership; conversely, the ones to short are those with heavy institutional ownership.

7. High Short Interest

Anyone who shorts a stock will eventually have to buy it back. If there are a great number of short sales outstanding on a stock (the figures are published monthly) you know a lot of pent-up buying power is lying in wait to make itself felt. For that reason, stocks with a heavy short interest are often among the best bargains.

A Time to Short

As should be obvious, the very factors that tell you when not to buy a stock can be used to tell you when to sell, or short-sell. I expect to be a heavy net buyer of stocks through most of the middle to late 1980s; but with the kind of titanic fluctuations the markets are sure to have, there will be good chances from time to time to play it both ways. But because of high inflation, it's going to be harder to sell short than it was in the classic bear markets of the 1970s.

There's no telling how high a tree can grow, so that even when you feel certain the market is overpriced by a factor of two it can just as easily become overpriced by a factor of four—wiping out premature short sellers.

As economic gloom envelops the financial landscape in the years ahead, there will be plenty of "good reasons" to sell short, but by that time they'll be so apparent to everyone it will be time to buy. The market of the 1980s will present magnificent shorting opportunities, but they will occur within a major bull market trend.

┌───┐
| —— *Buying Stocks for Maximum Profit* —— |
| |
| • *Stay long in the market.* |
| • *Favor stocks with low P/E ratios, high dividends,* |
| *high book value, mediocre price performance,* |
| *low institutional holding, high short interest; do* |
| *so when news is bearish.* |
└───┘

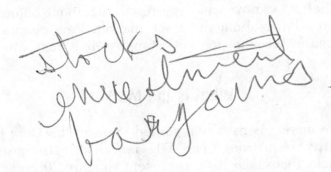

Chapter 21

Stocks: The Leaders of the New Bull Market

It helps to know what you're talking about before you start talking about the stock market. Few people who discuss "the stock market" stop to define the term.

Wall St

What Is the Market?

The market is usually assumed to mean the Dow Jones Thirty Industrials. The DJI is valuable because the stocks that make it up represent roughly 20 percent of the market value of all U.S. stocks, and even more of the dollar value of trading on any given day, but it's not "the market." The price performance of thirty stocks out of 40,000 doesn't give you anything but a vague indication of how the other 39,970 are probably doing. A familiarity with the other indices will prove helpful in deciding which stocks to buy in the years ahead, as well as supplying valuable clues about when to buy them. Let's start with the broadest and work down to the most narrow.

The Wilshire Index

This little-known barometer is the combined market value (price per share times number of shares outstanding) of the 5,000 biggest companies, and it represents 98 percent of the value of all companies. As such, it's a very realistic gauge of whether funds are flowing into or out of the market. It's directly comparable to the money supply figures, or the amount of money in money market funds, and is quoted at least weekly in major financial journals.

The Dow Jones Industrial Average

By far the most widely followed index, the Dow is also the oldest, dating to 1897. It's actually a rather odd, unscientific index where a fluctuation in one stock can have an inordinate effect. Allied Chemical, for instance, has only ⅟₅₀ the market value of IBM, but a one-dollar move in its stock affects the DJIA by half as much. The composition of the index is rather arbitrary, but only widely traded, heavily capitalized stocks are included.

The New York Stock Exchange Index

The NYSE is a composite index including all common stocks on the exchange, each weighted according to its market value (i.e., price per share times number of shares). The index is adjusted to eliminate the effects of capitalization changes, new listings, and delistings. The average was started on December 31, 1965, at a base of 50, and was calculated back to earlier years for statistical purposes. If the index is, for instance, 25, it means all NYSE stocks together have a market value half that of December 31, 1965. A value of 100 means it's twice the total value on that date. The value of the NYSE at year-end 1980 was $1,242 billion—about two-thirds of the value of all stocks.

The Value Line Index

This is an unweighted geometric index with a base date of June 30, 1961; it includes approximately 1,600 stocks that are followed by the Value Line Investment Survey, about 90 percent of which are on the NYSE, but the index includes about 150 heavily traded over-the-counter and American Exchange issues.

Unlike the NYSE Index, a 10 percent move in a minor stock has just as great an effect as a 10 percent move in a major stock on this index.

The Indicator Digest Index

This, like the Value Line, is an unweighted index.

The Nasdaq Index

Introduced in February 1971, the National Association of Security Dealers Automated Quotations also is weighted by the market value of its approximately 2,600 components, which include the largest and most widely traded over-the-counter issues. At the end of 1980, over-the-counter stocks equaled about $122 billion, or about 10 percent of total NYSE market capitalization.

The Standard and Poor 500 Index

Although started in 1923, the average uses the period 1941–1943 as a base equaling 10. Like the NYSE, it's weighted according to the market value of its components, the 500 largest corporations in the U.S.

The American Stock Exchange Value Index

Introduced on September 4, 1973, it's been calculated back as far as January 2, 1969. Like the NYSE, it measures the aggregate value of all common shares on the exchange based on 100 starting in 1973. The value of the Amex at year-end 1980 was $80 billion—about 5½ percent of all U.S. stocks.

All of these indexes have their own slant on "the market," because they compute different stocks, weigh them different ways, and often represent them on graph paper using different scales, although the charts I've included in Chart I and Chart II are all ratio scale. All of them, used one way or another, have significance, and are often used selectively by stock pundits to demonstrate almost anything they'd like, since some stocks are always going up, down, or sideways.

It's helpful to classify the most widely quoted indices by the "quality" of the issues that make them up. The Dow is made up of the biggest, most heavily traded stocks. The Standard and Poor's includes all the Dow stocks plus 470 of the next most important U.S. corporations, and fairly represents the secondary tier of the market. The Amex and Nasdaq indices are both fair indicators of the tertiary tier of the market, the unseasoned speculative issues. They're known as "cats and dogs" on Wall Street.

The relative values of these indices are useful in determining not only how mature a bull (or a bear) market is but which kinds of stocks you ought to be in for maximum profit.

When the lowest-quality stocks start to completely outrun the blue chips, it is one of the surest tip-offs that the end has come to a bull market. It happened in 1929, in 1968, in 1973, and it signaled the crest of the last bull market, starting in 1978, as well. The market had been going up steadily and strongly for six and a half years, but it was only in 1981, after the bull market had gone on for over three years, that stocks on the Amex and Nasdaq started to move. As happens toward the end of most bull markets, the "quality" issues started to weaken relative to the "junk," as the arithmetically drawn charts on pages 306, 307, and 309 show.

From 1978 to the top in 1981, the Dow stocks gained 33 percent, the S & P stocks 75 percent, and the Amex stocks 200 percent.

Chart I

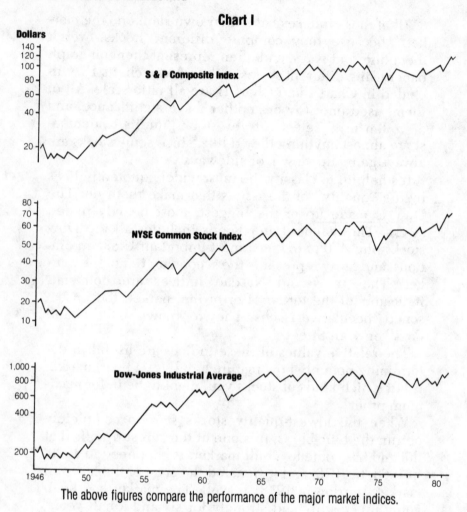

The above figures compare the performance of the major market indices.

Opposite: Notice how the blue chip stocks underperformed the secondary and tertiary issues during the last stage of the 1974–1981 bull market.

Chart II

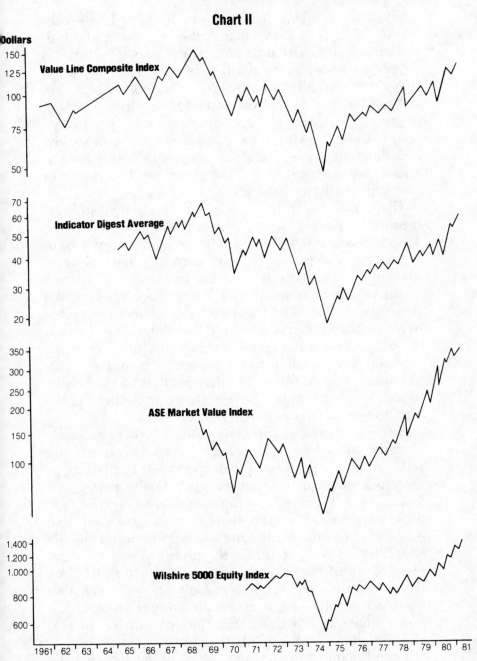

There are good a priori reasons why Dow Jones—caliber stocks usually move first at the beginning of a bull market and fade first at its end. After a crash, or during a depression, people are afraid to buy stocks at all; when they do, it's usually only the largest, strongest, best-capitalized companies that can attract them. In the type of depressed business climate that usually accompanies a bear market, the strong have the best chance of surviving. Relatively new, marginal companies with inexperienced management (the kind listed on the Amex or Nasdaq) are often casualties.

That's especially true in today's economy, and the business cycle analogy in Chapter 3 should predict the way the economy will react. The government will favor the biggest companies with its spending, both because it can only deal with the biggest, and because it's most afraid of the consequences of their not surviving the depression. They'll be the first to get the money created to restimulate the economy, and they'll be able to spend it early, before a tidal wave of inflation hits. The small companies, equivalent to the Gucci stores in the example, must wait for the restimulation effort to filter down to inflate their profits. There's a corresponding lag before investors regain interest in their stock.

If the government succeeds in its efforts to generate an inflationary boom, confidence grows that the future will continue rosy. Investors who reaped big profits on the stock of major companies early in the game start looking for leveraged "underpriced" issues. The fear they experienced at the bottom is transformed into greed at about the same time the government's dollars start filtering down to inflate the profits of small companies. Many of them take their profits in the DJI-class issues to redeploy them in Nasdaq-type stocks. That always causes the senior issues to drop relative to the junior ones; and at this stage they often drop in real after-inflation terms as well.

The phenomenon is exaggerated by the fact that the

market value of DJI-class stocks is so great. If only 10 percent of the money in the seniors flows into the juniors, the seniors may drop only a few percent in value, but the juniors could easily double because the market value of the senior stocks is many times that of the juniors. It's at this stage that promoters start entering the market, selling "new issues" to newly frenzied buyers. New issues are the most marginal of the junior stocks, and when they get hot it's an almost sure sign the market is about to turn—exactly when least expected by stock buyers. It's at about that time the business cycle has started to head down again as well, and the stock market will follow it in short order.

Take a close look at the charts and you'll see the pattern. The primary stocks are first to move up, then lose relative strength as the secondaries boom. When the secondaries fall, they fall much farther and faster than the primaries, just as they rose much farther and faster.

Chart III
ASE MARKET VALUE INDEX

Chart IV
NASDAQ - COMPOSITE

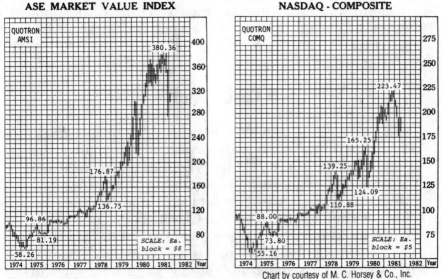

Chart by courtesy of M. C. Horsey & Co., Inc.

Although these tertiary stock groups moved up seven and five times respectively from the bottom in 1974, most of the moves came after 1978.

That will most likely be the order of events in the next bull market as well—first the Dow Jones stocks, then the S & P and NYSE issues, and finally the Amex-Nasdaq stocks. By the same token, by the time the bottom comes to the bear market that began in 1981 (and it may have come and gone by the time you read this), the secondary issues will have been devastated (as Charts III and IV show), while the blue chips will be relatively intact—relative, that is, to the secondary and tertiary issues.

Of course, looked at over the long term, the blue chips have already been devastated—by the 1966 and 1972 market disasters in dollar terms, and by inflation in real terms. They will be the leaders in the next bull market, after the Greater Depression sets the stage for them.

The Bible may disapprove of money (the "root of all evil" and such), but its comments to the effect that "the first shall be last, and the last shall be first" showed that the heart of a potentially shrewd speculator throbbed in the breast of the author.

There are a lot of practical ways you can use an application of the business cycle to your advantage in the years ahead. IBM is a case in point.

A Case History

IBM has been a growth stock since day one; it made legendary fortunes for early investors. Throughout the early '60s and '70s, it sold for P/E ratios between 30 and 50 to 1, yielding only a minuscule dividend. Investors were convinced growth would continue forever, and were willing to pay a premium for it. The whole world knew the computer industry was just starting its boom, and justifiably believed profits and dividends would grow apace. It seemed logical that stock prices would continue booming in light of the fine fundamentals.

As it turned out, they were only half right. IBM, the company, did just fine, but IBM, the stock, started dying a slow death as the financial markets and investment fashions changed.

Chart V tells the story. Even though its earnings have almost quadrupled and dividends have risen nearly *seven* times, the price of the stock in 1981 (at approximately $50) is off 35 percent from its 1968 high, and 45 percent from its 1973 high. Worse, in after-inflation real terms it's off by 67 percent; $50 in 1981 buys only what $25 would in 1968. That's something to think about when you hear bioengineering touted as the new computer industry.

By late 1981, the company's stock was yielding 7 percent, selling at only seven times earnings and only 150 percent of book value. While it's true the company has grown, it's also become less innovative, more unwieldy,

Chart V

INTERNATIONAL BUSINESS MACHINES

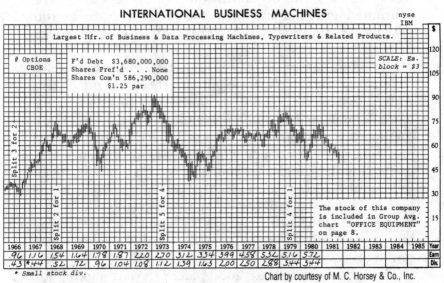

	1966	1967	1968	1969	1970	1971	1972	1973	1974	1975	1976	1977	1978	1979	1980	1981	1982	1983	1984	1985	Year
Earn	.96	1.16	1.54	1.64	1.78	1.87	2.20	2.70	3.12	3.34	3.99	4.58	5.32	5.16	5.72						
Div.	.43	*.44	.52	.72	.96	1.04	1.08	1.12	1.39	1.63	2.00	2.50	2.88	3.44	3.44						

* Small stock div.

Chart by courtesy of M. C. Horsey & Co., Inc.

Growth of earnings and dividends have only a limited relationship to higher stock prices.

more mature, and closer to its eventual demise. That doesn't mean its stock is automatically a bad investment. More likely the market just overestimated its performance twenty years ago, and is underestimating it today for the opposite reasons. In the long-term bull market, since World War II, the stock of IBM languished predictably as the market reached its late stage.

By the time the depression climaxes, much of the company's new competition will have been wiped out, while the government's action in trying to restimulate the economy will ensure a flow of dollars into IBM's coffers. And the stock will almost surely be one of the leaders of the new bull market that will soon get under way.

The Leaders of the Next Market

Fortunately there is a whole class of stocks like IBM— stocks that used to be darlings of Wall Street and have continued growing but have fallen from grace as the very long term post–World War II bull market for stocks matured.

During the early 1970s, there was a whole class of so-called "one decision" stocks, popularly called the "Nifty Fifty," that were favored by portfolio managers. They were "one decision" since you had only to decide to buy them and would never have to sell, because the companies that underlay them would just keep growing and increasing dividends. Of course, predictably, the stocks fell out of bed, but in many cases the companies continued making good progress as analysts predicted. As primary issues, the old "Nifty Fifty" and the traditional Dow Jones Thirty blue chips will probably lead the next bull market.

The following lists are good places to start looking for bargains when, perhaps by using a comparison of the various averages discussed a few pages back, you determine the bottom has come.

The great post–World War II bull market peaked in 1966 for the Dow Jones blue chips that led it up to that time. To put their prices in perspective I've indicated their 1966 highs and 1966 dividend yields as well as

Table I   DOW JONES INDUSTRIALS 1966

Stock	High in '66	Dividend Yield at '66 High	Jan. '82 Price	Jan. '82 Dividend Yield	Percent Increase/ Decrease in Nominal $	Percent Increase/ Decrease in Real $
Allied Corp	$51	4.8%	$40	5.9%	− 22%	−69%
Alum Co. Am	63	2.0	24	7.4	− 62	−86
Am Brands	41	5.3	36	9.0	− 12	−66
Am Can	60	4.2	31	9.2	− 48	−80
Am Tel & Tel	64	4.0	58	9.2	− 13	−64
Bethlehem Stl	42	5.5	23	7.6	− 45	−79
Dupont	81	3.1	35	6.7	− 57	−83
Eastman Kodak	71	1.6	71	4.3	0	−63
Exxon	42	4.7	30	10.0	− 29	−71
Gen Electric	60	2.6	57	5.5	− 5	−63
Gen Foods	42	3.1	30	7.5	− 29	−71
Gen Motors	108	5.5	39	6.5	− 64	−86
Goodyear Tire	29	2.7	19	7.4	− 35	−76
Inco Ltd.	40	3.2	14	1.5	− 65	−86
Intl Bus Mach	38	1.2	60	5.5	+ 58	−39
Intl Harvester	53	4.1	8	Nil	− 85	−64
Intl Paper	35	4.4	36	6.7	+ 3	−60
Johns Manville	31	4.3	14	13.0	− 55	−82
Merck & Co.	41	2.0	82	3.4	+100	−22
Minn Mng Mfg	43	1.6	54	5.5	+ 26	−51
Owens-Illinois	35	2.2	28	5.6	− 20	−69
Proct & Gambl	39	2.8	83	5.0	+113	−18
Sears, Roebuck	33	2.2	16	8.4	− 52	−82
Std Oil Cal	39	3.7	36	6.7	− 8	−64
Texaco	42	3.4	30	9.8	− 29	−71
Union Carbide	70	3.5	46	7.4	− 34	−74
US Steel Corp	37	4.9	26	7.6	− 28	−73
Unit Technol's	100	2.0	38	6.3	− 62	−85

Table II NIFTY FIFTY 1972

Stock	High in '72	Dividend Yield at '72 high	Jan. '82 Price	Jan. '82 Dividend Yield	Percent Increase/ Decrease in Nominal $	Percent Increase/ Decrease in Real $
Avery Prod.	$ 43	.7%	$24	3.3%	−44%	−72%
Avon	140	1.1	29	10.0	−79	−90
Baxter Travenol	56	.3	33	1.1	−41	−71
Black & Decker	38	1.1	15	5.1	−61	−80
Burroughs	126	.3	32	8.0	−75	−75
Clorox	48	1.6	11	7.7	−77	−89
Coca-Cola	75	1.2	30	7.6	−60	−80
Disney	106	.1	47	2.4	−56	−78
Eastman Kod.	150	1.1	70	4.3	−53	−77
Eckerd Jack	29	.5	23	4.0	−21	−60
Emery Air	30	1.0	12	8.3	−60	−80
Ford	64	3.8	17	0	−73	−87
Intl Fla & Fra	44	.6	19	5.2	−57	−78
Johnson & Johnson	44	.4	36	2.8	−18	−59
Kresge-K Mart	50	.4	16	5.8	−68	−84
Lilly Eli	80	1.0	52	5.0	−35	−68
Marriott	35	Nil	34	0.9	− 3	−51
McDonalds	77	Nil	60	1.8	−22	−61
Merck	90	2.2	82	3.4	− 9	−54
Polaroid	150	.3	20	5.0	−87	−93
Rite Aid	42	.2	27	2.9	−36	−68
Schering Plough	70	.8	28	6.0	−60	−80
Texas Inst.	95	.5	75	2.7	−21	−61
Xerox	172	.6	38	7.7	−78	−89

corresponding figures for January 1982 when this book went to press. The next column lists their percentage decline in dollar terms (i.e., nominal or current dollars); it averages 20 percent. In the last column is their percentage decline in real terms (i.e., after-inflation constant dollars); it averages 68 percent.

Table II is a selection of some of the old "Nifty Fifty" stocks, which generally reached their highs in 1972, six years after the Dow Jones issues. Figures correspond to those above, except with a base year of 1972.

The stocks in these two groups constitute the cream of American industry and, as such, should lead the next bull market.

There are, however, several other groups of stocks that should do at least as well—although for completely different reasons. One of those with the greatest potential is, perhaps surprisingly, the utilities.

Selecting a Winner

- *Become familiar with the different market indices; they're useful in picking tops and bottoms of the market.*
- *The time to buy stocks is fast approaching.*
- *Buy the "quality" issues first. Consider using a "no load" mutual fund for your basic position.*

Chapter 22

Utilities

Any investment policy followed by all naturally defeats itself.
Thus the first step for the individual really trying to secure or
preserve capital is to detach himself from the crowd.
G. M. Loeb

Utility stocks offer a textbook example of how the market dispenses justice to those who run with the thundering herd and slavishly believe the prevailing wisdom dispensed by their stockbrokers. Stated simply, it devastates them.

A Disastrous Investment . . .
For the Right Reasons

Throughout the 1960s and '70s, shares of electric utility companies were sold to the unwary as a surefire way to grow with America; everyone was sure the industry's revenues, profits, and dividends would inevitably rise with the level of prosperity. The odd thing is, the brokers were right on all counts, except their "logical" assumptions that utility stock prices would also go up. There were a number of reasons why they didn't. As usual, investors saw only what they thought were the direct and immediate consequences of prosperity. They didn't see the indirect and delayed ones. The stocks had a great track record. The Dow Jones Utility Average more than quintupled from 1947 to its peak in 1964.

By the time investors believed utilities were riskless growth stocks, the top, predictably, had already come and gone. People never stopped to think where the utilities were going to get the money to build the plants needed to generate all that electricity. The companies got it in the stock and bond markets; they floated new issue after new issue of their stocks, and the average utility more than tripled its outstanding shares from 1960 to 1980. The supply of the stocks far outpaced demand and, as a consequence, share prices dropped. Increased demand for power and national prosperity, the very things everyone counted on to send share prices up, were ironically the factors that knocked them down as the utilities were forced to scramble for capital. In the process, they also sold bonds for scores of billions, weighing themselves down with borrowed money. Starting with the credit crunches of 1970 and 1974, investors became very leery of debt-burdened companies, and perceptions of the utilities started changing.

The utilities joined the rest of the country in an orgy of expansion, financed by watering their stock and borrowing to the hilt. A lot of power plants have been built, but the expansion hasn't done investors much good. Early investors have lost about 60 percent in dollar terms and about 90 percent in terms of purchasing power. That's enough to start them worrying about the safety of their investments.

A Great Investment . . . For the Wrong Reasons

Investors sold on the idea that growth is good for the utilities now see the economy contracting. Worse yet, they see today's extraordinary interest rates and wonder how the utilities are going to float stocks and bonds. Once again, they have it completely backwards. Bank trust officers have put these stocks in widows' and orphans' accounts for decades. These slow learners are finally starting to figure out they're a "bad investment," twenty years too late.

It's time to buy them as high-potential speculations. There are four specific reasons this is true.

1. Depressed Prices

Of course, just because utility stocks have gone down from 50 to 90 percent in real terms doesn't mean they can't fall further, but all bear markets come to an end.

I've reproduced below a chart of Commonwealth Edison—in many ways a typical utility.

The stock traded as high as 58 in 1964, when it had a price/earnings ratio of over 21 and paid a dividend of less than 3 percent. Since then it's gone as low as 17½. That's a loss of 60 percent in dollar terms, and almost 90 percent in real terms, although the company has added thousands of megawatts of generating capacity—which

Chart I
COMMONWEALTH EDISON CO.

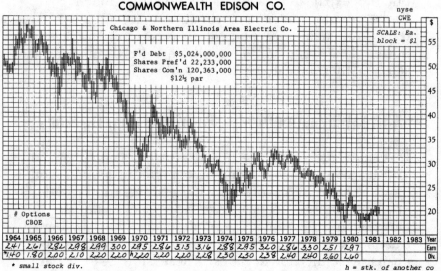

1964	1965	1966	1967	1968	1969	1970	1971	1972	1973	1974	1975	1976	1977	1978	1979	1980	1981	1982	1983	Year
2.41	2.61	2.82	2.98	2.99	3.00	2.95	2.86	3.13	3.16	2.88	2.95	3.20	2.86	3.30	2.51	2.97				Earn
*1.40	1.80	2.00	2.10	2.20	2.20	h2.20	2.20	2.20	2.28	2.30	2.30	2.38	2.40	2.40	2.60	2.60				Div.

* small stock div.

h = stk. of another co

© M. C. Horsey & Company, Inc.

is real wealth. In the meantime, while its stock was involved in a slow-motion crash, the company's dividends went *up* by 90 percent, so that today the stock sports a 14 percent yield and a 6 to 1 price/earnings ratio. You can now buy it for half of book value from all the losers who were scrambling to get in when it was selling for almost three times book twenty years ago.

2. Lowered Standard of Living

Among other things, the depression will force people to turn the lights out when they leave the room and reduce the setting on the air conditioner. As the standard of living drops, so will electricity consumption. This will be compounded by a second factor. Not only will the public be using less electricity but they'll actually be generating their own and selling it back to the utilities. They can do this economically with solar, wind, and hydro systems, as well as using the excess capacity of heating plants to run dynamos.

This phenomenon, known as cogeneration, was quite common around the turn of the century, when many buildings generated their own electricity. The idea made especially good sense where the excess heat from the boiler on the premises could be used to warm the building; in a public utility this low-grade heat is wasted or, worse, viewed as thermal pollution. It's probable that thousands of buildings all over the country will install the equipment needed to turn that waste heat into electricity and wholesale it back to the power company. Farmers will dam streams and erect windmills for the same reason.

Accordingly, the utilities won't need new generating capacity in the '80s, and that means utilities won't need to borrow more money and float more stock, and that's bullish.

3. Inflation

On the other hand, if the depression is going to reduce electricity consumption, how are the companies going to service the fantastic amount of debt they've taken on in the last twenty years preparing for demand that's not going to be there? Not to worry. Eventually, inflation is going to get much, much worse. And that debt is going to be inflated out of existence. About half of the total capital of the average utility is debt, and as inflation increases, the corporation's liabilities decrease proportionately. The devastating losses of the bondholders are going to accrue directly to the benefit of shareholders.

It's ironic that inflation, which has hurt these stocks so badly in the past, will ultimately redeem them in the future. There is a real danger that a hostile regulatory climate or severe cutback in electricity usage or a credit collapse could bankrupt some utilities. But, unfortunately, there is a safety net.

4. Governmental Action

There are several industries that the government will consider sacrosanct regardless of what type of trouble they get into, because of their size or prominence or lobbying power. The utility industry is one of these. The government realizes that the bankruptcy of any major utility could shatter the delicate balance of the financial markets. And besides, it just wouldn't do for lights to go out across the country. It would almost surely step in to bail out a troubled company, one way or another.

That, of course, is disastrous for the economy in the long run, but it takes a lot of the worry out of being a utility investor in the short run. Once again, government takes a lot of risk out of speculating.

How to Select Utilities

Almost any utility you buy in the early 1980s should present you with significant profits, in real terms, by the end of the decade; some, however, will do much better than others. In selecting utilities I once again suggest you attempt to buy those that are "low," because the thundering herd has assessed the facts incorrectly, as usual.

If you get hold of a report from your broker on how to buy utility stocks, it will be apparent that it's almost 180 degrees opposite what you're reading here. The shares I'm recommending are held in low repute by brokers, and sell at a substantial discount to their fellows.

It's a happy coincidence, although not at all coincidental, that I'd be willing to pay a premium, if necessary, for the very shares now selling at a discount. There are three reasons in particular why you should zero in on only ten, or at most twenty, of the hundred-plus major utilities in the U.S.: the future of nuclear power, current inadequate capacity, and depressed locations. It's no coincidence those are exactly the reasons no one wants the few stocks really worth buying.

The Future of Nuclear Power

The Naderites and eco-fascists had a field day in the '70s creating huge problems for companies attempting to build nuclear power plants. There are problems with nuclear power, of course, but they're insignificant compared with the problems of oil, coal, or hydro. First, oil is liable to a supply cut-off for political reasons. More important in the long run, the stuff has become too valuable to burn for power where substitutes are easily available. Its most economic use would appear to be as a petrochemical feedstock or transportation fuel, where substitutes are uneconomic or even technically unfeasible, at present.

Coal is incredibly dirty and polluting; the ash, sludge, and smoke created by burning this fuel probably result in thousands of long-term victims each year, in addition to the hundreds of miners who die in cave-ins or from black lung disease. The waste from coal-fired plants that doesn't go up in smoke is a very nasty sludge amounting to cubic acres per plant per year. Hydro power is clean, but whenever a dam is built thousands of acres are flooded, which may or may not be the most desirable use for that land. Moreover, when dams break, they can destroy billions in property and kill thousands of people.

Nuclear power, despite all the hysteria generated against it, gives every indication of being the safest, cleanest, and cheapest form of power generation available. Strictly speaking, it's hard to say it's the cheapest form of power, since the government has spent billions subsidizing its development at taxpayer expense to the benefit of the industry. But, on the other hand, fighting legal battles and regulatory delays has cost the industry billions on the other side of the ledger. It's extremely clean, as the few cubic yards of waste generated per plant each year can easily be transformed into glasslike rock and planted in geologically stable formations under the earth. Nuclear generates no more thermal pollution than any other power source.

And if the track record is any indicator, it's far safer. No one has ever been killed in thirty years of power generation, contrary to popular opinion, and despite the hysteria surrounding Three Mile Island, there was never a serious danger of a real disaster. A mistake was made and backup systems caught it. That's why they were built.

There's always a lot of resistance to any new technology from neo-Luddites, elitists, and everyone who has some interest in the status quo. My assessment is that reality is on the side of nuclear power, and reality usually overcomes. Nuclear power is probably the solution to the world's energy problem, at least until fission is mastered, or until orbiting solar collectors can send down the sun's energy by microwave, or some other technology is perfected.

Utilities with a heavy commitment to nuclear power tend to sell for a discount despite that, which is just fine for you as a speculator.

Current Inadequate Capacity

Some utilities can't generate enough power to satisfy the demands of their customers; they have to buy power from neighboring utilities with excess capacity and retail it to their own clients. This "purchased power" is less profitable than electricity they generate themselves, and it depresses their earnings.

At the same time, the market seems to believe they will have to build the extra capacity eventually, and believes (probably correctly) that they won't be able to do it at present interest rates. As a consequence the stocks of "purchased power" utilities are depressed relative to those with excess capacity.

The very things that make most people feel these stocks are a bad buy actually make them a great buy. As electrical usage drops in the depression, utilities with inadequate generating capacity will suddenly have just the right amount of capacity, while their well-heeled competitors will experience a surplus, which will result in lots of very costly dormant facilities. The decline in usage will be a problem for the utilities held in high esteem today, while those with inadequate capacity are the very ones best positioned to weather a depression. Which leads to a third clue as to which to buy.

Table I

Utility	Fuels/Generating Source
Boston Edison	oil 73%, nucl. 24%, pur.pwr. 3%
Central Maine Power	oil 55%, hydro. 15%, nucl. 30%
Detroit Edison	coal 83%, hydro., oil & gas 6%, pur.pwr. 11%
Duquesne Light	coal 92%, oil 1%, nucl. 3%, pur.pwr. 4%
Eastern Utilities Assoc.	oil 83%, nucl. 17%
Iowa Elec. Light & Pwr.	coal 30%, nucl. 44%, pur.pwr. 24%, other 2%
Iowa Resources	coal 61%, nucl. 38%, gas & oil 1%
Long Island Lighting	oil 60%, gas 14%, pur.pwr. 26%
Northeast Utilities	oil 43%, nucl. 53%, hydro. 4%
Orange & Rockland	oil 38%, gas 41%, hydro. 3%, pur.pwr. 18%
Philadelphia Electric	oil 15%, coal 24%, nucl. 25%, hydro. 4%, pur.pwr. 32%
Portland Gen'l Electric	hydro. 15%, coal 5%, nucl. 27%, pur.pwr. 53%
Public Service E & G	oil 18%, coal 29%, nucl. 22%, nat'l gas 17%, pur.pwr. 14%
Rochester G & E	nucl. 42%, coal 32%, pur.pwr. & other 26%
San Diego G & E	oil 49%, gas 32%, nucl. 1%, pur.pwr. 18%
Toledo Edison	coal 69%, nucl. 25%, other 6%
Washington Water	hydro. 68%, coal 10%, pur.pwr. 22%

Current P/E Ratio	Current Dvdd. Yield	Recent Price	20-Year Range	Institut'l Owners	Book Value
5.0	13.0%	21	14–51	1.10%	32.25
6.4	14.8%	12	10⅛–22¾	2.99%	16.75
5.8	15.1%	11	7⅛–38⅝	4.99%	17.50
5.9	15.8%	12	11–36½	2.15%	16.75
5.4	14.8%	11	8–31¾	.39%	15.45
5.7	14.0%	12	8–34¼	1.51%	18.30
5.6	14.0%	20	15–45	1.53%	27.85
5.9	13.2%	15	9⅝–38½	3.21%	19.50
5.6	14.6%	8.3	5½–22⅛	5.68%	14.90
5.7	13.1%	13	7⅛–34⅞	1.10%	18.65
5.8	15.4%	13	11⅛–40½	5.61%	18.05
5.9	13.5%	13	10¾–29⅞	.83%	17.80
6.7	14.1%	18	—	11.82%	26.35
5.3	12.3%	13	8⅛–25½	7.73%	21.20
5.5	14.0%	12	9–28	2.92%	17.00
6.0	14.5%	16	15–41½	5.86%	23.80
5.4	13.8%	17	15⅛–27½	.74%	24.60

Depressed Locations

Most people live perpetually in the past; even those who think they are future-oriented usually just project past trends into the future. Sometimes that works out in life, but very rarely in investments, because prices reflect what everyone "knows," and that elimates the chance for profit.

Apropos of that, brokers tend to tout stocks in growth areas of the country, such as the "Sun Belt." As a result, utilities located in that part of the country sell for about 50 percent higher price/earnings ratios, and for about 30 percent less yield than those in depressed areas of the country. After a trend has been in motion long enough to award such distinctions to stocks, about the only thing that can happen is that it will reverse, catching the trend followers in a lurch and rewarding the contrarians. With their large pools of unemployed workers, relatively cheap land costs, and local governments that are so strapped they're forced to be accommodating, places like Detroit, Chicago, and Buffalo could have a renaissance. Whereas it's hard to see how things could get much better in Florida.

As an extra bonus, the institutions (mutual funds, pension funds, and banks) have loaded up with the expensive stocks you don't want and have few of the depressed ones you do. As explained earlier, the institutions are great contrary indicators, and the utilities to buy are the ones they don't own. It all fits together into a neat package.

___ *Speculations for Widows and Orphans* ___

- *Properly selected utility stocks (those listed in Table I in particular) should be big winners in the '80s.*
- *They offer a nice combination of current yield and high upside potential in a nice low-risk package. They belong in the portfolio of the wildest speculator as well as that of the most conservative.*

Chapter 23

Uranium Stocks

Each and every one of us should in the acquisitive period of our business lives take at least one chance for high stakes. Several, if one has the wherewithal and courage.

G. M. Loeb

The mining business is quite cyclical, and the profits of mining companies fluctuate radically with the prices of ore. That periodically presents buying opportunities to speculators with foresight. Whenever metal prices hit the bottom of a bear market, it looks like they'll never recover, for perfectly valid reasons. The prospects of gold, silver, and copper stocks all looked grimmest at the best moment to buy. The uranium industry is now at that point.

The rationale for nuclear power, which is the end consumer of almost all uranium, was presented in the previous chapter. If you accept the reasoning there, you may want to make a direct commitment in some uranium issues as well as the nuclear utilities, which are an indirect play on the fuel's prospects.

Since hitting an all-time high of over $43 a pound in 1978, the spot price of milled uranium ore (called "yellowcake") has fallen to $23—a six-year low.

In the meantime, costs within the industry have continued rising at over twice the rate of inflation in general, and the industry is in full retreat. Exploration is at a ten-year low, inventories of yellowcake are at all-time highs, 50 percent of workers have been laid off since 1979, and many companies are selling off their proper-

Chart I

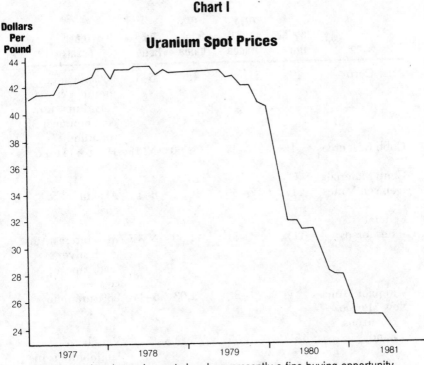

Uranium Spot Prices

Dollars
Per
Pound

44 –

42 –

40 –

38 –

36 –

34 –

32 –

30 –

28 –

26 –

24 –

1977   1978   1979   1980   1981

Uranium prices have plummeted and are presently a fine buying opportunity.

ties to generate cash. On the whole, there's every indication that it's a good time to buy.

It wasn't always this way. In the early 1950s there was
a uranium boom, and fortunes were made in the penny
stocks of small uranium exploration companies traded
mostly in Salt Lake City. The stocks did well again in
1979; since then, however, fortunes have been lost in
them. The charts tell the story.

Most American uranium (the U.S. mines over half the
world's supplies) is produced by oil companies, such as
Exxon (the biggest producer), Conoco, and Kerr-McGee.
Uranium contributes only a small fraction to their profits. The following companies, however, have a significant percentage of their activities devoted to the

Table I

Name	Jan '82 Price	1971–1981 Range	Book Value	P/E Ratio	Other Assets
Atlas Corp	19	5½–36	18	5–1	63% revenues uranium & vanadium. Low cost producer of uranium.
Cobb Resources	4⅞	2–11	.50	NMF	Has some oil & gas.
Conti Materials	6⅝		10	4–1	
Denison Mines	24½	4½–50	16	8–1	Also in oil & coal.
Federal Resources	1⅝	1½–11	1.50	NMF	Also interests in gold, silver, lead, zinc, & copper.
Midnight Mines	⅞	1–8	1.03	5–1	95% uranium
New Mexico & Arizona Land	15½	4–55	5	25–1	Very large landholdings in western U.S.
Ranchers Explor & Dev	25	4–65	15	32–1	Also in copper.
Reserve Oil and Min	1⅞	4½–52	1.50	NMF	
Rio Algom	31⅞		32	6–1	
Timberline Minerals	1	4–1	.10	NMF	Developmental only at present; also has gold, copper & molybdenum.
UNC Resources	6⅜	4–34	17	12–1	Attempting to diversify out of uranium.

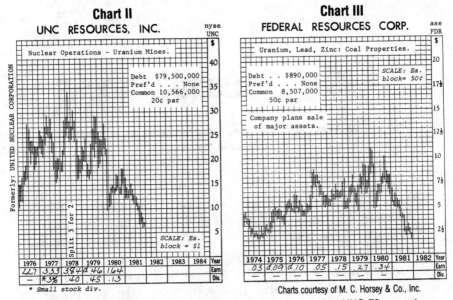

Chart II
UNC RESOURCES, INC.
nyse UNC

Nuclear Operations - Uranium Mines.

Debt $79,500,000
Pref'd . . . None
Common 10,566,000
20¢ par

SCALE: Ea.
block = $1

Formerly: UNITED NUCLEAR CORPORATION

Split 3 for 2

	1976	1977	1978	1979	1980	1981	1982	1983	1984	Year
Earn	2.27	3.33	3.84	d.46	1.64					
Div.	—	*.3%	.40	.45	.13					

* Small stock div.

Chart III
FEDERAL RESOURCES CORP.
ase FDR

Uranium, Lead, Zinc: Coal Properties.

SCALE: Ea.
block= 50¢

Debt . . $890,000
Pref'd . . . None
Common 8,507,000
50¢ par

Company plans sale
of major assets.

	1974	1975	1976	1977	1978	1979	1980	1981	1982	Year
Earn	.03	d.09	d.10	.05	.15	.27	.34			
Div.	—	—	—	—	—	—	—	—	—	

Charts courtesy of M. C. Horsey & Co., Inc.

Federal Resources has lost 85 percent of its value in the bear market, UNC 70 percent.

radioactive metal. Many of them are broadly diversified in other natural resource areas, such as coal, oil, gold, silver, and copper; but their stocks have been hammered down in the selling panic surrounding the collapse in uranium prices. The highs shown on the table were all reached in 1978 or 1979. They are sound values once again, now that uranium is out of fashion.

In addition to stocks on this list, Kerr-McGee, Homestake, and Phelps Dodge derive a fair portion of earnings from uranium.

───── *When Mining for Profits, Remember* ─────
• *Uranium stocks look like gold stocks did in 1971.*

Chapter 24

Penny Stocks

*The most important single factor in shaping security markets
is public psychology.*
G. M. Loeb.

It is the daydream of every investor to find another IBM, Polaroid, Xerox, or McDonald's while it is still unknown and unwanted by the masses, to buy it for pennies a share, and sell it for hundreds of dollars a share. Unfortunately 99 percent of the stocks with that kind of potential—or seeming potential—will wind up worthless. That shouldn't come as a surpise; nearly all situations that offer high rewards are attended by high risks. But the intelligent speculator always looks beyond the obvious, and today the very things that look riskiest are often the safest. Things like penny mining stocks.

In the upside-down world of the '80s, the most conservative blue chips will become crazy speculations, and the craziest speculations will become the most conservative blue chips. *U.S. penny mining stocks are probably the finest long-term speculation of the decade.* There's every reason to believe these stocks could move upward fifty or a hundred times as a group while some individual issues go one thousand for one.

Background

U.S. penny gold and silver stocks are literally in a class by themselves, direct descendants of the old days when the public had a chance to grubstake a prospector looking for the Lost Dutchman or the Seven Cities. Many publicly traded penny stocks represent scores of claims, sometimes comprising hundreds and even thousands of acres of land. The land is generally leased from the state where it's located, and underlying minerals are owned by the prospector so long as he continues making inputs of labor and capital to the land.

Almost all American gold mining companies are located in seven Western states: Colorado, California, Nevada, Washington, Utah, Idaho, and Alaska. Their shares are traded largely by brokers who are members of the Spokane Stock Exchange in Spokane, Washington, or the Intermountain Stock Exchange in Salt Lake City, Utah.

The typical penny gold stock represents a share in a marginal exploration company, not an active mine. Many companies were going operations as late as the 1930s, but were closed down during World War II by the government as "non-essential" industries. They were never reopened after the war, because costs skyrocketed while the prices of precious metals were controlled. With very little cash (few have any current income), all that such a company can do is keep tax assessments in order, comply with government regulations, and hope that a larger company with more financial resources will take an interest. For the most part, the larger companies have looked to the small miners to do most of the prospecting.

Should an established company take over operation of a property in return for royalties, it is quite possible for a stock to literally explode in value. Should that happen when there is a gold boom under way, the results would be phenomenal.

Why They Will Boom

There are at least nine characteristics surrounding the penny stock market that set it up as a once-in-a-genera-

Chart I

Dollars

Spokane Stock Exchange Averages

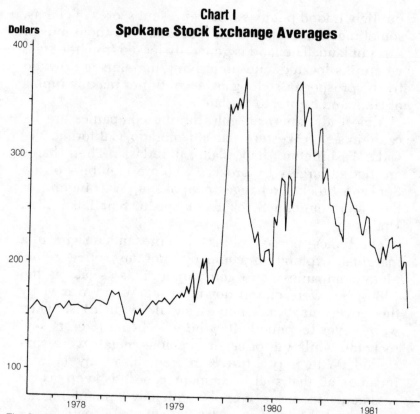

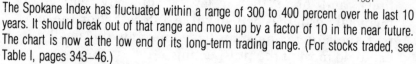

The Spokane Index has fluctuated within a range of 300 to 400 percent over the last 10 years. It should break out of that range and move up by a factor of 10 in the near future. The chart is now at the low end of its long-term trading range. (For stocks traded, see Table I, pages 343–46.)

tion opportunity. Any one of them could skyrocket the market, but all of them are probably going to act to-gether. A successful speculator always has at least one "backup system" to make it go right if his first line of reasoning proves faulty, but here you have nine.

1. A Very Thin, Inactive Market

There may be no public trading for weeks at a time in some of the penny mining stocks. Even the biggest penny gold companies often have total capitalizations (i.e., total number of shares outstanding times the price per share) of only three or four million dollars. The typical penny gold company has a capitalization of only $500,000 to $1,000,000, a trivial amount of money in today's financial markets. With a float that tiny, it takes only a small amount of buying to move the market. A single buy or sell order for a few hundred dollars may move the price by 10 percent or more. When the public moves in a few years from now, that same characteristic will put early buyers in the catbird seat. That's why it's critical to buy when the market is distressed and scraping bottom.

2. An Uninformed Market

When you buy most publicly traded stocks, you can at least read their annual reports or a research bulletin from an advisory service to help you make an intelligent decision. But this is not always an advantage. The material you see as a private investor has usually been filtered through several layers of professionals, and the stock price often already discounts the information that you receive. But this is rarely the case with penny mining stocks.

Most penny mining companies don't even mail annual reports to their shareholders, and institutions and advisers don't even know the companies exist, much less conduct research on them or advise their purchase. The average investor has, therefore, as close to an even break as he's likely to get in the market. Inside information doesn't affect penny stocks, because there is none to be had—at least none that's any good.

3. An Unknown Market

Not only is information within the penny mining market sketchy, but few people even know the market exists, because it isn't widely promoted. What people don't know about they can't buy. By the time brokers are touting the profits in a group of stocks and the press is covering it, everyone who might have any intention of buying has already done so, and all he can do is sell. Penny mining stocks are still in the "you'll find out" category for most people, and that is when the successful speculator likes to buy.

4. The Psychology of Present Holders

So far these stocks have been bought mostly by serious, long-term speculators who see the possibilities and are putting away their certificates for the long haul. As the rationale for penny mining stocks gains credence, the number of buyers will grow, putting gradual upward pressure on the market. Even those people who just "take a flyer" on this market on a tip or on a whim rarely sell. After all, if you buy 1,000 shares of a five-cent stock for $50 because you expect them eventually to be worth $500 or $5,000, you're hardly going to bail out if it drops to $45 or $40 or even $5. The amount of money involved just doesn't justify the transaction costs. So most people buy them, often in large blocks because they are so cheap, and forget them. In the parlance of the stock market, these stocks are in an accumulation phase.

5. A Leveraged Play on Precious Metals

As the gold and silver markets take off in their final runs to the climax of a long bull market in the mid-1980s, anything related to them will be carried along. Mining stocks are a leveraged way of playing the market.

A mine that is earning only $1 per ounce at $300 gold (because its costs are $299) would earn $301 should gold only double to $600; that's the kind of leverage that will attract buying when the gold market gets hot again. Established companies with good earnings have the least potential. Stocks with no earnings at all—like most penny issues—offer the greatest leverage. That's because no one can really be sure how much metal can be recovered from the company's property. A strike, when it occurs, could transform an abandoned hole in the ground into a new Golconda. That makes them good takeover candidates.

6. Takeover Possibilities

Many of these small companies are ideal merger or acquisition candidates for large mining companies flush with cash and desiring more property to exploit. In addition, large industrial users of precious metals, like Eastman Kodak and Polaroid, may decide it's cheaper to buy silver in the ground than on the open market. Ownership of mining properties would assure them a constant-cost supply in the future. If a takeover craze ever hits these small natural resource companies the results should be breathtaking.

7. A Speculative Arena

That prospect of speculation will draw buyers into the market after a few plots of moose pasture inevitably do turn into viable mines. Unsophisticated markets in Spokane and Salt Lake City are natural rumor mills, and rumors are the stuff of wild feeding frenzies when other conditions are right. The class of speculators bred by terminal inflation should flock into penny mining stocks if only because the stories associated with them make such good telling.

8. Foreign Exchange Control

America is a large importer of both gold and silver. When foreign exchange controls are imposed, their import would cease or be curtailed. The controls would also close off investment in South Africa and possibly even Canadian mines, leaving these junior Americans as the only game in town.

9. A General Stock Market Boom

From 1960 to the peak in 1968, the average Spokane silver stock skyrocketed by a factor of 100. The best-performing penny silver stock was Coeuer d'Alene Mining. In 1960 the stock could have been purchased for two cents. In 1968 it could have been sold for $20. A $1,000 investment would have turned into $1,000,000. Coeuer d'Alene was by no means unique. Taking three stocks at random from an alphabetical list, we find Abot ranged from $.04 to $1.60, American Silver from $.03 to $7.50, and Atlas Silver from $.06 to $5.25 over the same time frame.

The price of silver doubled—from $1.29 to $2.50—from 1960 to 1968. There were periodic gold crises, but the government was still able to keep that metal's price at $35. That shouldn't have caused the kind of explosion that took place, and it didn't. It only acted as an ignition point; the main propellant was the sentiment in the U.S. stock market as a whole.

The 1960s were the greatest sustained speculative boom era since the 1920s. Players were always looking for the next hot stock group, the next high flyer; they raced from computer stocks, to high technology stocks, to leisure stocks, to conglomerates, looking for something "cheap" they could sell for a fortune to a greater fool. With the doubling of silver in 1968, the penny mining issues fitted the bill nicely. They were ideal: a thin undiscovered market with a hot story behind it. The explosion had nothing at all to do with hedging against inflation, devaluation, or depression. Just greed.

The reason the penny stocks boomed in the '60s, then,

was not so much because the metals markets were moving (that was a necessary condition, but *not* the cause); it was because the U.S. stock market was at an all-time high and some of the enthusiasm spilled over into the mining stocks.

If you accept my analysis that the stock market will boom shortly, then you can see these stocks as a double play on both precious metals and securities. The stock market in general should get very hot, and the metals even hotter. Owning shares of small companies that mine them should be a bonanza.

How to Buy

It's hard to say exactly what market conditions will be when you read this, so it's hard to give timely advice; that's the function of a newsletter, not a book. The most important thing is to start buying these stocks, whether the market is flat on its back or already heating up as you contemplate the thought. Even if you wind up buying on a temporary bulge, look upon it as an insurance policy on what may develop into the greatest bull market of the decade.

The market in these stocks is very illiquid. There's not a lot of trading in them from day to day, and that means prices can fluctuate radically with only small changes in supply and demand. Your call to a broker to buy $5,000 worth of a thinly traded $.03 stock could double its price, simply because there may be only $1,000 available at the price he's quoting. The reverse is true of selling. That is part of the reason why some of the stocks quoted later in this chapter have spreads of 50 to 100 percent between the bid price (the price you sell for) and the asked (the price at which you buy).

The spread is so wide because a market maker has to tie up a certain amount of capital in inventory. A heavily traded stock may have only a 2 percent spread; the market maker can "make it up on volume." A dealer requires a bigger spread in the penny mines precisely to compensate for the low volume. And since few brokers make markets in these stocks, the competition to narrow the spread isn't very fierce. That's why patience is so important in buying these stocks. Sometimes a dealer will find himself overloaded with inventory of stocks and will be forced to hold a fire sale—just like a clothing store would.

Some ways of getting into this market are better than others. The trick is largely to use limit orders whenever you can.

Since fluctuations in the market can be so great, and the spread between bid and asked so wide, you must be careful of buying "at the market." If a stock is quoted at $.07 bid and $.10 asked and you place a market-buy order, you'll pay $.10. If you prudently place a "limit" order to buy at $.08, however, you may very well get it. Experienced players place limit orders at some lower figure in hopes of catching the dealer in a moment of weakness. It also acts as a good discipline and keeps you from "chasing" the stock.

Brokers

Attempt to place an order for a specific penny stock with the average broker and you'll be greeted with an expression of disbelief followed by one of consternation. He won't believe that anybody would do anything so silly. The consternation will arise from several facts.

1. He hasn't the slightest idea what you're talking about.
2. He wasn't aware that such stocks really existed.
3. He doesn't know how to buy them, or where to find out how.

4. He hates to take orders for penny stocks because of SEC rules. A broker selling, or even passively order-taking, for stocks such as these could be "deemed" (that quaint seventeenth-century word the SEC likes to use) to have violated the "due diligence" rule, the "know your customer" rule, the "prudent man" rule, or numerous others that exasperate the customer and bedevil the broker even while they employ the bureaucrat.

For that reason you'll do well to use a broker who's sympathetic and knowledgeable; I've listed a few in Chapter 33 whom I've met personally.

Which Stocks?

All this inevitably leads to the question of which stocks to buy, since there were several hundred, more or less, of the little wonders at last count.

It's a hard question to answer for stocks in general but an almost impossible one for penny mining shares in particular. From time to time you may hear one stock or another touted for various reasons, but in this market any "news" is almost tantamount to rumor and hearsay, and should be treated as such.

What do I recommend? Quite simply: *random selection.* Unless you're a mining engineer, know the company's management personally, and are willing and able to put on jackboots and venture out into the goat pasture yourself, you have no real basis to choose one stock over any other. That's entirely apart from the fact that there are so many opportunities in the world it's almost certainly a misallocation of your time to try to puzzle out geology surveys, and what annual reports are available. They all talk about things like "sinking the number two shaft to the Klerksdorf Reef," the number of tons of air conditioning they're installing, and why we'd all be millionaires if only the mule hadn't died while they were searching for the treasure of Sierra Madre last winter. Most information is highly technical, far too detailed for an investor who wants to watch the big picture, and frankly, pretty incomprehensible and boring. So unless you consider yourself an expert already, you've probably got better things to do than clutter up your mind with all the gruesome details unless you think it will make good trivia on the cocktail party circuit. Using it to make investments will, chances are, only be counterproductive. Casual "research" will often lead only to stocks that have already been inflated in price by promoters hoping to unload to a credulous public, especially when the market heats up.

Random selection, therefore, is both the best hope for profit and the best defense against loss—even though it's contrary to the way stocks "should" be selected.

A perfect example to underscore the point comes to mind. In a little book called *Prospecting in the Coeuer d'Alene*, the author, apparently a grizzled prospector, gave his opinion on a company called Quad Metals. The stock, which sold for as low as $.02 in 1975, was deemed worthless and its managers branded as scoundrels. Despite this seasoned, well-researched "expert" opinion, the stock subsequently sold for $.40—a 2000 percent movement. It's a good idea to disregard touting on these stocks, regardless how sage or well-intentioned.

Diversification

When you buy U.S. penny gold and silver stocks, you're actually buying a concept—not an individual stock. Your strategy, therefore, should be to buy as many different issues as you can, for two reasons. The only way you can increase your odds on getting one or more really big winners is by having as many different issues as possible. At the same time, diversification protects you against one company's untimely bankruptcy (a rather common occurence with this class of stocks). With most share prices in the $.03 to $.25 range, you'd be much better advised to buy $500 each of ten different stocks than $5,000 worth of one stock.

If legions of mutual fund managers who read volumes of economic reports can't choose New York stocks any better than a randomly thrown dart, it's hard to see how you can do much worse in Spokane. I hesitate to suggest that you even use some method as mechanical as choosing every fifth stock on the list, since a lot of people may accept that as "inside information" and do just that.

Somebody will probably endorse that technique once the boom gets under way, and you'll see the prices of every fifth stock double overnight. Therefore, I'll simply suggest that you choose twenty stocks whose first initials correspond to those of your mother's maiden name.

Here are the stocks from which to choose. The first column gives the stocks previous high *bid* price (generally in 1968, 1974, or 1980), the second column gives the stocks current *ask* price in January 1982.

Table I SPOKANE STOCK EXCHANGE—TRADED STOCKS

Over-the-Counter Stocks	Previous High Bid Price	Jan. 1982 Ask Price	Over-the-Counter Stocks	Previous High Bid Price	Jan. 1982 Ask Price
Aberdeen Idaho ..	.85	.25	Atlas	5.25	1.60
Abot Mining	1.60	.70	Beacon Light	.25	.20
Admiral	.41	.05	Bismarck	6.25	.45
Alice Cons	1.50	.15	Bonanza Gold	1.25	.32
Amazon Dixie	.35	.30	Bullion Lode	.25	.08
American Silver ..	7.50	2.10	Bunker Chance ..	.31	.08

Table I   (continued)

Over-the-Counter Stocks	Previous High Bid Price	Jan. 1982 Ask Price	Over-the-Counter Stocks	Previous High Bid Price	Jan. 1982 Ask Price
Burke Mining	.20	.15	Mascot Silver	1.75	.20
Caledonia	.65	.04	Merger	5.00	.80
Callahan Con	.80	.18	Midnite Mines ...	5.25	1.25
Canyon Silver	4.75	.23	Nabob Silver	.95	.12
Capitol Silver	.17	.40	Nancy Lee	4.50	.35
Center Star Gold .	.57	1.00	National Silver ...	1.00	.15
Champ Gold Sil ..	.60	.13	Nev Stewart	1.10	.08
Chester	5.50	1.00	Niagara Mining ..	.20	.70
CDA Crescent ...	2.00	.90	North Star	.52	.04
CDA Mines	22.50	8.75	Oom Paul	.48	.18
Conjecture	3.10	.35	Painted Desert ...	.10	.02
Cons Silver	5.75	2.00	Placer Creek	.40	.25
Daybreak Mines .	.50	.08	Plainview	2.85	.50
East CDA	1.00	.07	Rock Creek	1.00	.65
Eastern Star	.26	.05	Royal Apex Sil ...	.25	1.10
Empire Expl	.40	.35	St Elmo Silver ...	1.75	.50
Evergreen	.50	.10	Signal Sil Gold ...	.57	.08
Gold Bond	.40	.08	Silver Beaver	.31	.08
Gold Placers	2.65	.20	Silver Belt	.95	.25
High Surprise	.85	.20	Silver Bowl	.71	.11
Hunter Creek	.81	.20	Silver Buckle	1.10	.25
Idaho General ...	.50	.15	Silver Crystal	.70	.39
Idaho Leadville ..	.70	.18	Silver Hill	.40	.05
Idaho Mont Sil ...	.65	.10	Silver King	.25	.15
Idaho Silver	.60	.40	Silverore	.72	.20
Inspiration Lead .	.60	.10	Silver Scott	.40	.20
Jenex Gold	.20	.08	Silver Seal	.30	1.10
Judith Gold	.60	.25	Silver Star	1.80	.18
Keystone Silver ..	.75	.05	Silver Surpise	3.00	1.35
King of Pine	.34	.07	Silver Trend	.23	.08
Lookout Mt.	.40	.07	Square Deal	.75	.20
Lucky Fri Ex	1.25	.23	Sterling Mining ..	3.10	.50
Lucky Star	.38	.06	Summit Silver ...	.25	.10

Table I (continued)

Over-the-Counter Stocks	Previous High Bid Price	Jan. 1982 Ask Price	Over-the-Counter Stocks	Previous High Bid Price	Jan. 1982 Ask Price
Sunset Minerals ..	.07	.04	Verde May	.65	.08
Superior Silver ...	.55	.08	Vindicator	3.00	.80
Thunder Mt	1.25	.36	Virginia City Gold	.07	.04
United Mines	.41	.10	Western Energies	.10	.07
Utah Idaho Cons .	.18	.04	Yreka United	1.15	.13

Registered Stocks	Previous High Bid Price	Jan. 1982 Ask Price	Registered Stocks	Previous High Bid Price	Jan. 1982 Ask Price
Allied Silver	1.65	.50	Mineral Mtn	1.45	.35
Callahan	36.50	13.00	Nesco Mining	.50	.15
Clayton Silver ...	2.80	1.50	New Hilarity	.53	.12
Fourth of July	.40	.10	Princeton	1.80	.20
Gladstone Res. ...	2.50	1.25	Quat Met	1.25	.06
Grandview	.52	.10	Sidney	1.00	.20
Gulf Resources ...	41.00	15.00	Silver Butte	1.30	.20
Hecla	40.00	10.50	Silver Ledge	2.25	.15
Helena Silver	.50	.20	Silver Mtn	1.40	.30
Homestake	71.00	31.00	Sunshine	35.00	8.00
Indep Lead	3.40	.60	Western Gold	.21	.15
Little Squaw	1.05	.85	Western Silver ...	.80	.20
Met M & L	.48	.12	Western Sil A	.80	.20
Metropolitan	2.05	2.25			

A Home Run

Buy these stocks as a long-term speculation. Because of the high commissions (sometimes ranging to 9 percent), and the traditionally large spread between bid and asked prices, the pennies are not good trading vehicles. But successful speculators tend not to be traders anyway. You're looking to hit a home run for ten or a hundred times your money, so considering the steep transaction costs, it's just silly to try jumping in and out. You might decide to take short-term profits on a run-up rather than wait for a reaction to buy them back that never comes. Buy them and put them away until the points covered in Chapter 17 tell you it's time to sell.

The penny stock market will give a whole generation stories to regale their grandchildren with as it makes multimillionaires of early buyers.

Ultimate Advice

• *If you engage in no other speculation recommended in this book, buy a selection of these penny mining stocks as soon as possible.*

Chapter **25**

Gambling Stocks

Speculation means taking a calculated risk on an intelligent estimate of future possibilities. Practically every great success in this world of a national as well as a corporate and personal nature has come from intelligent and successful speculation.
G. M. Loeb

The best long-term speculations capitalize on the great swings of the economy and the nature of society itself, as well as investor psychology. The penny mining shares and the utility stocks are both in that class. And so are the gambling stocks. They should prove a low-risk way of profiting from the unfortunate decline in the work ethic that invariably accompanies high inflation.

Inflation turns people into gamblers as they desperately attempt to stay ahead of the depreciating currency; it makes life seem unpredictable and seem as if there is little to lose by taking big risks. It appears pointless to plan and save prudently, and that's the type of atmosphere that gambling itself thrives in. That means higher volume for the gambling industry, and casinos are very leveraged to volume. Twice the gross can mean quadruple profits; a halving of the gross can mean no profits at all. As Everyman troops to the casino hoping for Lady Luck to solve his financial problems, there will be a high proportion of inexperienced and desperate players as well. The legal gambling industry should do almost as well in the 1980s as the underground illegal gambling industry did in the 1930s. It all adds up to profits for the house for at least three reasons.

First, inflation creates an attitude of "eat, drink, and be merry today, for tomorrow we die"—exactly the type of attitude casino owners try to cultivate.

In addition, local governments nationwide will rapidly approach wholesale bankruptcy in the years to come as locals join the welfare roles and demand more services in face of a declining standard of living. It will be hard to raise traditional taxes, so it's quite likely these governments will legalize gambling, as they have recently in Atlantic City, for the extra revenue that will bring in. There's no fundamental reason why the growth curve of Atlantic City casinos won't be duplicated in every major metropolitan area. Parimutuel betting (horses, dogs, and jai alai) is now available in thirty-four states, off-track betting is legal in three, and there are now fourteen state lotteries, but only two states have casinos.

The companies that are already established in running casinos will best be able to capitalize on the trend. If the

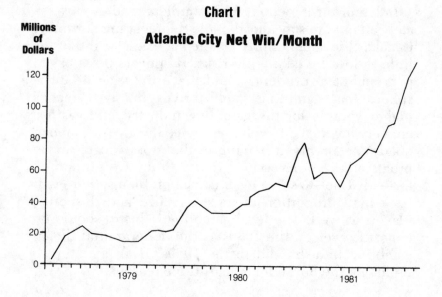

Chart I

Millions of Dollars

Atlantic City Net Win/Month

demand for local casinos goes up as quickly as it should, local governments may even have to offer concessionary terms to bring in the needed capital and expertise to take advantage of it.

A third fundamental reason for investing in gambling stocks is that the stocks themselves have shown the potential for a tremendous run-up in the past. Gambling is the type of industry that can catch investors' fancies, and since there aren't many companies in the business, the bidding for them could be fierce. They had a speculative blow-off and have substantially retreated from the highs that they set in 1979, although earnings have continued to climb. Despite their potential, they've fallen from fashion since the price bust.

It's true, of course, that the industry is heavily infiltrated by organized crime and is regulated by local government; but, as with any other investment, whether a risk is worth taking is strictly a function of the price of

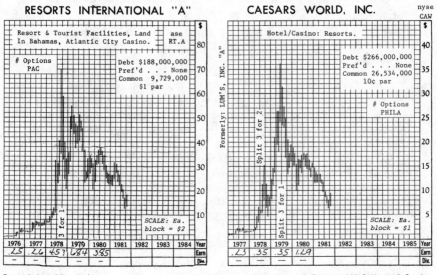

Two typical gambling stocks.   Courtesy of M. C. Horsey & Co., Inc.

admission and the potential reward. If every American gambled with the frequency of Nevada residents (full-time residents, not visitors) the profits of the industry could increase by ten.

Like the liquor, tobacco, drug, and weapons industries, the gambling business has a long track record and should prove to be contracyclical. The best way to gamble is to own the house, and now is a good time to buy your share. As a bonus, the worse things get, the better they'll all do. You and I may not approve of any of this —we might prefer to see that capital directed to food or hospitals or solar research—but we don't make the rules, we just play the game. If buying these stocks makes you feel uncomfortable, give a portion of your profits to the Salvation Army; they offer soup kitchens for those who guarantee your success because they are on the "wrong side of the table."

There are no sure things in the investment world, but as a long-term hedge against hard times, the gambling stocks will do nicely. If nothing else, they teach an invaluable lesson on not mixing moral ideology and investment.

The following stocks are among the most prominent in the industry:

Name	Symbol	Jan. '82 Price	1974–'81 Range	% of Book Value	Jan. '82 Dividend Yield	P/E Ratio
Bally Mfg. Corp	BLY	$24.0	$1.9–48.6	158	0.7%	8.3
Caesars	CAW	6.8	0.5–18.9	106	Nil	5.1
Golden Nugget	GNG	21.0	0.8–44.6	141	Nil	5.3
Hilton	HLT	39.0	2.2–52.3	192	4.6%	8.9
Holiday Inn	HIA	25.0	4.3–32.8	108	3.2%	7.4
MGM	GRH	8.9	1.4–25.9	169	5.4%	8.2
Playboy	PLA	7.8	2.0–32.8	60	1.5%	4.8
Ramada	RAM	6.1	2.0–17.0	100	Nil	NMF
Resorts Int'l	RTA	17.0	0.3–69.5	72	Nil	9.4

Chapter 26

South African
Gold Stocks

*There is no rule about anything in the stock market save
perhaps one. That rule is that the key to market tops and
bottoms or the key to market advances or declines will never
work more than once. The lock, so to speak, is always
changed. Therefore, a little horse sense is far more useful
than a lot of theory.*

G. M. Loeb

The South African gold stocks have been very kind to
their buyers over the last ten years; most have returned
their original purchase price to shareholders many times
over in dividends alone. They've established a great
track record, and this whole group of stocks seems to
have been legitimized as an investment. They've been
in the limelight for so long that they're no longer considered exotic; people have gone into them from fear of
inflation, anticipation of even greater profits, desire for
their high dividends, and international diversification,
among other reasons.

But just as gold isn't the same investment it was in
1971 or 1976, neither are these blue chip gold mines.
The group has been fully discovered by the investment
world, and can no longer be considered a high-potential
speculation so much as a long-term growth industry
whose product is more or less indexed to inflation. The
earnings, dividends, and share prices of the companies
should grow reliably—but gradually—in the years
ahead, although punctuated by explosive rallies and
sell-offs.

The character of these stocks has changed. That doesn't mean there won't be great profits to be had in the years to come; it just means it's a little late in a long-term bull market to buy them for that purpose, unless you can do so at bargain basement levels.

In a nutshell, the South African gold stocks should be looked at as being everything that American utility stocks are supposed to be but haven't been for twenty years—secure yield-with-growth stocks. It's the type of paradox that will be so typical of the 1980s, that rabid speculations will become suitable for widows and orphans, while dull conservative stocks will prove fodder for the wildest speculators.

The transformation of the South African mines shouldn't come as any surprise, however. In a free market, everything about these stocks would be predictable and they would be considered dull consistent-yield vehicles; the price of gold, the cost of mining, ore grades, and such could be conservatively discounted years in advance. Although neither the U.S. nor South Africa is a free market society, the biggest variable—the gold price —has had ten years to reach an equilibrium level and should no longer have the type of 5 to 1 fluctuations it's had in the past, at least in real terms. That relative stability will give gold stocks the characteristics utility stocks are supposed to have.

Which Mines?

These gold stocks fulfilled the potential I explained in *Crisis Investing*, but that doesn't mean they should be discarded, any more than it means gold should be sold just because it has reached an equilibrium. The gold stocks simply merit a different place in your portfolio; for that reason the type you hold should be different as well and conform to the new conditions in the economy.

In the past I've always recommended the highest-cost, shortest-life, most speculative mines in order to get the most leverage from each investment dollar. But because gold has "caught up" with other prices, you might do well to buy only the longest-life, lowest-cost conservative mines instead. They pay dividends that are almost as high as the leveraged stocks, and with much less risk. The following thirteen mines are the blue chips of the approximately forty-five issues in South Africa:

Name	1974 High	1976 Low	1980 High	Jan. 1982 Yield	Jan. 1982 Price
Buffelsfontein**	36¾	6⅜	168½	17.4%	$29.50
Driefontein	18	4¼	41	9.7%	20.50
Free State Geduld	37½	10¼	97¼	16.1%	29.75
Hartebeestfontein**	41¼	6⅞	113	15.3%	44.00
President Brand*	40	8¼	82¾	15.3%	29.75
President Steyn*	40	5⅜	72¼	15.4%	26.25
Randfontein**	59¼	14	112½	10.9%	49.00
St Helena	50½	9⅛	60	16.7%	27.00
Southvaal**	24⅛	3⅜	46½	11.5%	27.75
Vaal Reefs**	63¼	9	109	14.9%	58.25
Western Deep**	37	6⅜	84⅛	15.2%	30.00
Western Holdings*	56¾	12⅜	117¾	20.5%	40.75
Winkelhaak	25⅞	3¾	45½	13.1%	24.00

A quick comparison of the highs of '74 and '80 will show how popular these stocks became over the last market cycle. The lows of 1976 give some idea of how cheap "cheap" can get before they can be considered good speculations.

I've marked mines with some uranium reserves with an *, those with substantial reserves with **. If you accept the reasoning in the section on utilities for nuclear power, these will tend to offer a lot of extra potential on the upside. Since their earnings and dividends are based almost wholly on gold, with uranium prices very depressed, there's little additional downside risk.

One downside risk in the mines is the increasing prospect of terrorism or serious political turmoil in South Africa. It's always been a risk, but I consider it minor for the near-term future. The prices of the stocks have always discounted the danger of a blow-up. See it from the Baron Rothschild's point of view, as an opportunity.

There's a riot or some other type of civil commotion or political turmoil in South Africa every few years, and that's always been an excellent time to go bargain hunting. Patience is important; buy these stocks only when there's a whiff of cordite in the air, not when prospects look rosy.

There are five open-end mutual funds that have all or most of their portfolios in gold and silver stocks.

The Way to Buy

The various mutual funds specializing in gold stocks were never a very attractive way to invest in the past, because their portfolios tend to be made up almost exclusively of those on the list above. They did well throughout the 1970s, but astute speculators selected highly leveraged stocks, such as Durban Deep, East Rand Proprietary, and Grootvlei, which ran three or four times faster and farther.

The portfolios of the funds are still quite conservative, but, like the broken clock on the wall, it's now the time when they are going to be right. You may want to dispense with picking stocks and simply buy shares in any of these open-end funds, which offer both diversification and dollar cost averaging.

United Services Fund
15748 Interstate Highway
P.O. Box 29467
San Antonio, Texas 78229
Toll-free (800) 531-5777
or in Texas, (512) 696-1234

Golconda Investors Ltd.
111 Broadway
New York, N.Y. 10006
Toll-free (800) 523-9250
or in New York, (212) 267-5100

International Investors
122 East 42nd Street
New York, N.Y. 10168
(212) 687-5200

Research Capital Fund
155 Bovet Road
San Mateo, California 94402
(415) 574-8800

Strategic Investments Fund
10110 Crestover Drive
Dallas, Texas 75229
Toll-free (800) 527-5027
or in Texas, (214) 530-2960

United Services and Golconda are "no load," so 100 percent of your money is invested; you have to pay a salesman a 9 percent-plus commission with the others.

International Investors, the oldest and largest fund, has a good assortment of U.S. and Canadian penny stocks, as well as blue chip South Africans; hence it is the best-rounded portfolio.

Research Capital has a policy of trading the market, which increases expenses and substitutes their judgment for yours.

United Services has exclusively conservative South Africans, and the management doesn't try to trade the market. For those reasons—and the fact it is a no load—it's probably your best choice.

Golconda's management tries to trade and second-guess the gold market, something which they haven't done well at; the fund has had the lowest performance of the group.

Strategic Investments Fund sticks to mostly the leveraged South Africans, and is probably a cycle behind the market for that reason—something which, however, is typical of mutual funds.

An Alternative

Perhaps the best choice, however, is ASA (known solely by its initials), which isn't on the list because it's a closed-end investment trust traded on the New York Stock Exchange. It's been a poor choice in the past, because it's the best-known way to play gold stocks, and that popularity with the unsophisticated has tended to make it overpriced. In the past, there were three good reasons to stay away.

First, as a closed-end fund it can sell for either a premium over or a discount to its asset value, but historically, it has usually sold for a premium of 25 percent to 75 percent to the shares in its portfolio. There was no reason for such a premium except the ignorance of those who bought it at those times.

Second, its dividend has usually been only one-third that of the dividends of the mines in its portfolio, because it retained them internally. When the fund was selling at a premium anyway, that did the shareholder no good at all.

Third, it invested exclusively in long-life low-cost shares, which have themselves usually sold at a premium and were the wrong type to own over the last ten years.

Things have changed, however. ASA now often sells for a 10 to 25 percent discount to its assets, currently yields a 15 percent dividend, and the stocks in its portfolio are just the ones to be in for the years ahead.

If you want South Africans, consider ASA. As a further hedge, and to increase income, it's an excellent candidate for covered writing of both put and call options. If you're unfamiliar with that technique, any of the brokers listed in Chapter 33 can explain it in detail or send you literature from the various exchanges that explain it.

Investing for Secure Yield ——— *with Growth Potential*

- *The best place for South African gold stocks, especially with the tremendous yields they offer, is in your pension, Keogh, or IRA plan. It's important to tax-shelter yields, which can range to 40 percent periodically.*
- *The mutual funds in particular offer a convenient way to play this game; the right fund in these stocks offers as trouble-free low-risk a method of preserving capital as you're likely to find in the 1980s.*

Chapter **27**

Convertible Bonds

*Your investment results are going to vary a great deal more
because of your personal influence than whether you buy a
security rated "AAA," "B" or even "X."*
G. M. Loeb

Convertible bonds offer another option that is even
lower in risk, and just as high in potential as South African gold stocks, while offering approximately the same
current yield.

Low Risk and High Reward

Ordinary bonds were, perhaps, the most consistently disastrous place for capital during the 1970s. Convertibles,
however, have held up much better. They now offer one
of the best risk and reward combination of any security.

Convertible bonds are bonds that can be exchanged
for a predetermined amount of the issuer's common
stock. They're usually issued by second-tier companies
that need to offer a bonus of some kind in order to raise
capital. Convertibles can offer the best characteristics of
either stocks or bonds, and they offer several advantages:

Guaranteed Yield

The interest rate coupon on the bond is guaranteed,
unlike the dividend of a stock. This can be most impor-

tant in a depression, when earnings fall rapidly and dividends are liable to be cut.

Reduced Risk

Bonds are senior securities and in the event of a liquidation have first claim on assets. Many companies will be bankrupted in the years to come, and common-stock holders will simply be out of luck. Bondholders have some protection.

Upside Potential

Because these bonds are convertible into stock at some price, they can appreciate either because interest rates drop (like any bond) or because the underlying stock goes up.

Convertibles first became really popular in the '60s because they seemed to offer the best of both worlds; bond prices were more or less stable, and stock prices appeared to be going up forever. Investors were wrong on both counts, but they were still much better off buying the convertibles than they were with either pure stocks or bonds at the time. No matter how bad the stock market might get, at worst a convertible can be looked on as a pure bond. And no matter how bad the bond market might get, at worst convertibles are a play on the underlying stock. The bond portion of a convertible acts as a hedge against a possible deflation on the way to eventual hyperinflation. As a result, the convertible presents lower-risk investment than either stocks or bonds over the next decade, while they can offer the upside of both.

The trick, as with any other investment, is to buy at the proper time, depressed. The years 1970 and 1974 were classic bottoms for both stocks and bonds. Sometime by late 1982 another double bottom should occur and offer a third chance to buy these securities for very low risk, super upside potential, while locking in a high current yield to boot. A speculator's dream come true, and as close to a situation like buying gold or silver in 1971 as you're likely to get.

There are several hundred actively traded convertibles. Rather than go into a discussion of such things as conversion terms and conversion premiums and recommendations of specific securities, I suggest you investigate two services listed in Chapter 33 that specialize in these securities. I could take four or five pages here to explain the technicalities, but it's more important that you just be aware of the opportunity, and alert to the times to take advantage of it, than be presented with another stock-buying list; various newsletters can supply a rationale for certain companies that are "special situations" from time to time. Convertibles are available from companies in dozens of vastly different industries, and it's impossible to analyze all of them here. In this book I've attempted to pinpoint "one-way street" situations like the penny mines and the utility stocks, rather than those that will move up and down erratically. One word of advice, though: Investigate this area thoroughly, and before you buy any stock check to see if it has a convertible which may offer better value.

Instead, the rest of this section will cover commodity convertibles, an area few are familiar with, and where little information is available.

Commodity Convertibles

What stock convertibles do for stocks, commodity convertibles do for commodities. They are a new phenomenon. The first of the breed were issued in 1980, and they were convertible into silver. Gold- and petroleum-related bonds followed.

By the end of the 1980s, it's reasonable to believe it will be possible to buy bonds backed in some way by copper and other metals, as well as some agricultural commodities. Just so no mistakes are made, the only bonds in this group I can recommend are the silver issues, particularly the Sunshines. The reason for that should be apparent as you read on, but the main distinction between these issues is the way they relate to commodity prices. The silver bonds are true convertible bonds, trading like other fixed-interest debt obligations, only with the "kicker" of being converted into silver at a fixed ratio per bond. The gold bonds are not "convertible" as such; they are indexed directly to the price of the metal. The oil notes, on the other hand, have only their interest payments linked to the price of the fuel.

Silver Bonds

The Sunshine Mining 8½s of April 15, 1995, and December 15, 1995, and the HMW Industries 8s of May 1, 2001, are particularly interesting because silver has the potential of reaching $50 or $100 an ounce in the years to come. They offer a way to profit directly from that while earning a current income in dollars. The rationale I gave in *Crisis Investing* for silver in 1979 (when the metal was $7) is just as valid in 1982 (when silver is about $8—at least at the moment). In after-inflation terms, the real price is the same. So is the potential, and I wouldn't be surprised to see $100 silver by 1985 as inflation and the financial markets both go wild.

The Sunshine Bonds. There are two series, those issued April 15 of 1980, and those issued December 15 of 1980. They're identical in all respects except the eight months' difference in maturity date. Terms are as follows:

1. Each bond is convertible into fifty ounces of silver. That means when silver hits $20 per ounce the bond's

$1,000 face value equals their conversion value. For each dollar silver rises thereafter the bonds gain $50 in intrinsic value. If silver, for instance, goes back to $50 an ounce, where it was in February of 1980, the bonds should trade for $2,500.

2. There is a 7 percent mandatory call provision each year. This means that Sunshine is required to retire 7 percent of the bonds each year, and each year the floating supply will become correspondingly smaller. At the same time any holder may redeem up to 7 percent of his bonds (in round lots, of course) for silver in any given year. Sunshine should be able to make good on its pledge because it's one of the largest independent silver mining companies in the U.S.

The bonds traded at 145 when silver was at about $20 and interest rates about 13 percent, and as low as 70 when silver was about $9 and rates 17 percent. Like all convertibles, these usually sell at a premium above their conversion value because of their other advantages.

The bonds are B-rated, and with silver selling for $9 to $12, offer about 7 percent less current yield than a similar quality straight bond. The reduction in current yield is a trivial price to pay for their upside potential. At the same time, the bonds allow the company to save that much in interest, which amounts to $3.5 million per year on the $50 million issue. That interest savings, of course, is why any company issues convertibles.

HMW Industries 8½ of May 1, 2001. HMW, the old Hamilton Watch Company, does a substantial amount of fabricating with silver, and these bonds, in effect, allow the company to borrow against its operating inventory and finance it at about half market rates. These bonds were initially sold at a discount in the summer of 1981 at prices of about $80, because of a combination of weak silver prices and high interest rates.

These bonds are redeemable into only forty-three

ounces each—less silver than the Sunshines, so silver must trade at a fraction over $23 before they are "worth their weight" in the commodity (23.25 × 43 = $1,000, the bond's face amount) and at that point the bonds will advance $43 in price for every dollar silver gains in value. The HMW bonds are B-rated, and sell for about the same price and current yield as the Sunshines. As they offer less silver in conversion, they would appear overpriced at first glance. As long as the bonds sell for a substantial discount from par (i.e., $1,000 per bond), however, their "yield to average maturity" is somewhat higher, and as long as silver stays in the doldrums, it balances out. There are $19,000,000 worth of the bonds outstanding, and HMW is obligated to retire 10 percent of that amount (i.e., $1,900,000) of the bonds at par value ($100) each year starting in May 1983.

That means if you buy one with a $10,000 face value you might pay about $8,000, but regardless of what happens to their market value, there's a chance HMW will pay you full par value for your position come 1983 should your bonds be among those randomly redeemed. That provision is compensation for the less favorable silver conversion terms. The HMWs have a higher yield to average maturity than the Sunshines, but also less upside potential. Take your choice, but since you're buying these issues as a play on silver, hoping to hit a long-ball home run while keeping your risk down, the Sunshines are superior.

With silver under $15 in a bottoming area, and long-term rates at 18 percent, these securities are an excellent low-risk, high-reward double play, paying over 10 percent current interest in the bargain.

Gold-Backed Bonds

There are numerous gold-indexed bonds issued before ownership of the metal was made illegal in 1934.

Although suits have been filed with the intention of forcing the issuers to make good on their promises to redeem their bonds in gold, the huge increase in the metal's price makes it unlikely the courts will ever enforce the original contracts. Gold-backed bonds issued before 1934 should be treated as ordinary bonds because, until the ethical climate of the country changes radically, that's all they'll ever be.

There is, however, an alternative: the Refinemet International N.V. 3¼ percent Gold Indexed Bonds of February 1, 1996. These are Eurodollar bonds, and because of U.S. securities laws they were not originally offered here in February of 1981, when they were issued. They can now be purchased like any other foreign bond, however.

The bonds are issued by a newly formed Netherlands Antilles company, which is the wholly owned subsidiary of Refinemet International, whose stock is traded in the U.S. Refinemet is a full-service metals company, that is, it trades, brokers, refines, and reclaims precious metals. The proceeds of the 100,000-ounce offering were used to purchase gold the company must carry as inventory; like the HMWs, it is to allow the company to finance its inventory at a below-market rate. The company doesn't want to bear the risk of carrying 100,000 ounces of gold, or financing it at 20 percent dollar interest rates, as it's in the business of fabricating, not gold speculating. At the same time, its bonds allow gold investors to reap a current return from a position in the metal.

The bonds are substantially different from the silver bonds, because their principal amount is in gold (ten ounces), not dollars. The silver bonds are denominated in dollars, and convertible only into silver. These bonds, on the other hand, always trade for exactly their value in gold—unlike the silver issues, which trade at a premium to their conversion value until silver goes beyond it. That accounts for the low 3¼ percent coupon on the

Refinemets—3 percent was the historic long-term yield when currency was backed by gold.

The ten-ounce bonds were offered at $5,190 each when gold was trading at $519 an ounce and have since fluctuated with the metal. The interest of .325 ounces of gold is payable each year on February 1, in U.S. dollars, based upon the gold price for the ten trading days ending on the fifth business day prior to the payment date.

Because the interest is paid in gold, your actual return will fluctuate with the gold price. For instance, if you buy them when gold is $400 an ounce and the interest falls due when gold is $800 an ounce, your interest payment in gold has remained .325 ounces, but it has doubled in dollar terms, much the way it might with a gold stock. The silver-indexed bonds, by contrast, pay a fixed rate of interest.

The bonds have two other features of note.

1. If gold goes to $2,000 and stays there for more than ten consecutive trading days, the company can, at its option, redeem them in full.

2. The company has provided a sinking fund to retire 10 percent of the original issue per year from 1991 to 1995.

If your U.S. broker is unwilling or unable to acquire them for you, a Swiss or Austrian bank will gladly comply.

In essence, these bonds solve the perennial complaint of novice gold buyers that they need an income, and their gold coins don't pay one; these bonds do. But there's a price for the income, and that is that you are only holding a piece of paper, not the gold itself. Once again, you pay your money and take your choice. I have no recommendation; the cost-benefit tradeoff is one only you can make, but you're probably better off with the South African gold stocks.

Oil-Indexed Notes

The Petro-Lewis International Finance, N.V. 9 percent Guaranteed Oil-Indexed Notes of May 1, 1986, are issued by a wholly owned subsidiary of the U.S.-based Petro-Lewis Corporation and offer a low-risk way to play possible increases in the price of crude oil. On May 1, 1981, $20,000,000 of the notes were issued on the Eurodollar market. These securities are a little odd in that the principal ($1,000) of each is constant, no matter how high or low oil goes, but the interest payable fluctuates with the price of oil. Since the notes are due in 1986, there's little downside risk unless Petro-Lewis, a B-rated company, goes into default. But there's not much upside potential either, because only the interest, not the principal, is indexed. Should we have a runaway inflation, holders of the gold and silver bonds would do nicely; owners of these securities would be wiped out. The interest on each note is indexed to 18½ barrels of petroleum, and, at the time the notes were issued, oil was $36 per barrel. A bonus (contingent) interest payment becomes due at maturity, so that owners benefit from any increase above $36, and they'll need every bit of it, as the notes carry only a 9 percent coupon—half the market rate for a straight note. There are, however, some gimmicks which may be used profitably.

Any holder who cares to redeem his note between August 15, 1983, and September 14, 1983, can do so for an automatic $1,182. That, together with previously paid nominal interest, gives a total of 14 percent yield to maturity if they were purchased at par, more if they were purchased at a discount.

The contingent interest is payable in a lump sum at the note's maturity, and only on the increase in oil prices over the value of 18½ barrels at $36. That means it's the greater of the following:

1. The *average* crude price for 18½ barrels for the three months ending February 28, 1986. If the price of oil goes to $68 by maturity, bondholders will receive an additional $592 of interest (18½ × 32 per barrel increase). If oil prices stay stable or drop, note holders get only their principal. The bonus varies proportionally in between.

2. If greater, interest bonus is payable on the highest *average* crude price up to a maximum of $68 for any calendar quarter through December 31, 1985. It's not a very exciting proposition, since if you buy the notes at par, best case is the equivalent of only about 14 percent compound interest.

The bonds are clearly only a good speculation if the price of oil averages close to $100 a barrel in the first quarter of 1986. Anything other than that, or less than that, and you're getting a market yield at best, and if oil is stable at $36, you may get as little as 9 percent, depending on what you pay for the bonds. Even in the best case, with $1,000 oil prices, the company needn't pay a total of more than $2,500 to redeem a note.

The notes are a way to play the upside of oil (to a limited degree) with little downside. As the only chance for meaningful profits occurs if oil averages a very high price in the first quarter of 1986, I wouldn't consider them. Notes are traded in bearer form on the Luxembourg Stock Exchange, and therefore have no withholding tax.

If you want a better way to play oil prices, I suggest you either invest in an oil drilling program or consider oil stocks such as those listed on page 115 of *Crisis Investing*. Like any other commodity, oil is limited, and higher prices reduce demand and increase supply. It's not a one-way street; it's gone from $2 in the early '70s to $36 in 1982—an 18 to 1 increase. Hardly the kind of speculation to make you wealthy at this point.

My point in discussing these convertibles is to point

out the different types, and their dangers, not—certainly in this last case—to make a recommendation. Appearances are often different from reality, and that's something that many companies are going to take advantage of, especially as this class of convertible proliferates. Brokers will be selling the "sizzle" of these securities even if sometimes the steak itself lacks appeal. It can be somewhat bewildering.

For straightforward simplicity, however, there's nothing like playing with commodities in their pure form, the subject of the next chapter.

Convertibles

- *Whenever you purchase a stock, check first to see if the company offers a convertible which may be a better value.*
- *There will probably be more bond issues in the future which are related to commodities, not stocks. The bonds can be convertible into commodities (e.g., the Sunshine Silver bonds), backed by them (e.g., the Refinemet Gold bonds), or indexed to them (e.g., the Petro-Lewis oil notes).*

Chapter 28

Speculating in Commodities

Deliberate, planned speculation is, in my opinion, the best and safest method to improve one's chances of preserving the purchasing power of capital or maintaining its constant convertibility into cash without loss.

G. M. Loeb

Commodities should be a significant part of your strategy to emerge from this depression very wealthy.

The twelve different exchanges in North America enable you to buy and sell at least fifteen different kinds of grain, five types of meat and livestock, six foods and fibers, five metals, two types of wood, seven foreign currencies, five financial instruments, and two petroleum products. In other words, practically all the basic raw materials of civilization. And each of them presents cyclical opportunities to capitalize on the foolishness and knavery of government.

Still, the commodity markets have acquired a bad reputation in the eyes of the public.

They are viewed as dangerous to participants (true enough, since 90 percent of the players eventually get wiped out) and inimical to the "public interest," because it's believed speculators cause price fluctuations and generally drive prices up (complete nonsense). Most people, therefore, stay away from them. But that's because most people understand neither how to play the game nor what's ahead in the 1980s.

Unlike stocks and bonds, commodities don't just represent real wealth, they are wealth. That's part of the reason why the commodity markets are perhaps the most sensitive barometer of the economic climate. They mirror the financial markets and economic environment as a whole.

During the 1950s the markets fluctuated within narrow limits, as did inflation; the '60s offered a great deal more drama, and prices moved radically; price moves in the '70s, both up and down, dwarfed everything that came before; the '80s should be a grand finale, the climax of a long-term secular trend that's been going on for decades.

Because of an even more massive reinflation of the economy, I expect prices to explode again very soon. Both the frequency and the amplitude of changes are becoming greater and more unpredictable.

Prices have been higher, in fits and starts, for the last few decades, and the future should be more of the same. But while that trend is a basic key to profitability, you need more. You need a method, a systematic way of putting theory into practice.

There are a lot of basic questions to be answered before you can hope to trade profitably. Questions that are often answered in the following manner by the unsophisticated and imprecise trader:

When or at what price to buy? As soon as possible.

What is the price objective of this trade? The level where a profit is made.

What is the time frame for holding? As long as it takes.

What point to sell at if the market turns against you? When you get really panicked or your broker sends you a margin call, whichever comes first.

How to react to an unexpected (or, for that matter, an expected) item of news? Deal with that when it comes up.

Those are just a few questions of the scores of reasonable ones that should have well-defined answers before a commitment is made.

There's no way to give proper answers to those questions here. Market conditions are too fluid for pat responses. But there are methods of dealing with the problem that you can plan in advance; two in particular have easy practical applications.

One is short-term, technical, and mechanical; the other long-term, fundamental, and judgmental. Both offer a framework within which to trade profitably. I'll cover both methods fully in a moment, but first it's important to establish the general environment for commodity prices. Should you expect prices to go much higher—and hence trade from the long side— or much lower, and hence trade from the short side? It is of crucial importance in commodities to establish the long-term trend.

Why the Trend Is Up

In a free market, the natural trend of commodity prices would be down. In an unregulated society, if a farmer or miner wanted a larger income, he'd have to produce more; and that increase in supply makes for lower prices. This puts pressure on producers to increase efficiency, i.e., to be more thrifty and to use more sophisticated technology. If the money supply stays constant and there's ever more real wealth, then prices must drop. And in a free market society the supply of money, gold, would be constant, at least relative to other things, for the reasons I explain in *Crisis Investing*.

Commodity speculating would be a dull game, and not a very profitable one either. Fluctuations in price would occur, but mainly due to fundamental supply and demand factors that are easily discounted by the market, or accidents of nature, which are hard to predict and speculate on profitably. Unfortunately, we don't live in that kind of world. Most of the fluctuations in the markets are caused by political factors, such as taxation, regulation, and inflation. While it's true most individuals today do try to produce more, practice thrift, and employ technology, all of which tend to reduce and stabilize prices, there are other countervailing factors. Those factors, created by the state, are negative for society as a whole, but provide great opportunities for speculators.

First, the money supply isn't anything like constant. It fluctuates widely (which makes it hard for producers to plan), but mostly upward, which in turn drives prices upward. As long as the money supply is controlled by the government, it is politically smart to bet on higher prices.

Inflation makes people less apt to save, and that reduces the pool of capital available for research and the development of new technology. Less technology means less wealth and, everything else being equal, higher prices.

High inflation and high interest rates create an inherently unstable financial environment. Rather than being able to plan in a stable, calm manner for their future needs, corporations that consume commodities are alternately forced to buy huge amounts of inventory to hedge themselves against price increases, and then to unload inventory because of the high interest rates.

Further, in a politicized environment it is not necessarily the most efficient, thriftiest, and technologically advanced producers who survive, but rather the best-connected politically. Less tends to be produced than would otherwise be the case, and prices tend to rise because of the lower supply.

Commodity prices are going to fluctuate not only with natural forces of production and consumption, but with financial forces, such as how liquid a producing or consuming company might be, and whether it can afford to keep inventory, or whether its management speculates on higher or lower prices. Forces of inflation and deflation, the level of interest rates, and other economic factors have a direct and immediate effect on commodity prices.

And so do most of the problems that are widely perceived in society today, although in a more indirect and delayed way. Overpopulation, urban sprawl, and pollution, for example, tend to put upward pressure on commodity prices. So does the "scarcity economy" psychology so prevalent among opinion leaders, which advocates not producing wealth lest it all be used up. The elitists holding that view, however, are rarely pro-conservation, but usually just anti-consumption. Actually there is an unlimited supply of any commodity— at a high enough price level. All those things should lend a bullish bias to your commodity trading, over the long haul.

Within this overall bullish context, a combination of political and natural surprises should sporadically drive prices higher to compound any opportunity for profit. Wars, revolutions, pogroms, persecutions, controls, regulations, confiscations, fires, floods, hurricanes, frosts, droughts, heat waves, diseases, infestations, and acts of stupidity—among many other factors—periodically skyrocket commodity prices. And if things really start to break down, anyone with any sense would much prefer to own 5,000 bushels of wheat or 25,000 pounds of copper than whatever amount of paper currency it may take to buy them.

Eventually, when inflation starts getting totally out of control, there will be a wholesale panic out of dollars and into real things—including commodities traded on the futures exchanges. When that eventuality happens, I pity those who are caught short. Only hard work, thrift, and technology are on hand to create abundance and send prices lower. Unfortunately, all of those things are in short supply, and none of them is likely to appear overnight in any market and create a glut.

All of the bad things I listed have often created dramatic shortages in the past, and can be expected to do so even more in the future, as long as the world is structured more or less as it is. The long-term trend for commodity prices is up, and the only question is: How best to play the game and take advantage of it?

Methods of Playing Commodities

There have been hundreds of books written on commodities. Their authors revel in formulating complex methods of trying to second-guess markets, and there are literally thousands of trading systems available today, all of them claiming to be more profitable and unique than the next. Many of them surely have merit, but it's hard to determine which.

It is possible, however, for you to determine which general approach to the markets is most suitable for you. It's in great measure a question of your own psychology and world view. Trading methods tend to be either *long-term, fundamentalist, and judgmental* (LFJ) or *short-term, technical, and mechanical* (STM). Unlike stock trading systems, covered in Chapter 19, most of which have substantial similarities, the two basic approaches to commodity trading are antithetical. Paradoxically, they both can work very well, although in the environment ahead the LFJ is probably superior if you will acquire the knowledge and assert the self-discipline to apply it.

Let's look at the dichotomy of their elements.

Long Term vs. Short Term

The long-term trader tends to believe that short-term events are random and unpredictable. He believes that trying to take advantage of short-term movements results in "whipsaws," and that a lot of in-and-out trading benefits the broker more than the trader.

The short-term trader believes that the further out he looks, the more likely is the occurrence of some unforeseen event that will make him wrong. He believes that not taking advantage of short-term movements is throwing money away, and that commission costs are trivial relative to the amount of money that can be made or lost on the position itself.

Fundamentalist vs. Technician

The fundamentalist believes prices are determined by supply and demand factors. He attempts to analyze all known information, statistics, and opinions in order to determine whether something is "cheap" or "dear." He believes that in the long run the truth will out, and that it will be reflected in prices.

The technician believes there are so many factors determining prices that it's impossibly confusing, and even misleading, to try to analyze them all. Rather he feels that all known information, statistics, and opinion are already reflected in the price history of the commodity. He doesn't claim to know if something's absolutely cheap or dear, but just whether the market indicates it's going to become relatively cheaper or dearer. He believes that a lot of things can happen while you're waiting for the "long run" that can wipe you out in the short run.

Judgmental vs. Mechanical

A judgmental trader is willing to pit his accumulated experience against that of others in the market and bet he'll be right most of the time. He believes his sense of the market is more reliable than any fixed trading rules. He believes his perception of crowd psychology in manias and panics gives him an invaluable edge in picking tops and bottoms.

A mechanical trader believes that he can formulate everything he knows into general rules that can be proved over large, statistically valid numbers of trades. He believes it's hard not to become emotional when trading and get swept up in a crowd oneself, and so he relies on strictly mechanical rules to guide him.

Which Strategy?

Paradoxically there is no "right and wrong" between these different ways of trading; each is equally correct and valid. Different approaches are part of what makes a market. The key is finding the one that is most rewarding for you.

I prefer using a method of trading that doesn't involve me from day to day; always watching prices on the screen can clutter your mind, and it makes it hard to tell the forest from the trees, while taking a lot of time that could be more productively employed elsewhere. The two methods I employ are, perhaps oddly, the logical extremes, the concretization of the philosophies outlined above. Use either of them if you care to, or both at once (in different accounts), or do some reading and develop your own approach to the markets. But it's imperative to remember the most basic rules of all trading: First, have a plan. Second, follow the plan. Those rules apply to trading anything, but they are more important with commodities, because such tremendous leverage is available—and usually winds up being used.

Most traders err by not even formulating a plan. They have, at best, some vague notion that the commodity is going up (or down) for some nebulous reason, but questions such as exactly when or how are never considered. (Precision takes a lot of fun out of gambling; besides, precise thinking is hard work.) Neither of the following methods takes the thought or work out of trading, but both can make it much simpler and drama-free.

The Short-Term, Technical, Mechanical Method

How detailed and well defined must a trading plan be to be adequate? The answer is almost necessarily arbitrary and subjective, but this is where a computer can be used to advantage. There's nothing magical about a computer; it's simply a mechanical aid, and if your plan is bad ("garbage in") your results will be bad ("garbage out"). But although the computer can't in any way guarantee the quality of a plan, it does help you create a plan. And some plan, no matter how poorly constructed, is better than none at all. The fact that the plan must be formulated well enough to be understood by a machine at least ensures its existence.

If there's anything more important than making the plan, however, it's following the plan. This is hard because of emotional factors.

Emotions are the bane of commodity traders; they usually induce you to do exactly the opposite of what should be done. Emotions cause you to get swept up in the moment; when markets are moving radically it's very easy to believe you're missing the boat and jump on board a trend exactly when you should abandon ship.

The ideal trader is cold, rational, unemotional, and not given to "ad hoc" judgment—the perfect description of a programmed computer. A computer given predetermined buy and sell signals doesn't agonize over the reasons, it simply does as it's told.

But it will have received its instructions far from the heat of battle, when cool reason and not panicky emotion is in command. The big question is what instructions the computer will be given, and there are thousands of possibilities developed by analysts over the years. Most computer trading systems attempt to follow trends, and determine whether a movement is in fact a trend through the use of such things as moving averages, price channels, and accumulation/distribution indices based on volume and price figures. Some are swing systems attempting to sell on peaks and buy on dips.

Most people have neither their own computer nor sufficient knowledge of the markets to use it even if they do. But there are many managed account programs offered through the various brokerage firms and advisory organizations which utilize computers. Your task is to select the one whose trading methods seem best able to take advantage of future movements. I would prefer a method structured as follows:

1. The method should tend to trade from the long side of the market. Since the overall secular trend of prices will be up, it's going to be generally safer to be long than short in commodities in the years ahead. Most computer programs attempt to trade down markets as aggressively as up markets, and being "short" in the 1980s will load the odds against you. The programs should generally either have you long in a commodity, or out of the market while you wait for a chance to go long.

2. The method should utilize a trend-following technique. The amplitude of price moves in the future should grow tremendously in the years ahead. In other words, once a trend is in motion, it will tend to stay in motion for a long time. You want a method that attempts to capitalize on that. Some methods attempt to insinuate the programmer's subjective judgment of the tops and bottoms into them; you want a method that follows the market, not one that leads it.

3. The method should trade a wide variety of com-

modities both to diversify and to catch the ebb and flow of the market as a whole. Some programs restrict themselves just to metals or currencies or farm products, which is silly, since the computer can watch the actions of all markets.

A well-set-up fund that trades according to those rules should preserve capital and multiply it in the chaotic years to come. My only reservation is that by buying into a fund you're not controlling your assets personally, but are handing over that responsibility to someone else. There's certainly a place for specialization and division of labor in money management, just like everything else; but if you're going to have active control of your life, it helps to have actual hands-on control of your finances.

That is why you're probably better off trading your own account, and the following method lends itself to that.

The Long-Term, Fundamentalist, Judgmental Method

The long term is becoming much more predictable, while the short run is becoming increasingly unpredictable. As the government runs about trying to undo or defuse the consequences of its past stupidities by committing even bigger ones, the markets can be expected to experience titanic fluctuations. In the short run those fluctuations will have a random, unpredictable nature as regulations, taxes, inflation, interest rates, strikes, war rumors, subsidies, and innumerable other factors all pull the market in their own directions. Over the long run, though, the distortion that government action created is quite predictable, and a good economist/speculator can take advantage of this with the following method.

It's a very contrary method, in fact a purposely contrary method. If you discuss it with other traders—certainly with your broker—you'll be met with incredulous looks and negatively wagging heads. That should not only be of no concern to you, but positively reinforcing. It's a clear indication you're acting in a contrary manner and breaking free from the herd, an excellent idea when well over 90 percent of the independent players in the commodity markets walk away losers. Clearly, doing what everybody else is doing and approves of does not tilt the odds in your favor.

That's not to say you should always do the opposite of the crowd, because sometimes the crowd is right. But there are never any big profits to be made running with the crowd, unless you're leading it and are first in as well as first out of an investment. That is what the greater fool theory is all about, of course, and I'm quite partial to it as a technique of stock market operation. But commodities are a fundamentally different proposition.

The way to make money over the long term is to take not only contrary market positions (i.e., buy when others are selling, sell when others are buying) but—just as important though much less obvious—adopt a contrary method of trading as well. Such a method has three elements: Most commodity speculators trade short term; if you want to win, you should trade the long term. Most speculators trade nearby contract months; you should trade far-out contract months. Most speculators trade on the smallest possible margin; you should trade for near cash.

Trade the Long Term

Your main objective as a speculator is to capitalize on significant distortions in the marketplace. But just as it can take years for the government to distort the market, it can take a considerable time for the free market to unwind it.

The only way to hit home runs in any market is to participate in major price moves, not by jumping in and out of markets, desperately trying to second-guess them. Short-term price movements are almost random in nature; they can jump because of rumor or forced liquidation or the whim of a big trader. A speculator only moves when the odds are stacked heavily in his favor, when he can see a major distortion being created or about to be liquidated. He does not use the futures market as a legal gambling casino where the odds are 50–50 that either red or black will come up on the wheel. Of course, even that's a better break than the average trader gets. At least at a casino there's an entertaining floor show, a free drink, and the drama is over in a minute or so. Win or lose, his time and attention are liberated for other activity.

If a trader is just looking for action, a casino offers a better financial deal, because the typical short-term trader will generate commissions equal to the capital he puts up over the course of a year. Of course, the typical trader doesn't last a year, for just that reason. He winds up paying a 100 percent commission as an entrance fee. And again that's entirely apart from the huge intangible costs in time, attention, and anguish that come from trying to watch the markets daily.

If, instead, you use the futures market as a convenient mechanism for buying and holding over a long enough term for distortions to right themselves and inflation to make itself felt, you are in a completely different game. Consider yourself to be a white-collar farmer or miner when you buy commodities. You can own a flock of chickens, a herd of cattle, or a field of grain and profit from higher prices just as can the farmer, but you needn't buy the equipment, hire the help, and get up at 5 A.M. to milk the cows.

Right now, in early 1982, I'm confident that by 1985 wheat will be $10 or $15 a bushel, but I don't have the foggiest idea about tomorrow morning. And neither does anyone else. So if we can predict the long run with some accuracy (and we can) and we can't predict the short run (no one can), we should be trading commodities in a way that allows us to take advantage of price movements over a meaningful period of time.

By establishing positions only on those comparatively rare occasions when you perceive the odds as substantially in your favor, and planning to hold them over a period of months—a year or more, if necessary—you're tilting the odds back in your favor. Let everyone else second-guess the short run; we'll be looking a year or more into the future.

Trade Far-Out Months

Most traders buy one of the closest-in contracts—that is, they buy a commodity deliverable in, say, only two months instead of two years in the future—because there's more activity and more liquidity in the nearbys. There's little reason for buying nearby contracts, however, if you're playing the long term. You don't need liquidity, because you're not going to be trading in and out. It's generally in your interest, therefore, to buy a commodity for delivery as far out into the future as you feel your prediction will be valid. You pay one commission and wait.

A distinction should be made between different classes of commodity, however. Those with an indefinite shelf life—the metals in particular—are usually more expensive each contract month into the future by an amount equal to the cost of storage, insurance, and, most importantly, the current interest rate. They are called "carrying charge" markets for that reason. A contract of January 1984 copper might cost $1.00 a pound, when a contract deliverable a year later would be perhaps $1.22 if the interest rate were 20 percent at the time. If interest rates go up from the time you buy, the distant contracts will become relatively more expensive. If they go down, they'll become less expensive. The ideal time to go long on a far-out contract in a "carrying charge" market is when you expect not only the commodity but also interest rates to go up.

In this respect, agricultural commodities are more interesting to a speculator. Very often a contract for delivery in a year will be priced at less than the current one. If the commodity is depressed, and a fundamentally good buy at the present, and you anticipate a substantial amount of inflation over the next year, you're really getting a double discount—lower in dollar terms, and much lower in real terms.

Regardless of how good the long-term fundamentals look, you've got to have the staying power to wait them out. You must, therefore, have more than adequate capital when you go in.

Trade for Near Cash

A reasonable question to ask here is: How can I keep from going broke in the short run while I'm waiting for the long run? The commodity markets are actually less volatile than the stock markets in absolute terms. They have a reputation for volatility only because of the low margin requirements traders customarily take advantage of. It's possible to control $20,000 worth of a commodity for as little as $1,000 of "earnest money," 20 to 1 leverage.

Most traders take advantage of the low margin requirements offered by the exchanges to buy for 5 or 10 percent down. That means that while a short-term fluctuation of that amount in the right direction can double their money, one in the wrong direction can wipe them out. Lack of adequate margin is why many traders who would have been right in the long run never last long enough to see it.

People are more likely to get in trouble when they trade for very low margin. Trading for cash (or near cash), combined with the other rules, almost ensures you won't be wiped out.

One of the nice things about commodities, though, is that the long run occurs much quicker—and more surely —than with stocks because of the fundamentals.

Trade on Fundamentals

The essence of the method is to buy only when a commodity is selling for less than its costs of production, and when its price is at or near a historic low. Trading only when those conditions are present comes as close to assuring you of both low risks and large profits as anything can.

Unlike stocks, commodities have utility value; in other words, people can live without buying GM stock but they can't live without buying bread. For that reason (and many others), the price of GM can go to zero, but wheat can't sell for less than its cost of production for too long or farmers will simply stop growing it. At the same time the price of wheat clearly has an upside limit, because if it goes high enough, farmers will grow much more to take advantage of that while people will eat much less. The price of GM can go up indefinitely if the company's assets and profits keep rising.

The potential range of fluctuation, the volatility of any commodity, is therefore much less than that of a stock. A stock can easily become worthless, but a commodity will always have real value; commodities are self-regulating because high prices limit demand and create new supply, and vice versa.

That's why, if each is purchased for 100 percent cash, the commodity has inherently less risk, but the stock inherently more upside potential.

The truth, as in so many things, is exactly the opposite

of the conventional wisdom. Trading commodities can actually be among the least risky ways of making capital grow.

It's impossible to cover all of the commodities worth considering in the brief space available, but the following chapters should give you an idea of the explosive fundamentals that will tend to drive them up in price.

Profiteering on Shortages

- *Perhaps the greatest commodity bull market in history lies just ahead.*
- *Buy only distant contracts, with heavy margins, based on fundamentals.*

Chapter 29

Agricultural Commodities

Farm commodities in general, and basics like grains in particular, are in a long-term uptrend.

There are several fundamental market forces that should drive agricultural commodities higher in real terms as well as dollar terms.

1. Unprofitability of Farming

Net U.S. farm income is now at its lowest point in the last thirty years in constant dollars. When prices are low and farmers cannot grow profitably, they tend not to plant, just as when prices are at a high they tend to overplant to take advantage of it. That's why the market is self-correcting, and that's how the "invisible hand" of free market prices keeps supply and demand in balance. A look at the chart below shows very clearly that in real terms farmers are earning less now than they have since World War II.

Prices must go up in real terms (as well, obviously, in dollar terms) for farmers to make the investments necessary to increase production. As things stand, historically low farm income spells "grain shortage," and much higher grain prices to eventually solve the shortage.

For that reason, the lowest-risk commodities are usually those selling for less than their production costs. It's hard to figure exactly what the cost of growing any particular crop is; so much depends on how a farmer values his time, how quickly he depreciates his machinery,

Chart I
U.S. Net Farm Income

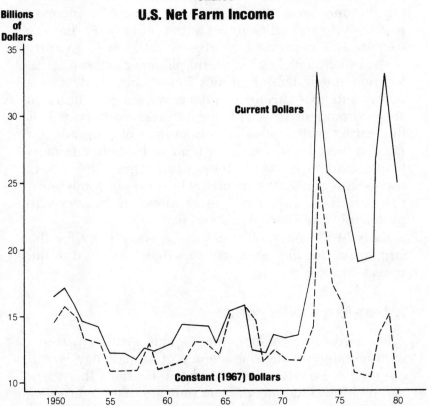

Billions
of
Dollars

Current Dollars

Constant (1967) Dollars

When farm income is low, farmers stop producing and prices then rise. 1982 prices are at a 30-year low in real terms.

whether he's using his own capital or borrowing money, and how he values the land, for example.

At the end of 1981, the cost of growing corn was estimated to range from $2.40 to $3.25 a bushel, wheat from $3.75 to $5.50 a bushel, and soybeans about $6.25 a bushel. The cost of raising a steer was about $.80 a pound. All were losing propositions.

An important contributor to costs has been the expense of buying, and financing, agricultural machinery. On the one hand, the farmer must have it to increase productivity and efficiency. On the other hand, income —at today's depressed levels—is inadequate to carry costs. Inflation makes long-term planning and capital allocation much harder, if not impossible. How can a farmer anticipate his needs for a new barn or combine in an environment in which the interest he must pay is fluctuating as dramatically as the prices of his products? He can't. And since farmers tend to be better farmers than speculators, most of them usually guess the wrong way—with disastrous results. The price of foods must rise if farmers are to stay in business; if farmers stop producing, however, prices will explode.

Early 1982 commodity prices are very risky for the farmer but, for the same reason, almost risk-free to the speculator.

2. Long-Term Weather Patterns

It's hard to make statements about weather patterns with certainty, since the science of climatology is still quite new. But there seem to be indications that there are not blue skies ahead. Data indicate that the last several centuries have been unusually warm and mild, and the good weather has presented farmers with crop yields much higher than is historically "normal." Temperature in the Northern Hemisphere has been in a clear downtrend for the last forty years as the following chart shows.

Notice that there's been an average decline of about .15 degrees Fahrenheit per year for a total of 6 degrees decline in average January temperatures. Thus in northern countries—such as Canada, the Soviet Union and Britain—the growing season has shortened by as much as two weeks per year.

One effect of this decline is that farmers in those countries will be forced to shift from high food value, long

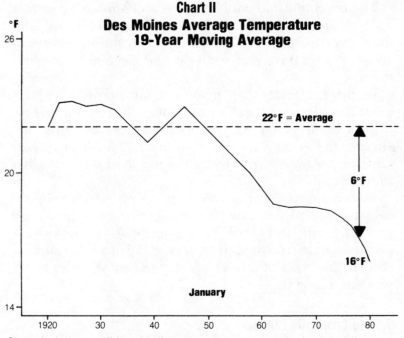

Chart II
Des Moines Average Temperature
19-Year Moving Average

Crops don't do as well in cold climates as warm ones; production may fall.

growing season crops, such as wheat, to low food value, short growing season (and generally less profitable) crops such as barley. One study shows that in Finland, a country whose climate is roughly comparable to that of Canada (one of the world's largest exporters) and the Soviet Union (the world's largest wheat producer), the production of barley increased fourfold in the last twenty years while the production of wheat has actually dropped. It's not that farmers preferred barley—which sells, on average, for about 25 percent less than wheat —it's simply that they couldn't grow wheat because of the shorter growing season.

As the cooling trend around the world continues, grain yields will be reduced and less desirable grains (such as barley) will be increasingly substituted for more desirable ones (such as wheat).

The cooling trend could also be accelerated by events such as the Mount St. Helens explosion of 1980. The dust layer that a volcano lays down in the upper atmosphere tends to reflect sunlight and decrease temperatures.

In brief, climate has been extraordinarily good for centuries. It could get even better, but when everything's been going well and prices are very low, it's smarter to bet on a spot of pestilence, war, disease, bad climate, volcanic eruptions, or some med fly look-alike to present itself.

By buying when prices are low, it's possible to simply rely on Murphy's Law: Anything that can go wrong probably will, and at the worst possible time. The worst possible time is when people least expect it; and, of course, they expect it least when things have been going well for a long time.

3. The Economic Climate

The economic climate is more important than the meteorological climate, and the outlook is for a cataclysmic hurricane. When times are good, a stable financial environment, reliable transport, the availability of capital to increase productivity, and compounding technological breakthroughs all work to reduce prices in real terms. That's all part of the past. The big gains in "green revolution" technology have all been made, but the practical effects of newly developed genetic technology are still years in the future.

World population is still expanding (especially in underdeveloped countries), but land speculation has buried millions of acres of prime farmland under expanding cities. There's nothing "wrong" with that, but it does deplete the amount of land available for agriculture. And, as cities have generally grown up in areas where farmland was best, it's generally been the most productive land that's been buried.

It's been estimated that the U.S. is losing over a million acres of farmland a year to urbanization. According to the General Accounting Office, even if present pasture and woodland were converted, there's probably only another 35 million acres of potential prime cropland remaining in the U.S.

These trends will reverse in time, but currently they're still in motion. The world could easily feed five or six times its present population as well as today's average American with the application of proper technology and economic freedom, but that's not the way things are going. Four hundred years ago, all of North America could support only about a million Indians on a most primitive level. As the world continues on the road to more government control, that means lower production of all types, especially food.

The key to greatest profits and lowest risks is getting in as close to the bottom as possible. And I suspect that early 1982 will prove to have been it.

4. Decreasing World Grain Stocks

Price fluctuations of any commodity vary not only with production in any given year but with supplies carried over from previous years. People have known since Biblical times that the more grain there was stored from previous years, the less danger there was of a famine in the future.

Unfortunately there's been a long-term downtrend in the amount of grain stored, both in absolute terms and as a percentage of consumption. That means when some shock hits the agricultural system there isn't a lot to absorb it. Over the past two decades worldwide grain production has grown at 2.8 percent per year, but consumption has risen at 3 percent.

This is true despite the fact that more grain has been coaxed out of every fertile acre. Yields have risen 50 percent per acre in the last twenty years because of in-

Chart III

Worldwide Grain Production

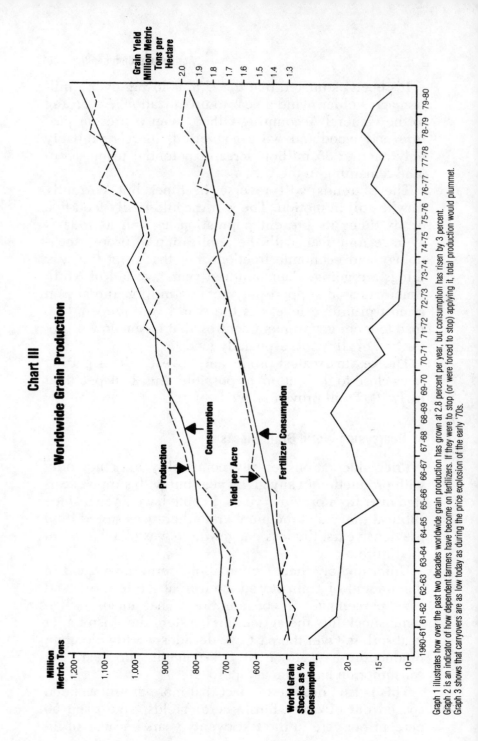

Million Metric Tons

1,200
1,100
1,000
900
800
700
600

Production

Consumption

Yield per Acre

Fertilizer Consumption

Grain Yield Million Metric Tons per Hectare

2.0
1.9
1.8
1.7
1.6
1.5
1.4
1.3

World Grain Stocks as % Consumption

20
15
10

1960-61 61-62 62-63 63-64 64-65 65-66 66-67 67-68 68-69 69-70 70-71 71-72 72-73 73-74 74-75 75-76 76-77 77-78 78-79 79-80

Graph 1 illustrates how over the past two decades worldwide grain production has grown at 2.8 percent per year, but consumption has risen by 3 percent.
Graph 2 is an indicator of how dependent farmers have become on fertilizers. If they were to stop (or were forced to stop) applying it, total production would plummet.
Graph 3 shows that carryovers are as low today as during the price explosion of the early '70s.

Table I LOOMING WORLD GRAIN SHORTAGE

Marketing Year Beginning July 1	(Million Metric Tons)		Ending Stocks		Price in Constant 1980 $	
	Production	Consumption	Amount	As % Of Production	Corn	Wheat
					—($ Per Bushel)—	
1960–1964 Avg.	703.5	705.6	168.7	23.9%	$2.76	$4.44
1965–1969 Avg.	839.7	835.3	171.0	20.5	2.53	3.07
July 1970–June 1971	892.7	933.1	146.3	15.7	2.58	2.58
July 1971–June 1972	978.9	958.5	166.9	17.4	2.00	2.48
July 1972–June 1973	954.4	990.5	130.8	13.2	2.79	3.12
July 1973–June 1974	1,043.3	1,040.2	133.9	12.9	4.28	6.63
July 1974–June 1975	985.8	998.5	121.2	12.1	4.68	6.31
July 1975–June 1976	995.9	997.6	119.3	12.0	3.59	5.03
July 1976–June 1977	1,125.1	1,070.1	74.4	16.4	2.89	3.67
July 1977–June 1978	1,085.0	1,091.4	168.0	15.4	2.56	2.96
July 1978–June 1979	1,200.3	1,177.3	191.0	16.2	2.66	3.52
July 1979–June 1980	1,161.3	1,185.6	166.7	14.1	2.72	4.16
July 1980–June 1981	1,147.9	1,189.9	124.8	10.5	3.40	4.10

1980 WORLD GRAIN CONSUMPTION

Grain	% Of Total
Wheat	37.1%
Corn	34.8
Barley	14.1
Other	14.4

Table I clearly points to the following:
1. Carryover stocks of grain (column 4) are nearly as low now in absolute terms as they've ever been in recent history.
2. Carryover stocks as a percentage of production (column 5) are lower than ever before.
3. Grain prices (columns 6 and 7), in real terms, are as low as they've ever been. It all points to much higher prices.

Table II COMMODITIES

	Average Price 1971	January 1982 Price (Feb 82/ Mar 82 Contract)	Percentage Change in Nominal Dollars	1982 Price in 1971 Dollars	Percentage Change in Real Dollars
BROILERS	27 cents/lb.	46 cents/lb.	170%	23 cents/lb.	−17%
CATTLE (LIVE)	34 cents/lb.	60 cents/lb.	176	30 cents/lb.	−13
COPPER	52 cents/lb.	72 cents/lb.	138	36 cents/lb.	−33
CORN	131 cents/bu.	271 cents/bu.	207	136 cents/bu.	4
COTTON	34 cents/lb.	66 cents/lb.	194	33 cents/lb.	−3
HOGS (LIVE)	18 cents/lb.	47 cents/lb.	261	24 cents/lb.	33
LUMBER	133 dollars/1000 bd. ft.	156 dollars/1000 bd. ft.	117	78 dollars/1000 bd. ft.	−41
SOYBEANS	305 cents/bu.	640 cents/bu.	210	320 cents/bu.	5
SUGAR (WORLD)	5 cents/lb.	13 cents/lb.	260	7 cents/lb.	40
WHEAT (KC)	156 cents/bu.	389 cents/bu.	249	195 cents/bu.	25

NOTE: 1971 was when the first great commodity boom started. In real terms, prices are lower now than they were then.

creased use of fertilizer and other "green revolution" technology. If fertilizer supplies were cut off for any reason (most are petrochemical based), total crop supplies would plummet. In the early '60s we could count on improvements in agricultural technology to depress food prices, but now, should any of that technology fail, prices could explode.

5. Low Real Prices

Speculators in Argentina, Brazil, Uruguay, Israel, and other perennially inflation-ridden countries don't pay a lot of attention to prices in the local currency. The price of everything "doubles" in the course of a year. To get a grip on values in real terms they monitor inflation-adjusted prices. The object is to buy cheap and sell dear, and it's helpful to keep things in perspective in real terms when trying to determine which is which. Table II inflation-adjusts important prices, and it's easy to see that late 1982 presents some great opportunities for low-risk speculation.

Of course, the five major factors we've just covered will not have an effect on the price of anything tomorrow morning or next month, but they are the underpinnings for a fantastic bull market in basic agricultural commodities over the next several years. People will panic into commodities to survive the destruction of the government's money substitutes.

Just as the market often overruns itself on the downside, it overruns itself on the upside as well. It wouldn't be a surprise to see prices triple across the board by the end of 1985.

Food for Thought

- *It's a very safe bet to buy positions in any agricultural commodity for the next several years.*

Chapter 30

Copper

Your overall plan for the 1980s should be to get out of dollars and into real wealth. Copper is another commodity which simultaneously presents low risk and high potential.

There are four related reasons why copper should reward early buyers handsomely.

1. Low Price

Two charts of copper prices are reproduced below, covering the last ten years. Chart I shows the metal's price in dollar terms, Chart II its price in real terms. In dollars, copper is selling for about half of its previous high, while in real terms it's at a historic low. Neither fact guarantees it can't go lower, but both charts tell the speculator that an opportunity is shaping up.

2. Low Stocks

In the past, the price of copper has often fallen to low levels because of simple supply and demand; a large inventory in the hands of users usually goes along with a low price. Chart II shows, however, that inventories are at close to the ten-year lows they set in the early '70s, a situation that usually corresponds to peak prices. At the same time, however, consumption has continued rising at about 3 to 4 percent per year for decades, so inventories will eventually have to be replenished. Al-

Chart I
Copper (New York)

Cents per
Pound

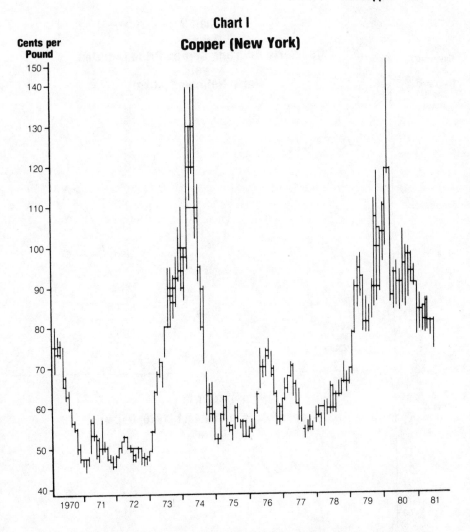

though the depression will substantially cut consumption of copper in many areas such as housing, autos, and electrical fabrication, the government can be expected to take up a lot of slack for military programs discussed below.

Copper speculators don't have the advantage of government price controls that guaranteed sure profits in

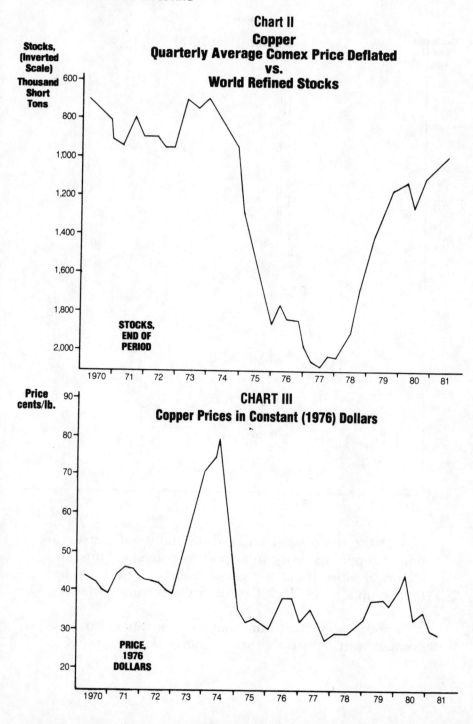

Chart II
Copper
Quarterly Average Comex Price Deflated
vs.
World Refined Stocks

Stocks,
(Inverted
Scale)
Thousand
Short
Tons

STOCKS,
END OF
PERIOD

CHART III
Copper Prices in Constant (1976) Dollars

Price
cents/lb.

PRICE,
1976
DOLLARS

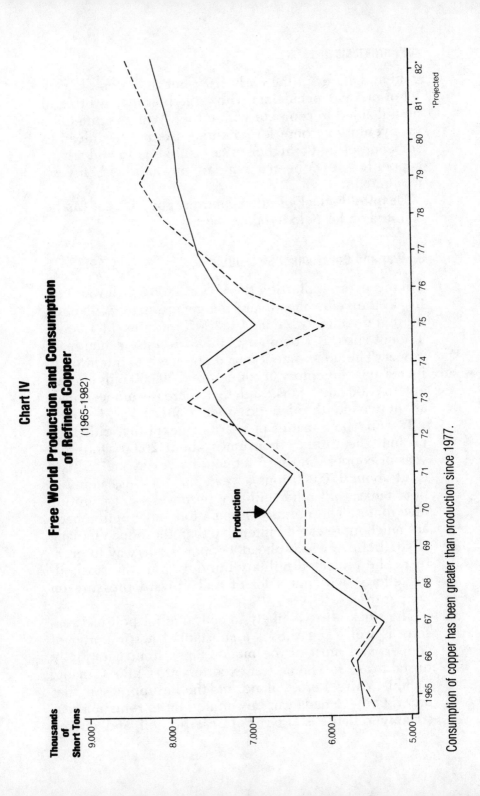

Chart IV

Free World Production and Consumption
of Refined Copper

(1965-1982)

Thousands
of
Short Tons

9.000

8.000

7.000

6.000

5.000

Production

1965 66 67 68 69 70 71 72 73 74 75 76 77 78 79 80 81* 82*

*Projected

Consumption of copper has been greater than production since 1977.

gold and silver in the early '70s; but they don't have a lot of private speculators with large holdings waiting to be unloaded to compete with either. Whatever metal is in inventory is there for potential use, not to unload to someone else at a higher price. Unlike gold and silver, copper has never been a popular "buy and hold" investment medium.

Despite the lack of price controls, government can be counted on for help in other ways.

3. War and Government Stockpiling

There's every indication the U.S. is going on a war footing in the years ahead, and the government will spend most of the money on matériel (MX missiles, M-1 tanks, Trident subs, B-1 bombers, and such) rather than manpower. The government has announced its intention to increase its inventory of copper from 30,000 tons at present to 1,000,000 tons, and that increase alone equals about two months of world production.

It won't be a matter of simple stockpiling, either. At present the military consumes about 20,000 tons per year of copper. During Vietnam, however, the military used about 170,000 tons a year, for missiles, ammunition, tanks, and other military purposes—not counting electronics. The military preparations now being made are much more capital intensive than those for Vietnam. If you believe war is ahead, copper is one way to profiteer. The projected military buildup, plus the stockpiling efforts, will put a lot of real upward pressure on copper prices.

The stockpiling is likely to continue for political reasons as well. The U.S. is a substantial net importer of copper, and most of the metal comes from potentially unstable areas. The largest exporters are Chile, Canada, Zambia, Zaire, Peru, Poland, and the Philippines, in that order. Only Canada can be counted on to remain a reasonably reliable source. Political turmoil and strikes could easily close down mines in Peru, Poland, Chile, and the Philippines; violent revolution and war are genuine dangers in Zaire and Zambia.

4. Producers Losing Money

The average cost of mining copper worldwide in 1981 was probably about $1.25 a pound—or about 40 percent more than its average market price. That's one of the reasons why there were so many takeovers and takeover attempts of copper companies like Amax, Kennecot, and Anaconda in the late 1970s. The miners were getting such a low return on capital that their stock was selling far below book as a result.

Copper mining isn't profitable, and all across the U.S., Canada and the Western World mines are being closed down wholesale. In Chile, the world's largest exporter, many hundreds of small mines have closed since 1978, in addition to two hundred medium-sized operations.

It's true that many of the countries will continue producing copper at any price, because labor is paid in local fiat currency and the copper must be sold to generate foreign exchange (Zambia, Zaire, and Poland are all classic examples), but even in socialist countries those mines will eventually collapse. Governments can't generate the capital to replace machinery and exploit new ore bodies if the mine is unprofitable.

It's estimated that no new mines can be brought into production unless the market price of copper rises to $2.25. Copper could actually suffer a supply deficit by the mid-'80s, since it takes years to put a new mine on stream, even if capital is available.

How to Buy

Copper is traded on the Comex in New York in 25,000-pound lots. It's not unreasonable to anticipate the metal going to $4 or $5 a pound by 1984 or 1985, especially if a speculative mania develops by then, as I expect. Because the metal can be purchased for delivery in 1984 for about $1, it offers a good return even if bought for cash. Bought for 50 percent margin, it could offer up to a 10 to 1 return; for 25 percent margin up to a 20 to 1 return. At the same time, it's hard to see copper falling more than 10 percent from the levels of early 1982. The upside potential outweighs the downside risk by a large factor, and that is the hallmark of a good speculation.

Your Road to Financial Security May Be Paved with Copper

- Copper may be bought as a strategic war metal.
- Supply-demand patterns are starting to resemble those of silver.
- A 1930s-style depression is the only thing that can cut copper prices below current levels; we're having a 1980s-style depression. Not to worry.

Chapter 31

Strategic Materials

War is the health of the State.
John Dublin

In many ways, the so-called strategic materials represent the most direct, obvious play on politically caused chaos. The very term "strategic" calls up visions of war and rumors of war, and that's probably the lowest common denominator for these materials. In this context, a strategic material is anything one country needs to ensure supplies for a successful war while denying it to the enemy. They include such obvious commodities as chrome, aluminum, oil, and copper, but perhaps even more importantly, rather obscure elements like tantalum, germanium, rhodium, and cobalt. These minor metals are the ones generally referred to as "strategic."

Theoretically, that definition could render almost anything "strategic," including horseshoe nails. As Ben Franklin would say: "For want of a nail the shoe was lost; for want of a shoe the horse was lost; and for want of a horse the rider was lost." General Buck Turgidson's "strategic mine shaft gap" in the movie *Dr. Strangelove* comes to mind. The military bureaucracy will seize on any pretext to swell its appropriations and power; that's reason enough to be suspicious.

Strategic materials, in the broadest sense, are those necessary for a society's basic industries to continue functioning. In the military, strategic bombing aims to destroy an enemy's cities, factories, the home population, and the ability to survive. Tactical bombing is a strictly front-line operation aimed to destroy the enemy's soldiers, war matériel, and ability to fight in the field. It's a question of degree at some point, but it's clearly of greater strategic significance to destroy a factory that makes tanks than the tanks themselves, and it's better yet to hit a factory making ball bearings without which the tanks—or any other machines—won't run. The most strategic act of all would be to deny raw materials to the ball bearing makers. Then the whole economy would wind down—for want of a nail, as it were.

What the *most* strategic materials might be is a moot question. Everything is strategic if you need it, but it's not feasible to cut off supplies of most critical materials. Most such materials, such as iron, coal, copper, and aluminum, are used in massive quantities and have such broad sources of supply that interdiction is a major undertaking. There are, however, some metals and materials that lend themselves to strategic cutoff.

Why Consider Them?

There are two real and compelling arguments for investing in such materials. *First*, they are war and high-technology materials, and there will be plenty of wars and rumors of wars in the '80s while technology maintains its strong momentum. Together, the demands of high technology and war industries should increase consumption. *Second*, strategic materials are in short supply in the developed countries of the West and the U.S. in particular. Through an accident of geology, most supplies come from the Soviet bloc, the underdeveloped Third World, and South Africa—any or all of which could stop exporting for numerous reasons, including a war, revolution, aggressive terrorist activity, or a serious break in international relations. In many of the primitive countries in particular, the gradual disintegration of society and the literal falling apart of plant and mining facilities could cut off supplies through entropy, even barring force majeure. Chart I shows the source of supplies of some major materials.

A Strategic Lesson

The arguments for buying the materials, as recited by a competent salesman, are tailor-made to incite greed and fear in the buyer while making him think he's being prudent. The price record they established in the '70s qualified them as a "good investment" in the eyes of unsophisticated would-be speculators who started buying them in 1979 and 1980, near the top. Most probably fancied they were preparing to capitalize on a "blood in the streets" opportunity in the making. And no doubt their rendition of the stories the salesmen told them held everyone's attention at cocktail parties, but they were the ones to get killed when the illiquid market for these minor metals joined the commodity collapse of 1981. See Chart II.

Any commodity that's gone up 900 percent in price in ten years is, almost by definition, a bad speculation. (It bears repetition that gold and silver, because of decades of price controls, are special situations.)

Every few years an investment proposition comes to the public eye that seems to offer all things to all people. Everything about the deal seems right.

Those, of course, are the deals to be most wary about. If they're that "hot," and everybody knows about them, then chances are the top has about arrived. Every time word on a hot investment gets out to the public, it appears "different" from the last one that burned them. It usually happens in the stock market. Microprocessor, movie, gambling, CB radio, conglomerate, and gold stocks all had their brightest "can't lose" day in the sun just before the monumental crash. It's happening in real estate. It happened in diamonds, and it happened in stra-

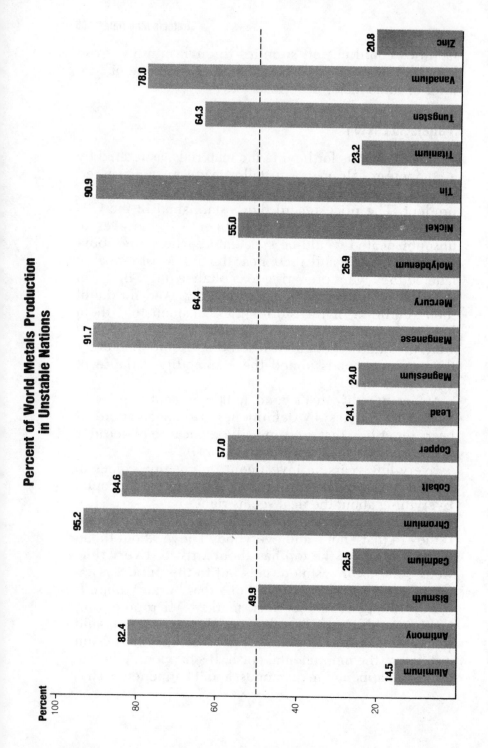

**Percent of World Metals Production
in Unstable Nations**

Percent

Aluminum	14.5
Antimony	82.4
Bismuth	49.9
Cadmium	26.5
Chromium	95.2
Cobalt	84.6
Copper	57.0
Lead	24.1
Magnesium	24.0
Manganese	91.7
Mercury	64.4
Molybdenum	26.9
Nickel	55.0
Tin	90.9
Titanium	23.2
Tungsten	64.3
Vanadium	78.0
Zinc	20.8

Substantial portions of the world's supply of minor metals come from politically unstable areas—the Soviet bloc, the Third World, and South Africa.

Chart II
1981 Value of $100 Invested
in Strategic Metals in 1972

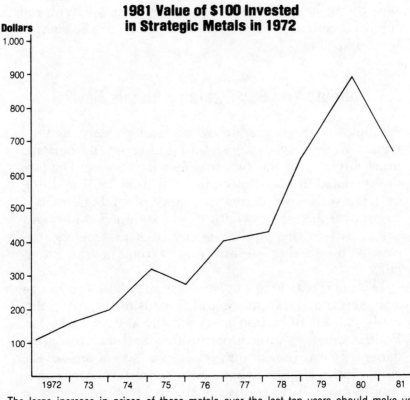

The large increase in prices of these metals over the last ten years should make you cautious.

tegic metals. Each of these things has real merit as a speculation, but that merit is entirely a function of its price level.

Once anything is popular, well promoted, and possessed of a good track record, the end has come. It eventually happens to absolutely everything that even looks like an investment. It's a lesson that can't be learned too well, because the chaotic environment of the Greater Depression will be rife with get-rich-quick schemes and overpriced "speculations" to trap the novice. And there will be millions of scared novices whom inflation and financial collapse will pull into the market, to be slaughtered like sheep.

Should You Buy Strategic Metals Now?

Although strategic metals are no longer cheap, as they were ten years ago, they should go higher and perhaps much higher, for the two reasons cited above. Despite the increase in speculative interest from 1979 to 1980, no large-scale speculative inventory of strategic metals hangs over the market waiting to be dumped at the right price. But as the public accumulates the metals, the price will be bid up—entirely apart from the fundamentals.

The main reason to buy strategic metals is as a hedge against war and a supply cutoff. That is the type of politically caused distortion a speculator always looks for. Politics creates those opportunities, and that is a great danger. If war breaks out, or supply cutoffs are severe enough, the country where your metals are stored may simply move in to confiscate them. Most are stored in bonded warehouses in Rotterdam or other international free ports, but that may become meaningless if the international situation becomes critical. It's no help if the metals are stored in the U.S. either; in fact, it's worse. As the property of a U.S. citizen, your investment is liable to be grabbed in the "national interest."

At the same time, the nature of the marketplace and the forces at work make it especially hard for the small player. There's no liquid market for these commodities, and you may have to pay a premium to buy and absorb a big discount to sell. Most sales are directly between the large corporations (or governments) that produce them and the end users. Up to just a few years ago, there was no open speculation interest at all to speak of, and prices were quoted strictly by producers. Strategics are probably a better market to take a lesson from than put money into, although the possibility does still exist for large gains. If you decide to invest in it, here are the fundamentals.

Strategic Metals: How to Buy

The answer to the question of "how to buy strategic metals" is what separates cocktail party trivia from usable investment advice. Write to each of the organizations below, and sift through their information carefully.

Strategic Metals Corporation
500 Chesham House
150 Regent Street
London WIR 5FA, England
Attn. Mr. Prasadam

Stock and Commodity Services, S.A.
10 Rue Bellot
CH 1206, Geneva, Switzerland
Attn. Mr. Roditi

James Sinclair Commodities
90 Broad Street
New York, N.Y. 10004

The Strategic Metal Trust
48 Atholl Street
Douglas, Isle of Man, British Isles
Attn. Mr. March

Leigh & Sullivan Group
Knights Pool, Windmill Street
Macclesfield, Cheshire SK11 7HR, England

Wogen Resources
17 Devonshire Street
London WIN IFS, England

There are a multitude of fees, commissions and general pitfalls in this market. For your reference, I've included the recent price ranges of some popular metals.

Table I

	High*	Low*	Recent Price
ALUMINUM	$ .83/pound	$ .39/pound	$ .83/pound
ANTIMONY	2.13/pound	1.22/pound	1.22/pound
BISMUTH	9.00/pound	1.70/pound	1.70/pound
CADMIUM	3.00/pound	1.11/pound	1.11/pound
CHROMIUM	4.25/pound	2.30/pound	3.75/pound
COBALT	25.00/pound	3.75/pound	12.50/pound
COPPER	1.34/pound	.61/pound	.73/pound
GALLIUM	400.00/kilo	250.00/kilo	375.00/kilo
GERMANIUM	1000/kilo	202.00/kilo	1000/kilo
LEAD	.61/pound	.19/pound	.31/pound
MAGNESIUM	1.34/pound	.82/pound	1.34/pound
MANGANESE	.70/pound	.35/pound	.66/pound
MERCURY	415.00/flask	115.00/flask	415.00/flask
MOLYBDE-NUM	17.80/pound	4.75/pound	4.75/pound
NICKEL	3.50/pound	1.97/pound	2.54/pound
SELENIUM	17.50/pound	8.00/pound	3.77/pound
SILICON	1,400.00/metric ton	600.00/metric ton	1,190.00/metric ton
TANTALUM	110.00/pound	15.00/pound	37.50/pound
TELLURIUM	23.00/pound	8.00/pound	12.00/pound
TIN	9.00/pound	3.03/pound	6.88/pound
TITANIUM	7.28/pound	2.70/pound	7.28/pound
TUNGSTEN	185.80/ton	128.00/ton	148.00/ton
VANADIUM	4.20/pound	2.80/pound	3.14/pound
ZINC	.40/pound	.29/pound	.50/pound
ZIRCONIUM	270.00/metric ton	75.00/metric ton	90.00/metric ton

* Average monthly highs and lows over the past five-year period.

NOTE: This will give you an idea of where the metals have been in past years.

I won't make any specific recommendations, because the market is too sophisticated and obscure to make them meaningful in a short chapter. Check with the sources on page 409 for more information.

_____ *Stratagems to Keep in Mind* _____

• Who *you buy from is as important as* what *you buy and* when *in this fragmented market.*
• *Don't forget the market is no longer near the bottom.*
• *This game really should* only *be played by high rollers.*

Chapter 32

Epilogue: The Cloud's Silver Lining

In every State the government is nothing but a permanent conspiracy on the part of the minority against the majority, which it enslaves and fleeces.
Michael Bakunin

Every great robbery that was ever perpetrated upon a people has been by virtue of an in-the-name-of-law.
Albert Parsons

Most people look upon a depression as a bad thing, and that's natural enough. They think of closed factories, bankrupt businesses, and failed banks. How can there be any good in destitute widows losing their last penny of savings and homeless orphans suddenly in dire financial straits because their trust funds go up in smoke? How can there be any good when families are thrown out into the streets, their homes repossessed; when businessmen contemplate suicide as the fruits of their lives' work wither; when students are unable to attend college; when lovers are unable to marry?

It's a long list and not very pleasant. I don't want to sound Pollyannaish and pretend every cloud has a silver lining, but in this case it's true. The prosperity of the last thirty years has in many ways been artificial, an illusion caused by people living beyond their means. Society's high standard of living has been an inflationary bubble, and like all bubbles it will burst.

A Change for the Better

A depression seems like a bad thing, but is it really? If a whole generation of people have built their lives on a foundation of sand, perhaps it's much better that the unsound structure collapse sooner rather than later. The sooner people start building on a solid foundation, the sooner they can plan for the future with confidence.

Most of the inequities, real and imagined, in society have been engendered by the government's inflation and regulation. As the depression washes away the old financial structure it will wash away many of the fortunes built around the old order.

Many of those people who have been most prosperous in the '60s and '70s will be hardest hit. And many of those who thought they would never get a break will become millionaires in the '80s. There's a certain justice to it.

There are some aspects of society that could stand a change, and a depression presents an opportunity for that. Perhaps with more drama, or trauma, attached than you might want, but change nonetheless. One of the problems with change is the moral overtones it carries. Some people feel change is good simply for the sake of change. Others feel the existing order (almost regardless of what it may be) is the way things ought to be, and they fight change. Others are a bit more discriminating and feel "change is good," if they approve of the direction it takes.

No one likes the prospect of a depression; even the thought is chilling. People naturally resist confronting it. The thought of society being turned upside down is somewhat emotionally draining.

But the more comfortable you can become with the idea, the better adjusted you are to it, the greater your prospects of success. Winning at life and the financial markets is 90 percent a matter of psychological attitude. The Greater Depression is not going to be pleasant, but it is a part of reality, and a psychologically healthy person is able to deal with reality, whether or not it's pleasant.

There's certainly no need to become terrorized, apathetic, or grief-stricken; those who are equipped to survive will in fact survive. Whatever it was that wiped out the dinosaurs—a shift in the earth's axis or a large meteorite strike—must have put a lot of pressure on the mammals as well. If they had a choice, the mammals would no doubt have preferred not to be a part of the catastrophe, but it was the best thing that ever happened to them, since it cleared the landscape of reptilian predators.

Most of the institutions that have grown up over the last fifty years, and the accompanying fortunes that have been made, were created during an era that's on the wane. As the economic climate that they thrived in is transformed, many will prove to be modern dinosaurs. The analogy is apt in a lot of ways.

Archaic Behemoths

Big government, big business, big labor, and the Establishment have become huge behemoths with pea-sized brains. Visualize the brutes thrashing about the landscape—slow and dim-witted, true, but also powerful and still very dangerous—sending small mammals scurrying away lest they be crushed, which many are.

An economic collapse will, with any luck at all, put an end to those four walking anachronisms, or at least to their worst excesses.

Big Government

There are plenty of people around who still see the government as "we the people," but the 1980s should disillusion them. Whatever it once was, the government today isn't the people ruling themselves, it's the people in power (and those who control them) ruling those who aren't in power, while keeping up the illusion that's what "the people" want.

It's important to get down to the basic principles involved when dealing with government, because it is the single most powerful organization in the world. It determines the value of the currency you save. It decides how much you may keep of what you earn. Its millions of regulations order your life. Its thousands of laws can jail you. There's no voluntarism about government; it is pure force, either revealed or concealed.

In many ways, dealing with the state is more dangerous than dealing with the Mafia. At least with the Mafia there is a code of honor that's generally adhered to, since the organization is outside the law. But when you're dealing with the state you are legally disarmed.

If the essence of government is force, and the use of force should be limited, then the government should be limited to protecting you from force, and should not be able to initiate it, as it now does. That would imply a police force to protect you from coercion and fraud inside the country, an army to protect you from criminals outside the country, and a court system for the nonviolent adjudication of disputes. It would not include public schools, social welfare, regulatory agencies, postal service, or national currency, among many other things.

A good case can be made that the government shouldn't even perform police services, if only because they're too important. If a criminal steals from me, I would much prefer having Mannix or Mike Hammer go after him than a government bureaucrat who puts away his tools at five o'clock. National defense today is a charade, since the Soviet Union can totally destroy the U.S. at will and there's not a thing that can be done about it, except to destroy the Soviets in return. The courts, ruled by politically appointed, arbitrary, and often corrupt judges, are impossible to get in to and, once in, impossible to get out of. In a free market society, arbitration agencies would compete with each other on the basis of their intelligence, fairness, speed, and cost effectiveness.

If government as an institution was ever viable, it was when mankind and his technology were still primitive. It was still possible then for a king or council or congress to tell farmers how much to grow of what, the oxen driver how much to charge for transporting it, and the merchant how much to charge for it. But now, with a complex society of billions of people conducting scores of billions of transactions daily, and technology rapidly expanding, it's impossible, and it has *always* been counterproductive. The question of the morality of some men setting themselves up to control the lives of others— whether they claim their mandate came from God, Dialectic, or The People—is something else again.

When government was a social institution (the way it was when the Declaration of Independence was signed) and the town meeting was the norm, it served a useful function. When the majority of the people saw a need, or a problem that required common effort to solve, people came together voluntarily to solve it. Laws weren't needed to punish those who didn't conform with the behavioral norms of the majority or who failed to participate in joint efforts. Peer pressure and social opprobrium were entirely adequate. The laws that were passed by the community were few and important, hence taken seriously and respected. Government, while it was still a social institution, was truly of, by, and for the people. People governed themselves without benefit of a caste of professional rulers. A government that controls itself is able to maintain the respect of its citizens; a government that controls only its subjects gains only their contempt.

The Collapse of the Super State

Even though the 1930s depression was caused by state intervention, it was used by government to expand its power base. It's impossible to tell exactly how the whole situation will unwind itself in the 1980s, but there's an excellent chance the process will reverse. Throughout the 1970s, when future expectations were still high, the state had trouble maintaining itself and its clients. It was forced to raise taxes and to borrow larger and larger sums, even while it inflated the currency to previously unheard of levels.

During the 1980s, popular support for government programs will evaporate; at the same time, the obligations of the programs will hit new highs. With massive unemployment, civil unrest, and bankruptcies nationwide, the government will attempt to command more of the country's resources than ever in order to pave over its past mistakes. But since it's already taking 32 percent of the gross national product—whereas it took only 10.0 percent before the last depression—the chances are good the government will levy a tax and nobody will pay; it'll pass a law and nobody will obey; it'll print more currency and nobody will use it.

I don't expect the state to take the situation lying down. Government bureaucrats equate themselves with "the country" and cloak their programs in "patriotism." They will beef up their enforcement arms—the IRS, FBI, SEC, and CIA, among others—to force citizens to comply. And they will have the help of all those who've been living at the expense of their fellow citizens. America may become a dog-eat-dog society for a while, as the non-producers desperately attempt to continue living off the labors of the producers. But I have every confidence that the average man will act in the best interests of himself, his family, his friends, his community, and his country, in that order. The will of 250 million individuals acting as individuals can overrule the will of the collective. The good guys can win.

Once people find the state isn't a cornucopia, they'll have no choice but to start running their own lives again. Those who were depending on the state for sustenance will have some hard times, but in the long run they'll be the greatest beneficiaries. Society will continue, but it will be restructured so that the individual has ultimate responsibility for his own success or failure. The depression we're now in offers the prospect of the super state's collapse, and that's a major reason why the depression may change things for the better.

And if big government collapses, so will its "running dogs" (as the Marxists say), those other nemeses of the average man: big business, big labor, and the Establishment.

Big Business

Giant corporations are such a fashionable target that I genuinely hesitate to pick on them. After all, they are responsible for many of the things that make life worth living: movies, airplanes, autos, computers, popcorn—anything, in fact, you can buy off the shelf of any store.

A corporation is a natural way for people to organize in a free society. It's a voluntary association. If you work for one and don't like it, you can quit and start your own shop, or go over to the competition. If you vote your shares, with all but the largest corporations, the number of other holders is small enough so that you can meet and influence them personally. If you want more power, you can get it by buying more shares. If you don't like the way the corporation is being run, you can sell your shares and eliminate the bother.

A corporation is just a group of people banded together to make a profit by producing goods and services for other people. When its services are no longer desired by the market, everyone simply parts company (through a return of capital, or a bankruptcy) and goes off to find something better to do with his time and money.

Although corporations are a natural way for people to relate in the business of business, a problem can arise when they get too big. At that point they tend to become impersonal, bureaucratized, hierarchical, and stagnant. There's an optimal size for most things, and bigger doesn't always mean more profitable in the case of business. After a certain point it just means more long-term obligations, operating policies etched in stone, a higher profile for antagonists to shoot at, less involved management and shareholders, and much slower reaction time to change. It's just the nature of a large organization, and in a free market few would get "too" big, and none would stay that way for long.

Most corporations today got big not because of success in a free market but because of government protection and aid. The marketplace is dispersed, diffuse, and diverse, with many local variations.

When 30 percent of the wealth produced in a country flows into one organization (i.e., the federal government) each year, the wealth of the country is being centralized. The corporations that cater to the government tend to behave like it; they operate inefficiently on a "cost plus" basis and are increasingly insulated from the market. Only the big corporations can hire the lawyers and the lobbyists to get laws passed and grants delivered in their favor. And only they have the clout to get in to see an important legislator or regulator at will. They're certainly in a better position to offer him a prestigious, high-paying job in return for his goodwill when he leaves the "public service." That's part of the reason I suggest you invest in the blue chip companies listed on page 313. They are in a position to make sure the state keeps their nests feathered.

That's also a main cause for the widespread resentment against big business. It's unfortunate that big business has somehow become confused with free enterprise, when the opposite is nearer the truth. "Big" business tends to be that way not so much because of the free market, but because of government intervention. That's what the "military-industrial complex" is all about. Big business and big government support each other, even if from time to time the dog bites the master (or the master kicks the dog, depending on how you perceive who's who).

By the time the depression we're now in is over, many big businesses will have gone under despite their advantages; that's why the stock recommendations I'm making here will only be valid till the mid or late '80s. Regardless of what happens to the corporations, their assets will still be there, though, waiting to go back into production however the free market sees fit. The death of these unproductive dinosaurs is another major way this depression will be a very refreshing experience, certainly for the average worker. But not nearly as good as the demise of big labor.

Big Labor

A worker's union, in principle, is no different from a gathering of stamp collectors or a touch football club. Each is a group of people who associate because they share common interests and common goals.

Today, however, unions are not a free association of co-workers, but a coercive monopoly that can deny a worker a job while polarizing employees against employers.

Big labor is big for the same reason that big business is big: the state. Without the state's laws, which grant unions the exclusive authority to represent workers and force workers to join them, unions wouldn't have grown to their present size.

Unions act against the interest of the worker in virtually every way. By fighting the introduction of labor-
saving devices (on the false assumption they're "saving
jobs"), they reduce productivity—the ability of the
worker to produce more in less time, something which
makes him more valuable as an individual while increasing the wealth of society as a whole. Union's constant harassment of management—an activity they feel
justifies their existence in the eyes of the worker—further decreases productivity while eating into corporate
profits, profits which add to society's wealth. Unions'
static, calcified structure buries a worker in a given job
description with little hope of lateral or vertical movement. This makes it hard for the competent to rise, and
decreases the risk of the negligent falling. Unions rob
the individual of responsibility and incentive. The
worker's hard-earned dollars support a bloated hier-
archy of empire-building bosses. Because of big labor,
the entrepreneurs often don't have the staying power to
compete in an "organized" field, and this works to the
advantage of big business. Big business and big labor
may be antagonists, but they always join forces against
any innovation that can disturb the established order
over which they rule.

In 1981, for the first time in decades, unions were
forced to accede to benefit cuts or give up jobs. When
Chrysler threatened to fail, workers found their union
powerless to help; as times get tougher, organized labor
will break ranks and collective bargaining will be replaced by individual bargaining. The collapse of whole
industries will obviate large unions. Big industries are
centralized and lend themselves to dealing with big
labor, but as workers are unemployed, many will go
back to work in the alternative economy or for small
business. Workers and owners will prove quite capable
of sitting down together—or as individuals—and deciding what is in each's best interest.

With the end of the unions, every man will have much

greater ease of entry to and exit from any job he pleases. Everyone will be, in effect, self-employed.

The depression should act as a catalyst to shatter the concrete casts in which big labor has embedded the working man. Surprisingly, the depression will have the best effects of all on the worker for that reason.

The Establishment

The depression will not only overturn the giant bureaucratic organizations that suppress the individual but change the country's social structure as well. It could mean the end of the "Establishment."

Throughout the last fifty years the rich have gotten richer while the poor have gotten poorer because of taxes, regulations, debt, and inflation—the very factors underlying the depression itself. Only the rich can afford the legal counsel it takes to weave and dodge through the laws that restrict the masses. The rich can afford the accountants to chart a way through loopholes in the tax laws. The rich can hire the experienced investment counsel* to capitalize on distortions in the market created by the state. The rich have the credit to borrow, and borrowers gain during an inflation. They have the money to acquire quality items that tend to appreciate during the same inflation that wipes out the few dollars the average man has scrimped to save.

Many of the people who are wealthy today are wealthy because of the evils of society; they're counting on more state action to maintain their wealth and compound it. The Establishment counts on big government and big business to keep them on top. The depression may topple them all; it offers a rare opportunity for justice to be done.

* Most investment counselors are no smarter than the market in which they're investing. But with the possible exception of bank trust officers, they're at least bright enough to do something other than leave money in a passbook account.

Justice is defined as each getting what he deserves. A problem usually arises with differing opinions as to who deserves what. I would answer by saying no one deserves anything except that which he produces, or trades for, himself. The spirit soars in anticipation.

Welfare recipients, who give nothing for what they get and therefore don't deserve it, will be cut off, perhaps cold turkey. As they're forced to go back to work the crime rate should drop precipitously (although probably not before large-scale riots and protest disturbances) as these people regain self-respect, responsibility, and job skills. This includes Soviet bloc and Third World countries, which are simply international welfare bums. A cutoff of loans and free food to them will no doubt precipitate violent internal revolutions in authoritarian countries, which is probably necessary to create conditions for growth in the future. Each of them has its own Idi Amin.

The whole class of people who've become wealthier solely because they had it to start with will probably be wiped out in the new environment. Inherited Establishment wealth in particular will change ownership as the old, protected order crumbles.

A whole new class of millionaires will arise, because that wealth won't vanish; it'll just change ownership. The new millionaires, starting from scratch, will prosper only by creating goods and services for other people.

The myth of the omnipotence of government should be destroyed, and that might pave the way for a new Golden Age.

Vast numbers of people who have despaired of ever owning their own home will have the chance to pick and choose as prices (in real terms) tumble. Those who despaired of ever getting out of the rat race will have no choice but to get out when it screeches to a halt and their non-productive jobs disappear. The reason why people feel caught in a rat race is that they don't perceive their jobs as productive. And if they don't, chances are they're right. Non-productive jobs are the first to go in a depression.

A whole class of people who have grown up living perpetually above their means, as well as the cynics who think that's just the way the world works, will be chastised. They'll probably be unable to change their lifestyle to adjust to new conditions; and if they can't, they'll get exactly what they deserve. The thrifty, hardworking, and prudent should once more have their day in the sun.

The small, bright mammals will replace the lumbering, suppressive dinosaurs on all fronts.

Gloom and Doom?

The depression is certainly going to mean hard times for some people, probably for most people. The media are fond of characterizing that type of prediction as "gloom and doom," depicting those who assert it as eccentrics dressed in sackcloth, who roll in ashes and carry little signs saying the end is near.

Speaking for myself, I have a low threshold of boredom and the '80s show every prospect of being, as the Chinese would say, "an interesting time," so the decade will at least keep me involved.

It may be that you don't like some of the predictions I've made in this book. But then if there were a fire raging out of control in the living room of your house and someone predicted the house was going to burn down, you wouldn't be very pleased by that prediction either. Consider the predictions as a warning to haul out the garden hose and start fighting the fire before it's too late.

Regardless of whether your neighbor puts out his house fire or not, you can certainly extinguish your own.

And you don't have to count on the fire department, the government, or the Easter Bunny to do it for you. The strategy is simple: Liquidate, Create, Consolidate, and, then, Speculate.

There's no reason why you shouldn't be among the new class of millionaires that will arise in the years to come. Gloom and doom need be nothing but a headline in the newspaper if you follow the proper plan. The depression doesn't have to be a bad thing for you and yours. Rather, it's an opportunity to gain all the things you really want in life as the suppressive institutions that may have been keeping you down are overturned.

Good luck and good hunting!

Chapter 33

Further Helps

The government has no mysterious ability to do things that can't be done in the free market.
Harry Browne

The instant formal government is abolished, society begins to act. A general association takes place, and common interest produces common security.
Thomas Paine

The purpose of this chapter is to make it easy to pursue the subjects in this book in detail. I've listed addresses and telephone numbers wherever possible.

Consulting Services

For those of you who feel that some of the points in the book need further clarification or that a lot has changed since the book was written (a lot has changed since yesterday morning, actually), or that you'd like to have a plan for your own personal circumstances, I'm available for private consultation on a fee basis, and can be reached at P.O. Box 40949, Washington, D.C., 20016, telephone (202) 462-3574.

I also manage funds on a discretionary basis, through International Fund Management, Inc., P.O. Box 40948, Washington, D.C. 20016, telephone (202) 298-7381. The minimum account is $100,000.

You might wish to subscribe to my newsletter, *Investing in Crisis*. In each issue I attempt to update the subjects in this book, as well as stock, currency, and real estate markets, and related subjects dealt with in my other books, *The International Man* and *Crisis Investing*. My newsletter attempts to give very specific investment advice, along with reasons *why* I believe it's correct. One thing is certain—the world is changing quickly, and markets will be presenting some magnificent opportunities.

If you are on the West Coast and want to speak to a competent financial planner, I recommend the services of Harry Browne's associate, Terry Coxon. He can be reached at 330 Primrose Road #201, Burlingame, California 94010, telephone (415) 343-7161.

Those who look to Europe will find the services of Robert Doorn, a close associate of Harry Schultz, most helpful. He can be reached at P.O. Box 137, 1815 Clarens-Montreux, Switzerland. Telephone: (021) 62/5518; telex: 25848.

Those of you who might be interested in some unusual opportunities in South America (and around the world) should contact Dr. Jose Pascar at Edificio Comercio de Bolsa, Sarmiento 299, Piso 6, Of. 655, Buenos Aires, Argentina. Telephone: 32-0739; telex: 18749.

Books by Mail

If you can't find the books I recommend in your local bookstore, it is simple to order by direct mail. Write to the following publishers for their catalogs. Although one would never know it from the statements and actions of Establishment economists, there are many fine books available on economics, finance, and related topics. If some of the books seem a bit radical to you, consider that all the more reason to explore them. It never hurts to broaden one's horizons.

Laissez-Faire Books, Attn. J. Muller, 206 Mercer Street, New York, N.Y. 10012. A must catalog for anyone with a libertarian bent.

Loompanics, Attn. M. Hoy, P.O. Box 264, Mason, Michigan 48854. Self-liberation books of all types, including an excellent selection of books on the alternative economy.

Eden Press, Attn. B. Reid, P.O. Box 5410, Fountain Valley, California 92708. For those seeking alternative lifestyles, get in touch with Eden Press.

Paladin Press, Attn. P. Lund, P.O. Box 1307, Boulder, Colorado 80306. For the physical survival buffs in the audience.

Common Sense Press, Attn. E. Ray, 711 West 17th Street, G-6, Costa Mesa, California 92627. A catalog of investment books compiled by John Pugsley.

Alexandria House Books, Attn. J. Fouse, 901 N. Washington Street, Alexandria, Virginia 22314. Financial books.

Part I: What Lies Ahead

Although I've outlined the economic theory that underpins the rest of my conclusions with a broad brush, you may want to pursue it in more detail; it certainly would be worth the effort.

Books

Crisis Investing, Douglas Casey (Pocket Books, $3.50.) I've referred to this book a number of times. It's as valid now as it was in 1979, and contains a lot of data not in this book.

America's Great Depression, Murray Rothbard (Nash Publishing). Just in case you're wondering why the last one happened.

Society Without Government, Linda and Morris Tannehill and Jarrett Wollstein (Arno Press, $14.95). This is one of the two most important books I've ever read.

Looking Out for Number One, Robert J. Ringer (Fawcett Books). The book lays out a rational philosophy on why you should do just that.

Restoring the American Dream, Robert J. Ringer (QED/Harper & Row, $12.50). If you have time to read only one book on philosophy, make it this one.

None of the Above, Sy Leon (Fabian Press, $7.95). An excellent antidote for those who are politically involved.

How You Can Profit from the Coming Devaluation, Harry Browne (Avon, $1.75). Perhaps the best popular explanation of money and inflation ever written.

How to Prosper During the Coming Bad Years, Howard Ruff (Times Books, $8.95). A clear, usable plan for living with high inflation. One of the biggest selling financial books ever written.

Defending the Undefendable, Walter Block (Fleet Press, $9.95). A brilliant, important book which uses extreme examples to refute all manner of commonly accepted rubbish.

Economics in One Lesson, Henry Hazlitt (Manor Books, $1.25). This is absolutely the best short presentation of free market economic theory available.

Understanding the Dollar Crisis, Percy L. Greaves, Jr. (Western Islands, $4.95). Greaves was a close associate of the late Dr. Ludwig von Mises, dean of the Austrian school of economic thought, and his book is a good summary of Mises's theories.

The Coming Currency Collapse, Jerome Smith (Books in Focus, $12.50). Presents the definitive argument for the probability of runaway inflation in the United States.

The Coming Credit Collapse, Alexander P. Paris (Arlington House, $7.95). The definitive argument for a deflationary credit collapse. Many good statistics.

Human Action, Ludwig von Mises (Henry Regnery, $19.95). This is the magnum opus of economics; its depth and breadth are unrivaled, although it is rather slow reading.

Atlas Shrugged, The Virtue of Selfishness, Capitalism, The Unknown Ideal, and, in fact, all of Ayn Rand's books. The cult that surrounds Ms. Rand and her works proves that she remains one of the most dynamic intellectual forces today, and that Western civilization's values can survive only if

grounded in philosophy. *Atlas Shrugged* is a novel about
the Greater Depression, although it was written in the
1950s.

For a New Liberty, Murray Rothbard (Macmillan). This book
amounts to a libertarian manifesto.

The Machinery of Freedom, David Friedman (Arlington
House). Excellent practical discussion of anarcho-capitalist
economic theory.

Periodicals and Newsletters

The following offer a good economic overview, as
well as a perceptive analysis of the political climate.

The American Institute Reports, Great Barrington, Massachu-
setts 01230 (25 times a year, $50). The oldest and still one
of the best researched newsletters around today.

Barron's, 22 Cortlandt Street, New York, N.Y. 10007 (52 times
a year, $32). The best financial weekly that America has to
offer, with incisive and penetrating editorials that give valuable insight.

Common Sense Viewpoint, 711 West 17th Street, G-6, Costa
Mesa, California, 92627 (12 times a year, $75). For the
smaller investor and self-employed businessman, Jack Pugsley's newsletter provides invaluable insights into how the
world works. Jack is a nexialist and his letter reflects it.

Alexander's Monthly Economic Letter, Box 54, Mechanics-
ville, Virginia 23111 (12 times a year, $20). Very libertarian
and philosophical—and quite clever.

The Ruff Times, Box 2000, San Ramon, California 94583
(about 26 times a year, $145). Howard Ruff's down-to-earth
letter is directed toward the small investor who wants to
preserve his capital rather than speculate.

World Market Perspective, P.O. Box 2289, Winter Park, Florida 32790 (12 times a year, $110). If long-term buying and
holding suits your temperament better than playing the fast-
moving markets, check out Jerome Smith's newsletter.

Part II: The Importance of Liquidity

I mentioned *Mother Earth* and *Co-Evolution Quarterly*, and both are worth subscriptions.

Mother Earth News, P.O. Box 70, Hendersonville, North Carolina 28791 (12 issues for $14.95).
Co-Evolution Quarterly, P.O. Box 428, Sausalito, California 94966 ($14 per year).

The most useful publication I know of covering interest rates is *The Bank Credit Analyst*, Butterfield Building, Front Street, Hamilton, Bermuda (12 times a year, $275). One of the most scholarly financial and economic services at any price. Every issue is an educational experience.

Regarding money market funds, you might want a copy of *Donoghue's Complete Money Market Guide* (Harper & Row, 1981, $12.95), or a subscription to *Donoghue's Moneyletter*, P and S Publications, Inc., P.O. Box 411, Holliston, Massachusetts 01746.

Part III: Creating Money

The best book on taking the proper psychological approach to life, business and investing is *How I Found Freedom in an Unfree World* by Harry Browne (Avon, 1973, $1.95).

Also very helpful is *The Psychology of Freedom* by Peter R. Breggin, M.D. (Prometheus Books, 1980).

My own contribution to the literature is *The International Man*, Douglas R. Casey (Alexandria House, $19.95). This is my first book. It explains in detail how to take advantage of financial opportunities and free-

dom around the world. It covers passports and foreign
real estate and black market operations, among other
topics.

Some worthwhile views on the subject of higher edu-
cation are contained in *Bear's Guide to Non-Traditional
College Degrees*, by John Bear ($19.95, P.O. Box 646,
Mendocino, California 95460).

You might consider joining the following organization
to keep up on business opportunities around the world,
and to meet others with similar interests:

The Merchant Brokers Exchange, Gary F. Scott, President, Suite 9, Westminster Palace Gardens, 1-7 Artil-
lery Row, London SW1P 1R1, England.

The tax laws are always changing, so books are
quickly outdated, but these are good usable texts:

How You Can Use Inflation to Beat the IRS, by B. Ray Ander-
son (Harper & Row, 1981, $14.95).
Taxpayers' Audit Survival Manual, by Vern Jacobs (Alexandria House, 1981, $19.95).

Each of these men publishes his own newsletter as
well:

The Taxflation Fighter, New Capital Publications, Inc., 468
Park Avenue South, Suite 1405, New York, NY 10016 (12
issues $195).
Tax Angles, Kephart Communications, 901 North Washington
Street, Alexandria, Virginia 22314 (12 issues, $48).

The following letter is also good, but more specialized:

Johnson/Marshall Estate Planning Report, P.O. Box 651,
Wheaton, Illinois, 60187 (10 times a year, $95).

There's not a big literature on the alternative economy, as such, but the following books are helpful.

How You Can Profit from the Coming Price Controls, Gary
North ($10). If you agree that federal price controls are just
around the corner, you'll need this book to survive.
Privacy: How to Get It and Enjoy It, Bill Kaysing (Eden
Press, $14.95). This book is as close to a guide to the new
economy as I know of; written with wit.
Mark Skousen's Guide to Financial Privacy, Mark Skousen
(Alexandria House, $14.95). To bring some privacy back
into your financial affairs, get this book. It's the best re-
searched one on the market.

The best book I've seen on starting, running, or taking
over a business is *How to Become Financially Successful by Owning Your Own Business*, Albert J. Lowry
(Simon and Schuster, $14.95).

A good magazine on entrepreneurial activity is *Venture* (12 issues for $9), P.O. Box 10772, Des Moines,
Iowa 50349.

Tax Shelters

Tax shelters not only save you money, but also de-
prive the government of harassment-producing revenue,
and that's a good reason to look at them. Tax shelters of
various types have been engineered by clever lawyers
to take advantage of loopholes in the tax codes' byzantine complexity. A lot of tax-preferenced investments
are simply bad investments, but some *do* have real
merit. For those of you with substantial assets, who are
also in at least the 50 percent tax bracket, I recommend
the following men. As far as I'm concerned, they are the
best in the business.

Lee G. Lovett, Esq., 1901 L Street N.W. #200,
Washington D.C. 20006. (202) 293-7400.

Larry Abraham, President, Larry Abraham and
Associates, 1914 64th Avenue West, Tacoma,
Washington 98466. (206) 564-3553.

A good newsletter on the subject is *Brennan Reports*, P.O.
Box 882, Valley Forge, Pennsylvania 19482 (12 times a year,
$100).

The people listed under "Oil and Gas Development"
and "Tax-Haven Counsel" are helpful in those areas as
well.

Oil and Gas Development

Domestic energy projects have treated investors very
well over the last ten years, and I expect that will remain
the case. An interest in a producing well offers tap advantages and a form of inflation-indexed income. But
there are pitfalls—not the least of which are the exces-
sive front-end costs many brokers charge. I recommend
the following company both for its fine record and its
mode of doing business:

Martin Truax, President, Cumberland Oil Corp., (404)
952-3999; mailing address: P.O. Box 720062, Atlanta,
Georgia 30358.

Tax-Haven Counsel

The government would like you to think it's illegal to
use a haven, but there are still some legal ways left,
despite their continuing efforts to close off so-called
"loopholes." The crux of the issue is for you to control a
foreign corporation (or assets or bank accounts) without
having either to pay taxes on income or to report your
ownership interest, while still observing the letter of the
law. Of course, the government can change the laws, or

its interpretation of them, unpredictably; that's why it's important you have competent continuing counsel in setting up an offshore entity and using it properly. Going off-shore is the ultimate way of protecting yourself from your government.

Although I've investigated the area in some detail, I'm not a specialist in tax havens. If you want further counseling, I recommend the services of David Fishman Esq., 16 Mary Street, Suite No. 4, San Rafael, California 94901, telephone (415) 453-9100.

Another man who's helpful in the practical, mechanical aspects of "going offshore" is Laban J. Quimby II, Quimby & Company Ltd., S.A., Post Box N-10717, Nassau, Bahamas, telephones (809) 325-7579, (800) 621-1466, #1140.

Part IV: Consolidating for Safety and Profit

There is no doubt what is the best book on a program of hoarding; it's *The Alpha Strategy*, by John Pugsley (Stratford Press, 1981, $12.50). Absolutely required reading for the small ($25,000 and under) investor, and valuable reading no matter how large your portfolio. If you follow the sound economic advice in this book, you can pave a road to an almost risk-free economic future. Consider it required reading.

A good newsletter to keep up on self-sufficiency is *Survival Tomorrow*, 901 North Washington Street, #605, Alexandria, Virginia 22314 (monthly, $60 per year). This letter is edited by Karl Hess.

One good source of storage foods and the type of practical equipment you'd want if you're reduced to eating them is SI Outdoor Food and Equipment, P.O. Box 5509, Carson, California 90749, (800) 421-2179.

There are several books on gold and silver available:

How to Invest in Gold Coins, Donald Hoppe (Arco Publishing, $2.95). Still one of the best books available on the subject, notwithstanding the fact that numismatic coins have already realized the potential the author anticipated.

Silver Profits in the '70s, Jerome Smith ($12.50). Everything you always wanted to know about silver.

Three newsletters cover gold and silver well:

Gold and Silver Report (one year, 24 issues, $78). P.O. Box 5500, Newtown, Connecticut 06470.

Gold Newsletter, 8422 Oak Street, New Orleans, Louisiana 70118 (monthly, $36). Published and edited by Jim Blanchard, director of the National Committee for Monetary Reform.

Remnant Review, P.O. Box 7999, Tyler, Texas 75711 (22 times a year, $95). Gary North's scholarly overview of investments and philosophy.

There's one book to buy on the subject of Swiss banks:

Harry Browne's Swiss Bank Book (McGraw-Hill, 1976). Everything you'll need to know on this subject.

Part V: Speculating for Maximum Profit

Several books offer a good overview of the way markets work and intelligent approaches to them in the '80s.

The Battle for Investment Survival, Gerald M. Loeb. I have an edition of this book from the mid-1950s and it's as timely now as it was then. The book could be the all-time investment classic.

Fiat Money in France, Andrew D. White (Foundation for Economic Education). Although written one hundred years ago, it's very timely today. It's about the collapse of an entire political system.

Extraordinary Delusions and the Madness of Crowds,
Charles McKay (Noonday Press). The South Sea Bubble,
Tulip Mania, and about fifty other similar aberrations are
analyzed.
Inflation-Proofing Your Investments (William Morrow, 1981,
$14.95). Co-authored by Harry Browne and Terry Coxon,
the book offers an intelligent overall strategy.

Real Estate

Most of the books you see on real estate maintain that
investing in it is a one-way street to certain wealth. A
book that takes a more reasoned approach is *The Coming
Real Estate Crash*, by Cardiff and English (Arlington
House, $10). A well-researched warning that the first
cracks in the real estate market have already appeared.

Another book is also excellent, but in a different way:
*How You Can Become Financially Independent by In-
vesting in Real Estate*, by Al Lowry. The book does an
excellent job of detailing the techniques to use in buying property when the time comes.

Two newsletters serve to update these books, and are
edited by the books' authors. They are:

Sound Advice (12 issues, $125). P.O. Box 487, Walnut Creek,
California 94596.
Winning with Real Estate, Al Lowry (12 issues, $195). New
Capital Publications, Inc., 50 Washington Street, Reno, Ne-
vada 89503.

Unfortunately, the nature of the real estate market is
such that it's not really possible to recommend any specific brokers. As I mentioned briefly, however, there are
some interesting possibilities abroad.

It goes without saying that a prudent investor with
substantial assets should get at least a portion of those

assets offshore. Real estate in certain foreign countries has reasonable upside potential, presents the same tax advantages as its U.S. counterpart, and should serve as one way of beating foreign exchange control's repatriation requirements. If you're interested, the subject is covered in my book *The International Man.* I also recommend that you get in touch with the following groups:

Eugene Jewett, President, Miller, Petersen, Kligman and Jewett, 505 Queen Street, Alexandria, Virginia 22314, (703) 548-4913. Gene's approach to international real estate differs from those above in that he forms syndications of properties, allowing wide diversification while solving the problems of management and selection. We've worked together for years.

David Galland, Vice President, Pacific Basin Advisory Group, The Conference Department, #4 Lovers' Lane, Suite A, Mandeville, Louisiana 70448, (504) 626-5641. I'm quite involved with this company, which syndicates real estate and manages securities in Australia and the Far East.

Stocks

The following are books I'd recommend on the stock market in general:

The Intelligent Investor, Benjamin Graham. The author was the dean of "fundamental" security analysis.
Total Investing, T. J. Holt (Arlington House, $8.95). A good overview of the investment world. Holt anticipates a deflationary depression.

It's easiest to keep up to date with a newsletter, however. Most of the letters below cover all aspects of the investment markets—including gold, commodities, and real estate—but have a bias toward securities:

Access to Energy, Box 2298, Boulder, Colorado 80306 ($18 for 12 issues). This is not an investment letter at all but gives excellent coverage of anything to do with energy—oil, nuclear, coal, hydro, and solar.

Deliberations (24 issues, $185), P.O. Box 182, Adelaide Street Station, Toronto, Ontario, Canada M5C 2J1. This very intelligent, well-thought-out publication by Ian MacAvity specializes in technical analysis of the stock market.

Growth Stock Outlook (24 issues, $95), P.O. Box 9911, Chevy Chase, Maryland 20015. The writer, Charles Allmon, has a fine record of picking companies whose earnings expand in both good and bad years.

Harry Schultz International Letter, P.O. Box 2523, Lausanne 1022, Switzerland (17 times a year, $258). Harry Schultz was one of the first hard-money financial consultants. His letter monitors world stock markets, precious metals, and currencies in particular.

Holt Investment Advisory, 277 Park Avenue, New York, N.Y. 10017 (24 times a year, $150). Offers perceptive, well-reasoned advice on the stock and bond markets.

Investing in Crisis, P.O. Box 40948, Washington, D.C. 20016 (12 times a year, $145). U.S. and world stock, bond, real estate, and commodities markets. This is my own newsletter, and I attempt to present what are literally the best investment prospects in the world.

Financial Markets Review, 633 Third Avenue, New York, N.Y. 10017 (12 times a year, $150). Although aimed at institutions and substantial investors, this letter can claim an excellent track record in the market and a number of specialized indicators.

Dow Theory Letters, P.O. Box 1759, La Jolla, California 92037 (24 times a year, $150). Editor Richard Russell has a superb track record. His may be the longest running stock market letter available.

Harry Browne's Special Reports, Box 5586, Austin, Texas 78763 (10 times a year, $275). Every issue of this letter is an education in economics and finance, with many practical recommendations. It is characterized by original research that usually can't be found elsewhere.

Readers interested in pursuing opportunities in convertibles might investigate:

R.H.M. Convertible Survey (published weekly, $125 per year, $72 half-year), 417 Northern Boulevard, Great Neck, N.Y. 11021.

Value Line Options and Convertibles, published by Arnold Bernhard and Co., Inc., 711 Third Ave., New York, N.Y. 10017.

Permanent Portfolio Fund

Most investments represent a bet on how the present era of inflation is going to end—whether with a runaway inflation, a deflationary crash, or a soft landing. Bets placed on the correct outcome may yield high profits; bets placed incorrectly will be lost.

Now there is a new mutual fund, the Permanent Portfolio Fund, based on the idea that no one can know just how the economic drama of our time is going to unfold. The Fund's strategy is to select the right mix of investments to avoid making the investor dependent on any particular outcome for inflation. Its goal is to protect the investor's purchasing power through good times and bad.

The Permanent Portfolio Fund commits a fixed percentage of its assets to each of the following investment categories:

Gold
Silver
Swiss francs
High volatility U.S. stocks
Real estate and natural resource stocks (foreign and
    U.S.)
Treasury bills, bonds, and other dollar assets

This diversity, together with strict adherence to a selected percentage budget for each investment category, is a formula for protection against economic uncertainty. Gold, silver, Swiss francs, and the stocks of real estate and natural resource companies should profit from continuing inflation; the gold will be especially profitable if inflation (or any other cause) leads to general disorder. The high-volatility stocks probably would appreciate many times over if inflation subsided gradually and the economy somehow escaped a depression. The dollar assets are a provision for a deflationary depression, when most investments would be selling at bargain prices but Treasury bonds would be soaring.

The Fund's management is not authorized to trade on the short-term zigs and zags of the investment markets. Its main jobs are to keep the Fund's actual holdings in line with the fixed percentages and to protect the Fund's investments from taxes.

Although this approach rates high in safety, it can be profitable as well. Because the Fund commits a fixed percentage of its assets to each investment category, there is a built-in tendency for it to sell off investments that have risen in price and to add to its holdings of investments that have fallen in price. Thus the Permanent Portfolio Fund, unlike most other funds, is designed to profit from volatility in the investment markets.

The minimum investment in the Fund is $1,000, which makes it practical for small investors to have the protection of a balanced portfolio. And the Fund can provide both large and small investors with the convenience of worldwide diversification and tax planning in a single package.

The Permanent Portfolio Fund is run by Terry Coxon (the co-author, with Harry Browne, of *Inflation-Proofing Your Investments*). Both Harry Browne and I serve as consultants to the Fund. Jim Benham, the founder and current chairman of Capital Preservation Fund, is also a consultant.

If you are interested in learning more about this investment, write to the Permanent Portfolio Information Office, Box 5847, Austin, Texas 78763, or call (512) 453-7558.

Brokerage Services

It's helpful to work with a sympathetic broker. I have confidence in the following individuals and organizations:

Bruce Greene, Vice President, Securities, Dean, Witter, Reynolds, One Northfield Plaza, Northfield, Illinois 60093, (312) 441-9319. I've worked closely with Bruce for many years, and he's fully versed in all the securities covered here—and a lot that aren't, since this is a book, not a 24-volume encyclopedia.

Darrell Brookstein, President, First Georgetown Securities, 1022 15th Street N.W., Washington, D.C. 20005, (202) 785-5000. Darrell does a lot with penny mining stocks these days, and they are his area of specialty.

Micky Fouts, Director of Corporate Finance, OTC Net, 3600 South Beeler Street, Denver, Colorado 80237, (303) 779-6721. This firm specializes in new underwritings, which should be a very hot market in the 1980s.

Regarding gold stocks, two books are worthwhile:

How to Invest in Gold Stocks, Donald Hoppe (Arlington House, $9.95). The book is now eight years old and a bit dated, but it provides excellent background. In addition, the first half of the book is a highly competent history of gold.

Small Fortunes in Penny Stocks, Norman Lamb (Alexandria House, 1982, $14.95). Just what the title says. I wrote the book's foreword.

There are several newsletters specializing in gold stocks, as well:

The Penny Mining Prospector, 1022 15th Street N.W., Washington, D.C. 20005 ($95). This is the one complete source for the penny mining stocks, and it will soon cover energy issues as well. I have a financial interest in this letter.

International Investor Viewpoint, 610 Southwest Alder Street, Portland, Oregon 97205 (13 times a year, $125). Good coverage of gold and silver stocks around the world.

The International Gold Mining Letter, 15 Wilson Street, London EC 2M ZTR, England ($160 for 12 issues).

Western Mining News, N. 3019 Argonne Road, Spokane, Washington 99206 ($35 for one year).

Commodities

The best book I've found on commodities trading is *Commodity Futures Game: Who Wins? Who Loses? Why?* by Tewles, Harlowe, and Stone (McGraw-Hill).

Four books might be worth reading on strategic metals. First is the unfortunately titled *Get Really Rich in the Coming Super Metals Boom,* by Gordon McLendon (Pocket Books, 1981, $4.95).

A more technical treatment is offered by *Guide to Non-Ferrous Metals and Their Markets,* by Robbins and Lee (Kogan-Page, 1981, $19.95).

Investing in Natural Resources, by Walter Youngquist (Dow Jones, 1980, $19.95). Covers the strategics along with many other resources.

The best practical treatment, however, is probably in *The Rare and Strategic Metals Report* (WMP Publishing, P.O. Box 2289, Winter Park, Florida 32790, $75). It's expensive but has some useful comments on the stocks of companies that mine them, as well.

I don't find most commodity newsletters very helpful, but these three are exceptions:

The Metals Investor (12 issues $195), edited by Jack Pugsley, 711 West 17th Street, G-6, Costa Mesa, California 92627.

Commodities Insider, co-authored by Maury Kravitz and Marshal Wright. Published by New Capital Publications, Inc., 468 Park Avenue South, Suite 1405, New York, N.Y. 10016.

World-Wide Investment Notes, P.O. Box 16041, St. Louis, Missouri 63105 (26 times a year, $145). This newsletter covers various investments around the world, but is very heavy on strategic metals.

As described in Chapter 28, there are two basic ways of commodity trading. Each of the following brokers has his (or her) own short-term systems that have shown good results; at the same time each is familiar with my method of long-term speculating. Do business with the one who offers you the best combination of services.

Bruce Greene, Vice President, Dean Witter Reynolds, One Northfield Plaza, Northfield, Illinois 60093, (312) 441-9319.

John Durkin, President, John F. Durkin & Co., Inc., 5848 Naples Plaza, Suite 204, Long Beach, California 90803, (213) 433-6727 or (213) 433-GOLD. Minimum investment is $5,000.

Richard B. Bermont, Vice President, Drexel, Burnham, Lambert, Inc., First Federal Building, One Southeast Third Avenue, Miami, Florida 33131, (305) 358-7750. The minimum account is $50,000.

Ron Miller, Vice President, Shearson, American Express, 41 Perimeter Center East, N.E. Suite 101, Atlanta, Georgia 30346, (800) 241-6900.

Susan Cole, Vice President, NCZ Commodities Inc., 49 West 57th Street, New York, N.Y. 10019, (212) 371-4656.

A Parting Thought

The thought occurred to me that you might want to do some further reading on the future—which is what this book, and especially the Epilogue, is about. Despite the

Greater Depression there's plenty of cause for optimism. The following books and periodicals are favorites of mine.

The best way to keep up with late developments in technology as well as libertarian thinking (they go together) might be a subscription to *Claustrophobia*, 5047-C Southwest 26th Drive, Portland, Oregon 97201. At $30 per year, it's a bargain.

The subject of space colonization has an expanding literature. The classic study is Gerard K. O'Neill's *The High Frontier*. I'd also recommend his more recent *2081* (Simon and Schuster, 1981, $12.95), for a technically competent look at how good the future might be.

If you are interested in the subject of life extension, the best book is *Life Extension: Adding Years to Your Life and Life to Your Years: A Practical, Scientific Approach* (Warner Books, 1981, $12.95), by Durk Pearson and Sandy Shaw.

The Third Wave, Alvin Toffler (William Morrow and Company, 1980, $14.95). A good overview of how technology is changing society.

The Next 200 Years; A Scenario for America and the World (William Morrow and Company, 1976, $3.95) and *World Economic Development, 1979 and Beyond*, both by Herman Kahn. Kahn's multifaceted mind expands on at least a dozen important theses in these books. They are brilliant works (although the first is flawed in its disproportionate attention to technology as opposed to economics).

The Last and First Men and *Starmaker*, both by Olaf Stapledon. These are actually science fiction books, but their breadth and depth makes them all-time classics on the future.

And finally, *Profiles of the Future* (Harper & Row, 1973) by the one and only, Arthur C. Clarke, a man ahead of his time.